On Global Accounting Standards
-Speeches by Hans Hoogervorst

汉斯·胡格沃斯特 (Hans Hoogervorst) 著
上海国家会计学院 译

论全球会计准则
——国际会计准则理事会主席
汉斯·胡格沃斯特演讲实录

上海财经大学出版社

图书在版编目(CIP)数据

论全球会计准则:国际会计准则理事会主席汉斯·胡格沃斯特演讲实录/(荷)胡格沃斯特(Hans Hoogervorst)著;上海国家会计学院译.—上海:上海财经大学出版社,2014.4

ISBN 978-7-5642-1841-6/F·1841

Ⅰ.①论… Ⅱ.①胡…②上… Ⅲ.①国际会计准则-研究 Ⅳ.①F233.1

中国版本图书馆 CIP 数据核字(2014)第 020903 号

□ 策划编辑　王永长
□ 责任编辑　江　玉
□ 封面设计　蔡　彦　倪亚辉
□ 责任校对　林佳依　廖沛昕

LUN QUANQIU KUAIJI ZHUNZE
论 全 球 会 计 准 则
——国际会计准则理事会主席
汉斯·胡格沃斯特演讲实录

汉斯·胡格沃斯特　著
(Hans Hoogervorst)

上海国家会计学院　译

上海财经大学出版社出版发行
(上海市武东路 321 号乙　邮编 200434)
网　　址:http://www.sufep.com
电子邮箱:webmaster @ sufep.com
全国新华书店经销
同济大学印刷厂印刷
上海景条印刷有限公司装订
2014 年 4 月第 1 版　2014 年 4 月第 1 次印刷

710mm×1000mm　1/16　20.5 印张(插页:1)　335 千字
印数:0 001—2 500　定价:45.00 元

译者序

一

改革开放以来，我国会计改革高扬接轨、趋同、等效的主旋律，实现了与国际财务报告准则(IFRS)的实质性趋同，改善了我国企业以及我国会计师事务所走向世界、深度参与国际资本市场的会计环境，增强了我国对国际会计事务的话语权。在中国会计改革开放的进程中，研究学习国际财务报告准则，全面参与国际会计准则理事会(IASB)各项活动，既是深化我国会计改革的需要，也是提升中国会计地位的需要。上海国家会计学院组织翻译国际会计准则理事会现任主席胡格沃斯特先生的演讲集，主要的目的就是学习借鉴国际趋同经验，主动把握国际会计发展大势。

本演讲集包括胡格沃斯特先生自2011年7月就任至2013年期间在世界不同国家、不同场合的22篇演讲稿。通过学习、研读、翻译胡格沃斯特先生的演讲稿，我们认识到，作为国际会计准则理事会的现任主席和第二任主席，尽管他本人并非一名职业会计师，但自他就职以来，国际会计准则理事会和国际财务报告准则呈现出许多值得关注的新变化。这些变化体现在：一是更加注重协调全球各方利益，通过建立会计准则论坛，畅通反馈渠道，认真倾听利益相关者的声音。二是更加突出国际财务报告准则作为全球唯一会计标准的地位，全力推进会计准则的国际趋同，提出"全球会计准则"新概念。三是通过各种场合，反复呼吁尚未实现趋同的国家尽快明确趋同路线图，特别是反复劝导美国，晓以利弊，给美国施加了很大压力。四是全力完成金融工具相关系列会计准则，及时回应G20关切，全面解决金融危机期间暴露出来的与金融市场、金融稳定、资本市场等相关的会计问题。五是突出强调会计透明、中立的重要性，重视概念框架建设，不断巩固国际财务报告准则的理论基础和理念创新。

胡格沃斯特先生的演讲，全面描绘了国际财务报告准则的发展蓝图，充分展现了他的会计理念。学习研读胡格沃斯特先生的演讲，深刻体会国际财务报告准则未来取向，可以帮助我们站在更高的起点，审视会计准则国际趋同的大方向，主动适应和准确把握我国会计准则趋同进程。

二

上海国家会计学院作为财政部直属事业单位，一直坚持"国际知名会计学院"的办学目标，以"一流培训基地＋知名商学院"为特色发展模式，在国际财务报告准则的研究、推广、人才培养等方面，孜孜以求，不懈努力，取得了许多有目共睹的重要成果。一是在科研方面，我们完成了国家自然科学基金课题"中国会计准则：国际趋同的经济后果与博弈"的研究，出版了同名专著，并保持力量持续跟踪国际会计准则变化趋势。二是在面向包括全国会计领军（后备）人才培养项目在内的诸多中高级会计人员培训中，嵌入了不同类别、不同层次的国际财务报告准则课程。上海国家会计学院远程教育网还面向广大一线会计人员，提供了国际财务报告准则的基础性、普及性课程，数十万人通过培训更新了知识、拓展了视野。三是中国会计视野网站充分发挥互联网平台优势和中国会计界领先的媒体导向作用，大力推介国际财务报告准则，持续跟进国际财务报告准则最新动向，全面、及时地翻译报道国际会计准则理事会的各项活动和国际会计职业最新动态。近期，中国会计视野网站还获得了 IASB 正式授权，翻译了 IFRS 的一些官方资料。

所有这一切，为上海国家会计学院组织翻译出版胡格沃斯特先生的演讲集奠定了基础、提供了条件。

三

2013 年 6 月 4 日，胡格沃斯特先生莅临上海国家会计学院，发表了题为"中国与全球会计准则"的主旨演讲。通过此次接触，我们更加坚定了组织翻译出版其演讲集的信心和决心。为确保译稿的专业性和准确性，我们组成了以上海市财政局会计处乔元芳先生为主、由中国会计视野网站的虚拟团队"视野瞭望社"人员参加的翻译团队，精心译校，反复斟酌，严把译、校、审三道关口,力求精准、传神地反映胡格沃斯特先生的演讲意图和传递的信息,前后历经半年,终于完成全部演讲稿的翻译与校审。

据了解,胡格沃斯特先生的会计演讲集在全世界范围内还是第一次结集出版。对此他特别高兴,欣然为本书作序,对中国会计事业取得的巨大成就给予高度评价。

在本书出版翻译过程中,我们要特别感谢国际会计准则理事会理事、中国证监会前首席会计师张为国教授。他通过面谈、电话和电子邮件等方式,不厌其烦地多次联络沟通,促成了胡格沃斯特先生同意授权出版,并对翻译、出版等具体事宜予以悉心指导。可以说,没有张为国教授的热情指点与无私支持,本书便不可能面世。

最后,我们还要衷心感谢上海财经大学出版社有限公司总经理黄磊先生和编辑江玉女士为出版本书而付出的努力和创造的条件。

刘 勤
上海国家会计学院副院长、教授
2013 年 12 月 25 日

前　言

在上海国家会计学院的大力支持下,上海财经大学出版社决定出版本人演讲集之中文版,我倍感高兴与自豪。由于演讲必须言简意赅、简洁凝练,演讲者对所要传递的信息不得不认真思考、字斟句酌,因此,在为公众服务的整个职业生涯过程中,我一直把演讲作为沟通信息、交流思想的重要途径与手段。对我来说,写作演讲稿不仅是沟通信息的手段,更为重要的是,写作也迫使我集中精力、专心致志地思考那些必须处理与面对的政策难题。作为进入会计大家庭时间不长的一名新成员,通过写作演讲稿,对我深入理解会计问题助益极大。我尽量以通俗易懂的非专业语言阐述问题,以使全球各地的读者能够更方便地融入复杂多样的会计世界。

现在,中国读者能以母语阅读我的演讲稿,我感到特别高兴。在过去的十多年时间里,中国会计事业取得了巨大进步,中国会计准则已与国际财务报告准则实质性趋同并不断取得新的进步。我在访问中国的时候,看到中国人民渴望学习、孜孜以求,印象特别深刻。中国参与会计准则制定与实施的人士(包括国家会计学院的师生)职业素养很高,我希望他们通过阅读本演讲集,能够享受阅读的快乐并有所裨益。

最后,我要感谢国际会计准则理事会沟通和外部事务总监马克·拜厄特以及理事会各位理事在起草准备演讲稿过程中所给予的帮助。

汉斯·胡格沃斯特
国际会计准则理事会主席
2013 年 12 月 17 日

Foreword

I am very proud that the Shanghai University of Finance and Economics Press has decided to translate and publish a collection of my speeches in Chinese, with the support from Shanghai National Accounting Institute. Throughout my career in public service I have used speeches as an important channel of communication. Because speeches have to be concise, they force the author to think carefully about the messages he wants to deliver. For me, writing them is not only a means of communication, but also an instrument to force myself to focus my mind on the policy issues I have to deal with. As a relative newcomer to accounting, writing speeches greatly helped me gain a deeper understanding of accounting issues. I hope that the fact that I have tried to write in a non-technical manner can contribute to making the complex field of accounting more accessible to people around the world.

I am particularly pleased my speeches are now available in Chinese. In the last decade, China has made tremendous progress in the field of accounting. Chinese accounting standards are now substantially converged with IFRS and further progress is on the way. During my visits to China I have been very much impressed by the Chinese eagerness to learn. The quality of those involved in accounting standard setting and implementation in China, and both students and faculty at the national accounting institutes is very high and I hope they will enjoy reading this collection.

Lastly, I would like to thank Mark Byatt, director of communications of the IASB, and my fellow board members for their help in drafting these speeches.

Hans Hoogervorst
Chairman, IASB
17 December 2013

目 录

译者序 ··· 1

前 言 ··· 1

Foreword ··· 1

财务报告的目标 ··· 1

中国与国际财务报告准则
　——主导全球财务报告的机遇 ·· 8

会计透明度与金融危机 ··· 17

美国在全球会计准则趋同进程中的使命与担当 ························ 21

美国全面采用国际财务报告准则是保护投资者利益的绝佳选择 ······ 28

纵论收入确认、租赁和金融工具 ·· 36

把国际会计准则理事会建设得更为强大 ·································· 44

国际会计准则理事会未来展望 ··· 51

纵论会计透明度与金融稳定 ··· 57

非精确的会计世界 ·· 63

审慎：消亡抑或生存？ ·· 69

1

会计协调和全球经济后果 ·················· 75

消除对国际财务报告准则的偏见与误解 ·················· 83

致力实现财务报告的一致性 ·················· 86

会计与长期投资:"买入并持有"并非"买入并期待" ·················· 90

国际财务报告准则与印度尼西亚会计准则:2013及未来展望 ·················· 95

国际财务报告准则趋同进展如何?
　——跟踪通向全球会计准则的世界进展 ·················· 105

打破披露程式 ·················· 111

欧洲与通向全球会计准则之路 ·················· 117

强化会计准则制定机构之间的协调配合 ·················· 125

期待美国尽快作出采用国际财务报告准则的承诺 ·················· 130

为什么金融业与众不同:金融业按现值计量的相关性 ·················· 134

A Time for Change? The Objectives of Financial Reporting ·················· 142

China and IFRS— An Opportunity for Leadership in Global
　Financial Reporting ·················· 151

Accounting Transparency and Financial Crisis ·················· 163

The Mission and Responsibility of America in the Process of
　International Convergence of Accounting Standards ·················· 168

Adoption of IFRS to Be the Best Way to Protect Investors
　in America ·················· 177

On Revenue Recognition, Lease and Financial Instruments ·················· 185

Building a Stronger International Accounting Standard Board ·················· 194

The Prospects of International Accounting Standard Board ·················· 202

On Accounting Transparency and Financial Stability ·················· 209

The Imprecise World of Accounting ·················· 217

The Concept of Prudence: Dead or Alive? ·················· 225

Accounting Harmonisation and Global Economic Consequences ······ 233

Dispelling Myths about IFRS ·· 243

The Search for Consistency in Financial Reporting ······················ 247

Accounting and Long-term Investment-"Buy and Hold"
　　Should not Mean "Buy and Hope" ······································ 251

IFRS and Indonesian Accounting Standards 2013 and Beyond ········ 258

Are We There Yet? Charting the World's Progress towards
　　Global Accounting Standards ·· 270

Breaking the Boilerplate ·· 277

Europe and the Path towards Global Accounting Standards ············ 285

Strengthening Institutional Relationships ···································· 294

Expectation of US Commitment to Adopt IFRS in a Timely Manner ······ 299

Why the Financial Industry is Different: The Relevance of Current
　　Measurement for the Financial Industry ······························· 303

财务报告的目标

2011年2月9日,欧盟委员会在比利时首都布鲁塞尔召开主题为"财务报告与审计——变革正当其时吗?"的会议。汉斯·胡格沃斯特出席会议并发表题为《财务报告的目标》的演讲。本文为演讲全文。

过去三年我参与过许多次会计问题的激烈争论,通常是两个问题唱主角:其一,财务报告应该主要针对哪些受众?是投资者,还是更广泛的普通大众?受众是否还应该包括那些态度审慎的监管机构?对此,人们常将其作为第一个问题提出来。第二个问题与第一个问题有关,那就是:会计准则的目标是仅仅服务于提升透明度?还是既要提升透明度,又要维护金融稳定?

我个人认为,这些问题的答案实在是明白无误、简单直白,但人们还常为此进行激烈辩论,这令我大惑不解。

首先,让我们尝试回答第一个问题:财务报告应该主要针对哪些受众?

财务报告的目的是尽可能忠实可靠地提供一个公司或者组织的财务状况,人们对此毫无异议。财务报表所提供的信息,应该尽可能不偏不倚、真实可靠。

毫无疑问,财务报表对投资者最具相关性。毕竟,财务报告天生的使命就是向投资者提供所投资公司全面、充足的信息。保护投资者利益,始终是会计准则制定工作的核心和焦点所在。

与此同时,我们应该认识到,如果财务报告的目的是尽其所能地忠实可靠,那至于谁是财务报表的使用者就无关紧要了,这一点很重要。要一家公司的财务报表做到尽可能准确,那就不能用十种不同的方法来编制。换言之用十种不同方法编制的财务报表,不可能同样准确。财务报表也不可能因为使用者的不同(如投资者、储户或是监管机构),而导致反映企业财务状况的忠实度有所增减。

此外,尽管不能否认财务报表对投资者的至关重要性,但在现代经济中,如此多的实体运用"他人钱财"进行经营,故财务报告对更广大的利益群体同样重要。总体而言,高质量的财务报告,对储户及作为其保护者的审慎监管机构、供应商、债权人都非常重要。

事实上,在全球市场经济中,可靠的财务报告是构筑信任和信用的重要因素,也符合公众利益。这就是国际财务报告准则基金会在其章程第一段中便提出"服务于公众利益"的原因。

要贬低国际财务报告准则在公众利益方面的作用也不容易。国际财务报告准则已经在100多个国家得以采用,成为一门通用的商务语言,事实上,它也是唯一一套可能在全球范围内得以统一采用的准则。国际财务报告准则是经济现代化的一个引擎,将工业化国家与世界各地的新兴市场联系起来。唯有国际财务报告准则才能释放一个真正的全球资本市场的全部潜力。它可以通过提高全球透明度和流动性,为经济增长作出巨大贡献。这符合全球公众利益,能为此目标工作和服务,我深感自豪。

广泛讨论的第二个热点问题是:财务报告的目标应主要是提高透明度,还是既要提高透明度,又要维护(金融市场)稳定?

在讨论这个问题时,人们通常将透明度和(金融市场)稳定对立起来,作为两个互相冲突的目标。而我认为,二者之间的矛盾和冲突根本不存在。依我之见,透明度是维护稳定的必要前提,这一点不言而喻。当前这场信用危机在很大程度上正是由于金融市场缺乏透明度而导致的。(金融机构的)资产负债表表内和表外业务累积了巨大的风险,却未被人们注意到。如果对隐含的风险没有适当的透明度,维护稳定最终将成为空谈。虽然维护稳定并不等同于提升透明度,但缺乏透明度,就不可能有持久的稳定。

因此,会计准则可以通过提升透明度,为金融稳定作出贡献。为此,会计准则制定机构近期做了大量工作,通常都是与审慎的监管机构进行密切磋商:收紧资产负债表表外融资业务条件;提出趋同建议以消除美国公认会计原则和国际财务报告准则在金融资产与金融负债抵消处理方面的差异;建议引入预期损失模型,以及时确认贷款组合的损失。

会计准则的规范能够避免对资产负债表和损益表的人为干预,也有助于实现金融稳定的目标,这也是国际会计准则理事会对金融工具继续采用混合计量属性的重要原因。如果一项金融工具具备基本贷款特征,并以合同收益率为基础进行管理,那么,这项金融工具就可按照摊余成本计量。人们深信,对于此类金融工具,成本能够提供比短期市场波动(的市价)更为相关的信息。这种方法确实可以阻断那些无用的"噪音",但这并不意味着市场预期无关紧要,稍后我将对此作进一步解释。

会计准则对影响损益表的"噪音"保持敏感,采取防干扰措施,对损益和其他综合收益加以区分也是一个例证。虽然其他综合收益的定义还需要一个更加坚实的理论基础,但是,把那些不能真实反映主体财务业绩的损益列入资产负债表来避免业绩波动,的确不失为一种务实的方法。

由此可见,会计准则通过提供最大化的透明度以及避免人为干扰,可以为维护金融稳定作出非常重要的贡献。

然而,我们必须牢记一点,稳定应该是更高透明度的结果,而不是会计准则制定机构的主要目标。原因很简单,因为它们缺乏相应的手段。例如,会计准则制定机构不能设置银行业的资本要求,因为这项(政策)工具属于审慎的监管机构,维护稳定是监管机构的主要使命。

此外,会计准则制定机构也不能在不稳定因素出现时还视而不见,假装一切如常。坦率地讲,这也是在有些时候会计准则制定机构与审慎监管机构之间的关系变得脆弱浮躁的原因。有时候,会计准则制定机构甚至怀疑,它们被强求给那些价值内在不稳定性的金融工具(通过会计处理)披上稳定性伪装。

追求透明度是会计准则制定机构的天然使命,但这并不必然是审慎监管机构的关注焦点。监管机构不得不遵循严格的保密条款,对于他们关起门来解决问题的方式,希望人们表示理解。毕竟,最大限度的透明化,并非总是防止银行挤兑的最好办法。

更为普遍的情况是,对金融部门这类脆弱的行业,透明并不可能总是自然而然地自发产生。目前,要找出一个比银行业风险更大的商业模式,还真不是一件容易的事情。这是因为,银行的资产和负债都极易波动。银行的资产不论是基于衍生工具、实体经济抑或主权风险,对经济周期都异常敏感,3A级金边债券都可能迅速恶化,爱尔兰就是例证之一。银行的负债也非常脆弱,可以说是臭名远扬,因为轻点鼠标,资金就可能在瞬间蒸发。

相关方面似乎觉得这些风险尚不足为惧,甚至允许银行业以最微薄的资本保证开展业务。20世纪,银行业的资本缓冲已急剧缩减。在本次危机爆发之前,绝大多数银行的有形普通股已低于2%,在许多情况下甚至接近于零!

这种商业模式在世界各地一再引发危机就不足为奇。危机发生后,在多数情况下,银行都需要政府的干预或大规模预算刺激来救助。更为常见的情况是,金融业必须依靠中央银行提供的免费"原料"(人为低利率)来起死回生。多数银行都喜欢政府作出或暗或明的担保,以便它们可以按低利率融入资金,从而事实上享受政府补贴。实际上,在世界经济体系中,金融业是享受政府支持力度最大的行业之一。

现有银行体系的诸多缺陷正在逐步解决:资本要求正得以提高;承销标准正在改进;衍生品市场的基础架构将得以加强。但是,许多漏洞依然存在。即使在巴塞尔协议Ⅲ的框架下,3A级主权债务的风险权重也依然为零。然而,我们现在都应该清楚,不存在毫无风险的债务。新的杠杆比率为3%,虽然比以前有了很大的提高,但是,与我们在当前危机中所遭受的巨大损失相比,依然过低。

审慎监管机构不得不为这个内在不稳定的体系负责,这不是一件让人羡慕的差事。因此,审慎监管机构往往不喜欢迫使问题公开暴露的会计规则,对此我们也能够理解。银行监管机构试图为银行系统争取更多的时间,以便它们能重新站稳脚跟,这么做也无可厚非。我们不得不承认,这种做法在过去也偶尔有效。史上最伟大的央行行长保罗·沃尔克,回忆起他在拉美债务危机的作为,至今仍倍感自豪,因为通过掩饰美国银行业基本破产这一事实,他为银行修复资产负债表成功争取了时间。

然而,对于这一套路在21世纪是否依然有效,我深表怀疑。时至今日,互联网引发的信息革命、媒体的密集窥探,以及机构投资者和激进股东的存在,使得真实问题不再可能被长时间掩盖。事实上,一旦人们意识到监管机构可能无法掌握问题的真正本质所在,就有可能引发市场不必要的动荡。

2010年7月欧洲银行业的压力测试就是一个很好的案例。市场马上意识到,压力测试不够严格。产生这种怀疑的原因之一是:许多主权债券在市场交易中已大幅折价,但在银行账簿上仍按账面金额计量。一些爱尔兰银行通过了压力测试,其后竟资不抵债而破产,这一事实无疑佐证了市场的怀疑。

我也想知道,压力测试到底向审计师们传递了什么讯息。在本次信用危机中,不少银行破产倒闭,但在此之前,审计师们却对这些银行的财务状况给予了健康评价,欧盟委员会就此提出了不少质疑。然而,当监管机构也认为那些大幅折价的证券不存在风险时,审计师们又能发挥多少应有的重要作用呢?

顺便说一句,审慎监管机构对预期损失模型翘首以盼、期望颇高,目的是更加及时地确认金融资产损失。但是,当前对于有明显迹象表明已经发生的资产减值都视而不见,预期损失模型能否发挥作用,可信度又如何呢?

只有及时记录减值的情况,按照摊余成本模式计量银行登记在册的证券才具有可信度。如果这些证券的市场估值与其账面价值之间始终存在很大的差距,最终,投资者就会强烈呼吁扩大公允价值的使用范围。

事实上,世界各地的投资者都不太相信,过去几年金融行业已经正视自身所面临的问题。在这种情况下,市场怀疑气氛浓重,往往导致过度反应。由此可见,缺乏透明度将直接导致稳定性的缺失。

我之所以认为会计准则制定机构和审慎监管机构都应该为提升透明度而全力以赴,还有最后一个原因,那就是通过提升透明度、全面揭示风险来防止危机的发生,其代价将显著小于放任自流、事后应付的做法。即使事后应付与整顿无可避免,我们也不应该试图掩盖问题、拖延时间,而应该采用更好的支撑和应对机制来管控这些问题。目前,这类机制正在研究设计之中。

我将自己的职业生涯全部贡献给了公众利益,并强烈期望能与所有利益相关者(包括审慎监管机构)紧密合作,共同致力于公众利益。在彼此合作的同时,我们也应该尊重对方的使命和责任。

会计准则制定机构应继续致力于透明度这一主要目标。通过提升透明度,会计准则制定机构为维护稳定作出巨大贡献。而让金融行业更加安全地进行运营,这项艰巨的任务则属于银行监管机构的责任。我深信,通过更有效地应用透明度指标,将其作为预防性工具,银行监管机构能够强化自身职能,维护稳定。银行监管机构应根据《多德—弗兰克法案》(Dodd-Frank Act)等的强制要求,进行更加严格的压力测试,并定期公布结果。此举作用极大,有助于监管机构完成强制金融行业提高自身资本充足水平这一艰巨任务。

最后,我想就另一个敏感问题,即会计准则制定工作的独立性与经管责任之间的关系发表一些看法。

当诸位阅读国际财务报告准则的那些基本原则时会惊讶地发现,大部分原则都以简单明了的经济常识为基础。尽管国际财务报告准则自身很复杂,但实际上它的经济推理体系却十分简练优雅,牢牢地植根于常识之上。

与此同时,我们必须认识到,财务报告并不是一门精确科学。在许多方面,资产估值更像是一门艺术,而不是科学。许多资产并不同质,并且通常没有一个活跃的流通市场,因而无法获取可靠的价格信息。在许多情况下,资产评估涉及大量的判断和(或)常识。因此,意见往往有所分歧,属于正常。

但通常,会计争论并非出于真正坦率的学术讨论目的,而是赤裸裸的经济利益纠葛。将以股份为基础的薪酬支付计入企业损益,并不符合企业首席执行官的利益,这也就是为什么当会计准则强制要求企业推行此种做法时,会遭到他们的极力反对。

同样,对于公司而言,在资产负债表上全面反映养老金负债并不是一件愉快的事情,因此,《国际会计准则第19号——雇员福利》曾受到强烈抵制。虽然会计准则变化迫使一些商业实务发生了改变,但很明显,这些改变是有益的,它们将隐藏的成本或者负债公之于众。

会计准则制定工作应该密切关注合理的商业诉求,但面对特殊利益要求时,却要立场坚定、保持独立。要维持社会公众对会计准则制定工作的长久信心,保持独立性是一个不可或缺的前提条件。

与此同时,我充分认识到,独立性并不会自主自发地形成。国际会计准则理事会不应该被视作象牙塔。只有当广大使用者以及认可准则的公共机构具备强烈的主人翁意识时,独立性才会得到尊重。这是一项巨大的挑战,尤其是对于国际会计准则理事会这样一个年轻的组织而言,尽管它在过去很短的时间内已经成功地开疆辟土。

要在世界范围内强化国际财务报告准则的主人翁意识,我觉得要从四个方面着手:

首先,国际会计准则理事会制定的会计准则必须始终保持一流的质量水准。我们也许对具体内容有不同的意见,但是,国际会计准则理事会的工作质量应该不容置疑。

其次,我们需要一个一流的应循程序。国际会计准则理事会一直非常严格地遵守相关规定,认真执行应循程序,在全球范围内不厌其烦地征询各方意见。国际会计准则理事会将审议和表决过程通过互联网进行网络广播,也因此成为世界上透明度最高的准则制定机构之一。不过,我们需要进一步加强外部宣传工作,以确保国际会计准则理事会能倾听到世界各地参与者的声音,恰如其分地考虑他们的意见。在日本设立国际会计准则理事会地区办事处,就是我们朝这个努力方向迈出的重要一步。

再次,对会计准则实施过程中可能面临的挑战,国际财务报告准则基金会需要有一个全面的认识。虽然会计准则需要与经济的快速发展保持协调,但在修改准则的时候,我们还应该考虑准则使用者的消化吸收能力。

最后,独立性需要一个强有力的经管责任机制来保驾护航。国际财务报告准则基金会的治理情况正由基金会本身以及监督委员会审查。我相信,对二者关系的治理能够得到进一步的加强,我期待相关的建议,以推动我们朝这个方向努力。建立一个更具包容性的治理结构是非常重要的,在这个治理结构下,所有采用国际财务报告准则的国家或地区都能享受到充分的代表权。

我们应该不惜一切代价避免给外界带来这样一种印象:国际财务报告准则基金会被一小撮国家所把持。作为一个全球性的组织,我认为让所有参与者都具有主人翁意识非常重要。显然,让一个年轻的国际性组织发展成为一个同质化的、所有参与者都具有主人翁意识的机构,是一项巨大的挑战。在服务于公众利益的职业生涯中,我遇到了诸多挑战,但我却喜欢挑战。因此,作为国际会计准则理事会的主席,我非常期待能在未来几年带领国际会计准则理事会走得更远。

(张翔 翻译;乔元芳 审定)

中国与国际财务报告准则
——主导全球财务报告的机遇

2011年7月26日,国际会计准则理事会新兴经济体工作组第一次全体会议在北京人民大会堂举行。汉斯·胡格沃斯特出席会议并发表题为《中国与国际财务报告准则——主导全球财务报告的机遇》的演讲。本文为演讲全文。

引 语

这是我担任国际会计准则理事会主席一职后首次造访中国,能在这样一个久负盛名的场合发表演讲,我深感荣幸。

首先,我要感谢中国财政部会计司杨敏司长及其同仁为召开此次会议所做的大量工作。其次,我还要向担任国际财务报告准则基金会受托人的刘(仲藜)会长以及我的朋友、同时也是国际会计准则理事会理事的张为国博士致以谢意,感谢你们为实现国际财务报告准则基金会的目标和宏愿所做的努力。

本次演讲所涉及的议题均经过深思熟虑和认真遴选。从制造业到学术研究等许多领域,中国已经或者正在成为世界的领导者,并正在迅速重拾其作为世界最大经济体之一的历史地位。正因为如此,全世界都重视中国的声音、听取中国的意见。在会计领域,注册会计师行业持续不断地与国际财务报告准则趋同,中国取得了巨大的成就,中国有理由为此而感到骄傲。欧洲证券及市场管理局(ESMA)、欧洲证券监管机构以及世界银行等重要的国际专业机构也赞赏中国会计事业发展所取得的成就。

然而,我认为,中国要想成为财务报告领域的全球领导者,还有很长的一段路要走。如果中国确有成为全球财务报告领域领导者的雄心壮志和远大抱负,国际会计准则理事会将全力支持并为此做好了准备。

接下来的 12~18 个月是明确国际财务报告未来发展方向的关键期,在座各位嘉宾的重大利益均与此密不可分。现在是时候畅所欲言,让世界倾听来自中国的声音,并积极行动起来,为我们的目标而共同努力。

在进入主题之前,作为财务报告领域的一位新人,我想有必要解释一下国际财务报告准则基金会受托人选择我作为戴维·泰迪爵士(Sir David Tweedie)继任者的原因。戴维·泰迪爵士在他的十年任期内取得了辉煌成就,我希望我也能够带领国际会计准则理事会迈向下一个成功的十年。此外,我还将与各位分享我对国际会计准则理事会在接下来几年时间内优先开展项目的分析。

我的职业背景以及对财务报告的兴趣

我首先介绍一下我的职业经历,这些经历激发了我对财务报告的兴趣,并最终使我当选国际会计准则理事会主席。

事实上,在过去很长一段时间内,我已亲身参与财务报告事宜。此前,我曾担任荷兰财政部部长,在就任国际会计准则理事会主席之前曾任荷兰金融市场管理局主席。该局类似于中国证券监督管理委员会,负责监管荷兰的证券市场。

在金融危机那段最黑暗的日子里,我就会计问题做了首次公开演讲,强调保持财务报告最高程度透明度的重要性。诚然,会计并非完美无缺,但我强烈地感觉到,某些人试图将会计准则作为引发金融危机的替罪羊。

这也许就是国际会计准则理事会和美国财务会计准则委员会于 2008 年邀请我担任金融危机咨询小组联合主席的原因所在,这是一次非常好的经历。金融危机咨询小组的成员分布广泛、具有很好的代表性,其中既包括公允价值会计的拥护者,也包括反对者。

在经过激烈的讨论之后,我们逐渐达成一致,撰写了一份广受好评的研究报告。

直到此时,我对于会计问题的兴趣被真正地点燃了。我发现,会计这门学科根本不枯燥,恰恰相反,会计极具智慧挑战;会计人坐而论道,通过观点来说服对方,结果是各方更加团结,这一点与官场有很大的不同。

上述经历引发了我个人对会计学的兴趣,但真正使我认识到会计工作对于全球经济重要性,并立志带领国际会计准则理事会继续成为全球会计准则制定机构的，是以下两个因素：

其一，无论怎样高估维持公众对于高质量财务报告信心的重要性都不过分。作为政策制定者和监管者，我职业生涯的绝大部分都在维护公众利益，而我们所维护的最重要的公众利益是为投资者和其他资本市场参与者提供财务信息，帮助他们作出投资决策。但是，会计准则所肩负的公众利益职责，远比上述内容更为深远。良好的经济体系有赖于真实可靠的财务信息，以便保持公众信心，确保资本流动，助推经济增长。

最近的这场金融危机提供了一个真实世界的样本，很好地说明了一旦人们丧失了对于已发布财务信息的信任，将会发生怎样可怕的事情。

在很大程度上，本次金融危机是因为诸如信用保证标准、信用评级机构标准以及被银行广泛操纵的巴塞尔资本比率等经济假定自身的诸多致命缺陷而引起。即便是会计准则，也为资产负债表表外融资、对大幅缩水资产免于计提减值准备提供了可乘之机，但相较于上述缺陷，危害程度要小得多。

这些问题长期以来一直存在，但当到了投资者感到无法再相信公开发布的财务信息时，心理恐慌便蔓延开来，进而触发资本市场自由落体式崩溃。这充分说明，高质量的会计准则是维持公众信心的先决条件，否则经济体系就不能正常运转。国际财务报告准则所提供的正是公共信任和信心。

其二，除了公众利益职责之外，高质量的国际财务报告准则也是经济发展的一种动力。如果一个国家采用了国际财务报告准则，那就表明它公开承诺将保持最高的财务报告水平。因此，对绝大多数国家来说，采用国际财务报告准则，能够促使其投资回流、资本成本降低、国力增强，进而提升全社会的生活水准。投资者的投资组合也将更加多元化，并从不断提高的财务信息可比性中获益。国际财务报告准则能够促进经济增长，为全球化市场提供一个高层次的竞技场。除了国际财务报告准则之外，没有一套会计准则能够将东方的新兴经济体与西方的成熟市场有效地连接起来。

正是由于这两个原因，我为能够躬逢其盛、参与其中而兴奋不已。

虽然我不是一名训练有素的技术型会计专家，但我希望能够凭借自己的经验以及我与纯粹财务报告界之外的广泛联系，帮助国际会计准则理事会成为全球金融系统中不可或缺的重要一员。幸运的是，我得到了曾任英国会计准则委员会主席的伊恩·麦金托什副主席的大力协助，在国际会计准则理事会全体同仁的共同努力下，我们将共同分享国际宣传咨询活动和技术工作的成果。

国际会计准则理事会的优先项目

接下来,我要讨论国际会计准则理事会近期拟优先开展的项目。这些优先项目在很大程度上是由我刚刚提及的两个因素决定的。作为一个服务于公众利益、旨在提升经济发展的组织,最终的产出和成果就是财务报告准则。因此,我们必须保证准则的最高质量。会计准则的制定程序必须健全,充分考虑使用者的需求,获得国际的认可、理解与运用。

在我看来,应该优先开展的有以下四个项目:

1. 完成趋同项目

第一,我们必须与美国会计准则制定机构一道完成剩余的趋同项目,吸收我们从全球财务报告界中收到的意见和反馈,尽可能制定出最高质量的准则。这些剩余项目涉及财务报告中最为复杂、最为重要的一些领域。

意在改进国际财务报告准则和美国公认会计准则收入确认要求的收入确认项目,已处于收尾阶段。在最后发布征求意见稿之后,共同制定发布的收入确认准则将取代国际会计准则理事会与美国财务会计准则委员会各自的现行准则。我们普遍认为,美国财务会计准则委员会的收入确认准则细致繁琐,而国际会计准则理事会的收入确认准则又略显粗略。

租赁会计准则的制定工作也在有序地开展。此项工作一旦完成,将为投资者提供更高质量的信息,帮助投资者更为全面地了解企业因租赁协议而享有的权利和应承担的义务。租赁会计准则是我们遏制资产负债表表外融资的重要举措。

完善和协调各自的金融工具会计准则,也是近期一项迫在眉睫的工作。国际会计准则理事会和美国财务会计准则委员会都提出了预期损失减值模型。就在上周,我们双方向达成共识又迈出了重要的步伐。

国际会计准则理事会正在根据收集到的公众反馈意见,重新考虑套期保值会计准则,而针对投资组合套期保值这一具有挑战性的议题,也正在提出建议与设想。

尽管国际会计准则理事会和美国财务会计准则委员会签署的谅解备忘录并未涉及保险准则,但该准则非常重要,是我们工作日程表上需要优先开展的项目。保险业是金融行业的重要组成部分,而规范保险业务的国际财务报告准则却是一项作为权宜之计的临时性准则,这种状况令人无法接受。

我们需要确保上述每项会计准则尽可能完善,确保我们在作出决定之前,清晰认真地倾听并理解各方观点。我们不可能让所有人都心满意足,而这也是为何准则制定程序必须无可挑剔的原因所在。

2. 咨询调查趋同完成后的工作安排

第二,我们将制定趋同完成之后的国际会计准则理事会工作日程。在接下来的几周内,我们将发布咨询文件,阐述我们的某些设想,更为重要的是,我们希望通过此举来收集反馈意见。

您将会发现,我们精心挑选了许多问题,希望得到各方面的宝贵意见。例如,亟待补救的工作有哪些?如何最大限度地利用有限的资源?除此之外,在未来的工作日程上还有其他的备选项目。各方都在要求我们完成概念框架,以夯实我们工作的哲学和方法论基础。

与此同时,我认为未来的工作安排应该清晰地表明许多司法管辖区都应成为国际财务报告准则的新成员,其中就包括中国。这些国家对国际会计准则理事会提出了合理要求,正在等待我们的回应。

咨询文件所提及的几个可能开展的项目都与中国尤为相关,包括同一控制下的企业合并、外币折算以及农业。

许多利益相关者认为,我们需要进一步夯实"其他综合收益"的基础,明确与此相关的"转回"问题。各方对利润和权益计量波动进行没完没了的讨论,而我认为上述问题与此密切相关,因此十分重要。

金融危机期间,有一种主流的批评声音,认为由于会计准则过于依赖不可靠的市场信息,因而导致市场过度波动。这些批评者认为,会计准则制定机构不应仅仅关注透明度,同时还要肩负稳定市场的职责。

我认为,这种将稳定和透明度相对立的论调,本身就是一个伪命题。在我看来,透明度是保持稳定所不可或缺的先决条件。金融危机之所以爆发,是因为金融系统本身所蕴含的风险缺乏透明度,不易被外界所察觉。所以,会计准则对金融稳定所能作出的主要贡献,就在于提供透明的财务信息。

对于避免引发会计波动这一问题,国际会计准则理事会密切关注。与此同时,我们也认为"其他综合收益"所依恃的方法论基础并不坚实,"其他综合收益"经常成为处理疑难项目的"垃圾桶"。

如果国际会计准则理事会能够就"其他综合收益"和"损益"给出一个科学合理的定义,那就是重大成就。我无法确定国际会计准则理事会是否能够完全平息有关稳定性和透明度的争论,但我能够确定的是:会计既不是市场波动的根源,更不能用来掩盖波动。

3. 推广全球适用的会计准则

第三,我们必须全力以赴实现 G20 峰会确定的、过渡到全球财务报告准则的目标,因为包括 G20 各国领导人在内,上上下下各个方面都大力支持采用一套唯一的全球财务报告准则。我们应该如何做到不负众望,实现目标呢?这是接下来几年内,国际财务报告准则基金会所面临的最为重要的一项挑战,我们将极力争取最为广泛的支持和帮助。

鼓励美国采用国际财务报告准则,是完成国际财务报告准则版图的重要组成部分。目前,在美国上市的非美国本土公司已经获批可以采用国际财务报告准则。美国证券交易委员会暗示,在今年的晚些时候,可能会就是否将国际财务报告准则纳入美国的财务报告体系,即是否允许美国公司采用国际财务报告准则作出决定。

美国拥有全球最大的资本市场,其公认会计原则极为成熟、复杂、严密。因此,在我看来,美国证券交易委员会花费大量时间来确定恰当的转换方法合情合理。与此同时,美国的企业也希望在不久的将来能够得到确定的答案,这种心情也可以理解。

我们必须清楚,对美国来说,作出抉择并非易事。欧洲于 2005 年决定采用国际财务报告准则,理由相对简单:在欧洲共同市场中,不可能采用 25 种会计核算方法处理相同的交易。

美国已经拥有了成熟且高质量的财务报告准则。事实上,一直以来,美国的专业意见对于国际财务报告准则的不断完善起到了非常积极的作用。所以,对于以转换成本过高以及主权丧失为理由的反对声音,需要谨慎对待。我认为,唯一合乎逻辑的做法是:美国签发一份国家认可协议,批准采用新制定及修订后的国际财务报告准则,因为其他国家也是这么做的。

尽管作出决定是困难的,但美国国会作出否定的决议是令人难以想象的。美国的投资者在全球进行投资,美国的企业也在寻求国际资本,采用国际财务报告准则符合美国的经济利益。作为 G20 公报的签约国之一,美国已经反复表示对全球会计准则的支持。

但现在的主要问题是:如果相信财务报告存在全球语言,则国际财务报告准则是唯一可能的选择。

我坚信,美国希望继续保持其在国际财务报告领域的领导地位,所以,我认为美国证券交易委员会不会作出否定的决议。

对于其他正在与国际财务报告准则进行趋同但仍未采用国际财务报

准则的国家来说，我们的信息也十分明确，那就是加快趋同进程，全面加入国际财务报告准则大家庭，助推国际会计准则理事会成为一个更为全球化的组织。

4. 强化与各大会计专业机构的联系

第四，在尊重和提升会计准则制定程序独立性的前提下，我们将继续强化国际会计准则理事会与其他会计专业机构的联系，深化合作，确保它们以一种主人翁的姿态，尊重国际会计准则理事会为全球投资者所制定的准则。

中国在财务报告领域的领导力

在概述了国际会计准则理事会拟开展的优先项目之后，今天我想探讨的最后一个议题与在座的诸位密切相关，那就是中国在国际财务报告领域的领导力。

自开启经济改革进程以来，中国就开始探寻将满足计划经济需要的会计体系，转换到基于市场经济原则的国际会计准则。2006年，中国财政部终于颁布了一套全新的、基本与国际财务报告准则相一致的会计准则。这套准则是中国向国际财务报告准则"持续趋同"的产物。虽然中国所施行的"公认会计原则"并非逐字照搬国际财务报告准则，但是，通过中国证券监管机构发布的分析数据，我发现在上海证券交易所（使用的是中国公认会计原则）和香港联交所（使用的是国际财务报告准则）同时上市的公司，所报告的利润差异平均仅为0.6%。净资产的差异更小，平均只有0.2%。

中国非常有机会成为财务报告领域的领导者，在我看来，这甚至是板上钉钉的事情。然而，我不得不说，在付出了巨大的努力之后，中国仍未获得应得的国际认可。综观国际财务报告领域的发展，可以看到是美国、欧洲以及日本走在了前列。

在中国成为世界第二大经济体，并为制定高质量的财务报告准则投入了大量的人力、物力之后，为什么是这样的一种情况呢？

我认为主要有三个原因：

其一，虽然也存在有利的相反证据，但是，国际财务报告界对于中国会计准则与国际财务报告准则之间的相近程度仍心存疑虑。"主要规定与国际财务报告准则一致"这样的表述，对中国毫无益处，这也是巴西这个几乎已经挖掘了全部经济潜力的国家决定全面采用国际财务报告准则的原因。巴西相信，要使巴西成为拉美地区主导的金融市场，就必须充分利用国际财务报告准则这一品牌带来的全部利益。一旦一家巴西公司的财务报表被贴上了"遵循国际财务报告准则编制"的标签,无论投资者身处伦敦、纽约、巴黎、法兰克福还是上海,他们都能够清楚明白地读懂该公司的财务报表。

我们尊重中国作出的关于国际财务报告准则的任何决策,中国有权根据自身的利益决定会计准则制定工作。但是,既然中国公认会计原则与国际财务报告准则之间的差异已经如此之小,为什么我们不共同努力来消除这些差异?尼尔·阿姆斯特朗登上月球时所说的那句名言可由此改述为:这是中国的一小步,却是全球会计界的一大步。会计准则的细微技术差异,不应成为阻挡中国成为国际财务报告领域领导者的障碍。

毫无疑问,在共同努力消除细微差异的同时,任何对于中国是否致力于高质量财务报告准则的质疑也将烟消云散,中国也将因此获得与其经济实力相匹配的会计准则制定的国际影响力。

为了实现这一目标,国际会计准则理事会将深化与中国当局的合作,制定旨在消除现有差异的路线图。需要提示的是,差异消除工作并非只是中国的单向行为,国际会计准则理事会将会在接下来的工作日程磋商中,充分考虑中国自身的特有情况。"双向互动"模式是财政部副部长王军先生提出的重要思想之一,他早在2005年就开始负责中国会计准则向国际认可的会计准则的转换工作。

其二,我认为,国际社会没有充分了解中国对于国际财务报告准则的承诺以及国际会计准则理事会对于中国的承诺。如果我们双方采取一致的行动,对于国际会计准则理事会与中国多年来的密切合作,就会获得更多的关注。国际会计准则理事会国际活动总监韦恩·阿普顿(Wayne Upton)造访中国的次数要远多于其他国家。无论是在国际会计准则理事会、国际财务报告准则基金会还是我们下属的各类咨询小组,中国的利益都得到了充分代表。

但是,这还不够,还有很多工作要做。

我保证,在国际会计准则理事会的各类讨论中,我们将充分考虑中国的利益,而中国也会因为其对国际财务报告准则的承诺而获得应得的声誉。在接下来的国际会计准则理事会工作日程咨询调查中,中国的反馈意见与要求将会成为一个重要的议题。相应地,国际会计准则理事会也希望中国像在全球经济合作以及金融监管改革方面所做的一样,对国际会计事务发表意见与声音。

其三,在技术层面,我们还没有与中国建立有效的联系,未将中国利益相关者的考虑纳入我们日常的准则制定活动。在对去年收到的征求意见稿进行大致地统计之后,我们发现,来自中国的函件还不到3‰。我们还需要做大量的工作,鼓励中国的利益相关者直接参与或者通过中国会计准则制定机构间接地参与国际会计准则理事会的准则制定过程。为此,我们将进一步增加在中国举办各类活动的数量。

此外,不断涌现的地区性会计准则制定机构也是可以依托的平台。"亚洲—大洋洲会计准则制定机构组(AOSSG)"的成立,为中国和该地区的其他国家提供了一个重要的媒介,使它们能够一道工作,共同分享各成员机构的经验和观点,并与国际会计准则理事会进行有效的合作。

在亚洲—大洋洲会计准则制定机构组成立过程中,中国扮演了领导者的角色,在强化地区声音、加强地区合作方面起到了非常积极的作用。我非常支持亚洲—大洋洲会计准则制定机构组的工作,并对中国为此所做的努力与贡献表示赞赏。

结　语

非常感谢诸位的出席。中国实施国际财务报告准则的前景是一个非常具有吸引力的话题。

我希望中国能够积极参与刚刚提及的四个优先开展项目:以最高质量完成趋同项目;规划后趋同时代的工作项目;处理国际财务报告准则版图中迷失的碎片,督促尚未采用国际财务报告准则的司法管辖区尽快采用;加强国际会计准则理事会与相关专业机构之间的联系,鼓励相关各方深度参与国际会计准则理事会的准则制定和实施工作。

此外,还有一项非常重要的工作,那就是中国应该在已经采纳国际财务报告准则的基础上继续前行,以获得国际社会的认可。完成这项工作,对于确保中国在国际财务报告领域获得与本国地位相匹配的影响力至关重要。

在任期内,我将为实现这一目标而竭尽全力。

(张晓泉 翻译;乔元芳 审定)

会计透明度与金融危机

2011年10月3日,汉斯·胡格沃斯特在欧洲议会经济和货币事务委员会(ECON Committee)发表演讲。本文为演讲全文,标题为译者所加。

引 语

尊敬的鲍勒斯主席及各位委员,能得此良机与各位进行交流,我深感荣幸。我已卸任荷兰政府公职很多年,此时此刻再次置身欧洲议会,勾起了我对往日的许多美好回忆。

各位如果对国际会计准则理事会工作有任何问题,我都将知无不言。在接下来的演讲中,我将主要关注两个议题:首先,我简要地阐述国际会计准则理事会与欧洲之间关系的重要性;其次是发表一些本人对会计准则应担当的角色与金融危机内在联系的浅见。

国际会计准则理事会与欧洲的关系

欧洲与国际会计准则理事会的战略合作关系对双方来说都至关重要。

2005年,在采用国际财务报告准则的过程中,欧洲投入了大量的政治和经济资源。此举有力地推动了国际会计准则理事会在全球会计准则制定机构的道路上大步迈进。

在是否采用国际财务报告准则的表决中,458张选票中绝大多数投了赞成票,欧洲议会也毫无悬念地批准了该决议[1]。此外,欧洲议会还呼吁让国际财务报告准则成为全球通用的财务报告语言。

欧洲议会的倡议得到了广泛的响应,越来越多的国家紧跟欧洲的步伐采用国际财务报告准则。在美洲,几乎所有的拉美国家以及加拿大已经全面实行国际财务报告准则。亚洲—大洋洲地区的澳大利亚、新西兰、韩国、中国香港以及新加坡已经或即将成为国际财务报告准则大家庭的一员,日本已经允许某些国内公司采用国际财务报告准则来编制报表,而中国正处于会计准则趋同的进程中。南非和以色列也已全面采用。再看欧洲,欧盟成员国之外的土耳其已经全面采用了国际财务报告准则,而俄罗斯也正在朝这个方向努力。大部分 G20 成员国已经加入了国际财务报告准则阵营。

美国证券交易委员会(SEC)也将在近期决定是否将国际财务报告准则纳入其财务报告体系,以及如何实施。就 SEC 对上述事宜的决策前景,我表示乐观。如果决策结果不利的话,无疑将给多年以来的趋同努力造成沉重的打击。不利结果会延缓趋同进程,但不会致其停滞不前,而我认为这种情况发生的可能性很小,几乎不存在。采用国际财务报告准则的势头是如此强劲,重要性不言而喻,这股势头已经形成滚滚洪流,不可阻挡。

国际财务报告准则在不到十年的时间里就能取得如此令人瞩目的成就,这主要得益于欧洲建立的财务报告国际领导者战略的成功。然而,这并不意味着国际会计准则理事会可以心安理得地接受欧洲的支持,坐享其成。

这就是国际会计准则理事会与欧洲利益相关方进行广泛磋商,共同制定新的国际财务报告准则的原因所在。我们与欧洲财务报告咨询小组(European Financial Reporting Advisory Group,EFRAG)及欧盟委员会建立了良好的合作关系,与各个欧盟成员国的国内会计准则制定机构积极互动,认真倾听欧洲投资者、财务报告编制者以及参与准则制定活动的利益相关者的心声。

尽管此类对话频繁且密切,但我们双方偶尔也有分歧。欧洲有其自身的核心利益,但与此同时,国际会计准则理事会也需要考虑其他国家和地区的意见。此外,即便是在欧洲内部,各成员国之间、欧洲投资者与财务报告编制者之间也常常就会计问题发出不同的声音。

当各方不能达成共识时,国际会计准则理事会就有责任和义务对自己所作出的选择加以阐述和说明,唯有如此,才能证明我们的会计准则制定工作是兼容并蓄的,所作的决策有理有据,遵循了恰当的程序和流程。

我们将一如既往地提升那些已采用国际会计准则理事会所制定的会计准则的国家和地区的信任感,按照我们与欧洲之外的国家和地区进行合作的方式,继续强化国际会计准则理事会与欧洲的合作关系,这是我们作为一家独立的全球会计准则制定机构进行工作的优先选择。

金融危机与会计准则

第二个议题,我想谈谈会计准则与金融危机的内在联系。这一议题值得我们花更多的时间进行探讨。今天由于时间所限,我先抛砖引玉,相信这对进一步讨论我们的工作细节将大有裨益。

本次经济危机的诱因是商业准则的崩塌和宏观经济政策的失误。巨大的风险以不易察觉的方式在集聚,而监管措施又未能跟上,当这一切爆发出来时则为时已晚。众多的事例表明,透明度的缺乏,致使投资者未能充分了解自身所面临的风险。

发生这种危机令人难以置信,我们不能允许此类情况再次发生。要实现这个目标,财务报告将大有作为。

透明是将会计准则制定机构从梦中唤醒的"起床号"。最高级别的透明度,能够帮助财务报表使用者穿透重重迷雾,洞悉企业真实的财务状况。

会计职业界对维持金融市场长期稳定能够作出的最大贡献就是提高透明度,它是保证金融市场长期稳定发展的先决条件。如果缺乏透明度,维持金融稳定的种种措施都只不过是装点门面之举,只能任凭风险毫无征兆地积聚,直到为时过晚而难以挽回。

然而,保持透明度,就不会总能描绘出美丽的画卷。目前的经济波动,大多根深蒂固。德意志银行的首席执行官日前表示,"波动是新的常态"。"无风险资产"即便存在,它的美好时代也早已一去不复返。

如果波动真的成为新常态,那么,会计准则制定机构应该如何应对?会计师应该阻止投资者吸取经济波动的教训,从而人为地保护投资者,还是应尽可能精准并透明地描述这种新常态?在我所接触的人群中,绝大部分人认为财务报告应该阐述事物的本质,而不是描绘我们心中所期许的景象。如果皇帝真的没有穿衣服,那么,即便人们对于皇帝的新衣视而不见,财务报告也应该责无旁贷地给予披露。

然而,我要提醒各位的是,要求财会人员描述经济波动是必要的,但是,我们必须小心谨慎,不能让财务信息成为经济波动的诱因。有鉴于此,在采用何种计量方法上,国际会计准则理事会总是秉持实用主义的观点。我们知道并不存在唯一正确的计量方法。因此,我们总是采用混合计量方法,将历史成本和公允价值相结合。这就是我们为何在近期对公允价值计量准则进行修订、为非流动性市场提供新指南的原因所在。我们对金融工具会计准则改革谨小慎微也正是源于此。即将出台的套期保值会计准则将有效阻止那些以对冲方式管理风险的公司因会计选择而造成的会计波动。会计处理不应该掩盖波动,但同样地,会计处理也不能成为波动的根源。

结束语

各位委员,十分感谢您的光临。我们生活在一个有趣的时代,需要大家齐心协力,共同面对根植于全球金融系统的诸多问题。

国际会计准则理事会承诺,将一如既往地与包括欧盟委员会和欧洲议会在内的欧洲利益相关方紧密合作,寻找进一步深入合作的机会,为增强金融市场投资者的信心贡献自己的力量。

受时间所限,还有许多议题我无法一一阐述。如果各位有任何问题,我都十分乐意予以回答。

谢谢!

---

[1] http://www.iasplus.com/resource/euiasreg.pdf.

(张晓泉 翻译;曹宇红 校对;乔元芳 审定)

美国在全球会计准则趋同进程中的使命与担当

2011年10月5日,美国注册会计师协会与国际财务报告准则基金会在美国波士顿举办大会。汉斯·胡格沃斯特出席会议并发表演讲。本文为演讲全文,标题为译者所加。

引 语

这是我就任国际会计准则理事会主席后首次在美国发表演讲。所以,我先简要地自我介绍一下比较合适。

在我的职业生涯中,大部分时间是为公众利益服务。在担任荷兰卫生部长和财政部长期间,我的主要工作是对荷兰福利体系进行精简,改变其臃肿状态。为此,我和我的同事们付出了很多努力,现在,荷兰是欧洲经济状况最好的国家之一。

所以,在2007年,我认为是我离开政坛的时候了。此后,我担任荷兰金融市场管理局(the Authority for the Financial Markets)主席,该机构相当于美国证券交易委员会(SEC)。我很高兴能够脱离纷繁复杂的政治世界,投身到相对理性的金融领域。

对于新领域,我的确知之甚少!

金融危机期间,有证据清楚地表明,像荷兰福利体系的客户那样,银行业越来越倚重政府。

一直以来,银行都是在微利的水平上运营。只有在政府和央行或明或暗的支持下,银行系统才得以维持。

我一直想知道,为什么资本市场花费了这么长的时间才发现"这个皇帝没有穿衣服"。答案显而易见,那就是缺乏透明度。金融危机爆发之前,衡量银行财务状况是否良好的依据是"巴塞尔资本监管比率"。这些比率依据风险加权资产系统而制定,事后被证明完全行之无效。某家银行的巴塞尔资本比率为12%,看上去非常健康,可实际杠杆倍数高达50倍,众多的投资者被这些虚幻的数字所误导。如果人们能够定期关注会计数据,他们就可以发现,绝大部分银行的资本金额仅占资产负债表中资产总额的1%或2%。

所以,我认为把会计准则作为金融危机的替罪羊有失公允。其中,公允价值会计处理最为人诟病。我极不赞同上述观点,因为上述观点忽视了经济本身存在的制度性缺陷。

有鉴于此,我与哈维·高兹奇米德(Harvey Goldschmid)共同执掌了金融危机咨询小组(FCAG),为国际会计准则理事会和美国财务会计准则委员会建言献策,协助它们共同应对金融危机。我认为,针对会计问题的热烈讨论,金融危机咨询小组能帮助大家取得某些共识。

金融危机造成的创伤使我深信,亟需提升透明度,保护投资者。透明度和投资者保护,如同一枚硬币的两面。复杂金融产品的错买错卖是金融市场中常见的"杯具",因此,投资者需要切实有效的保护。正因为如此,增强透明度对于保护投资者至为关键。

高质量的财务报告准则对提升金融市场透明度至关重要。

高质量的财务报告准则能使企业提供的经营成果信息逻辑严谨、条理明晰、可比性强,是市场经济的信任基础。因此,能够当选国际会计准则理事会主席一职,我深感荣幸并深受感召。

全球会计准则的重要性

下面,我想谈一谈统一全球财务报告语言的重要性。

首先,我承认,在国际层面,如果有现成的会计准则可以借鉴,那么,在制定新准则时就有更好的选择。金融危机咨询小组(FAG)、证券委员会国际组织(IOSCO)以及全世界的证券监管机构认为,如果我们致力于同一个目标,那么,我们就可以提升财务报告的国际标杆,而无需担心对那些按高标准行事的国家产生不利影响,这也是G20领导人一贯坚持的主张。

与此同时,所有企业均采用统一、高质量的财务报告语言,也能够产生良好的商业优势。稍后,我们将分享福特公司是如何将国际财务报告准则作为一个重要元素纳入其"一个福特"的战略中。

通过国际财务报告准则实现标准化,福特公司能够使用单一的财务报告语言来编制内部管理报告和外部全球业务合并财务报告。

单一财务报告语言能够消除福特全球子公司财务报表的重编和转换风险,从长远来看,能够节约大量的成本。

认识到上述好处的并不只有福特公司。近期,阿彻丹尼尔斯米德兰公司(Archer-Daniel-Midland)、纽约梅隆银行(Bank of New York Mellon)、凯洛格公司(Kellogg)、克莱斯勒公司(Chrysler)以及联合大陆控股有限公司(United Continental Holdings)与福特公司联名向美国证券交易委员会提交了一封公开信[1],呼吁美国采用国际财务报告准则。显然,对它们来说,这是一个非常重要的问题,其他大公司也秉持这样的观点。

对投资者来说,全球财务报告准则同样能够带来深远的影响。20世纪90年代后期,亚洲金融危机给投资者带来了如火烤手指般的锥心之痛,各大公司的经营成果看似靓丽,却瞬间崩塌,由此引发了各界对国际会计准则的反思。很明显,全球财务报告体系需要进一步完善。

现在,投资者对国际资本市场的依赖前所未有。

目前,美国占全球资本市场的份额超过30%[2],而在1996—2006年间,它所占的平均市场份额为45%。其实,美国的金融市场规模并没有缩减,只是因为其他国家和地区,尤其是亚洲金融中心,逐渐成为全球金融市场的参与者,从而瓜分了美国的市场份额。

资本市场的发展态势要求美国在全球会计准则制定过程中发挥出关键作用。美国最大的公共退休基金——加州公共雇员养老基金(CalPERS)在致证券交易委员会的一份信函中表示[3],它相信证券交易委员会会全面采用国际财务报告准则,并且给出了具体理由。该信函最后表示,"现在,正是证券交易委员会有效提升会计准则质量、重拾投资者信任、提振财务报告信心的大好契机"。

美国投资者、财务报告编制者以及资本市场的资本提供者坚信,所有人都使用统一的财务报告语言能够产生巨大利益。同样地,证券监管机构也确信,如果不能使用统一的财务报告准则,那么监管套利现象将无法根除。

综上所述,我坚信全球统一会计准则以及美国全面采用国际财务报告准则的浪潮将势不可挡。

美国证券交易委员会对国际财务报告准则的考量

下面,我想谈谈美国证券交易委员会就采纳国际财务报告准则可能采取的决策。与其他已正式采用国际财务报告准则的国家和地区一样,对美国来说,这也是一项重要的决定。在美国国内,对将国际财务报告准则纳入财务报告体系争论颇多,意见各异。在我看来,有些言之有理,另外一些则毫无依据。

关于会计准则的质量

让我们先讨论最为重要的"现行国际财务报告准则的质量"问题。一直以来,对于国际财务报告准则与美国公认会计原则(US GAAP)孰优孰劣的争论并未产生多大成效。学界认为,国际财务报告准则和 US GAAP 都是高质量的准则[4]。十年间,国际会计准则理事会与美国财务会计准则委员会共同协作,使得两套准则的质量大大改善并不断趋向一致,在主要资本市场上都得到了很好的应用。当然,它们也各有优劣。

我不否认两者之间存在的差异,但与此同时,我也不认为两套准则有高低之分。

所以,我确信对于质量的关注不会成为是否采用国际财务报告准则的重要影响因素。

关于国际财务报告准则的实际使用情况

我听到有这样一种说法,认为只有少量的主要经济体采用国际财务报告准则。甚至有人说,由于《国际会计准则第 39 号——金融工具:确认和计量》中的 9 个段落可由企业自行决定是否采用,因此,欧洲的上市公司不会采用国际财务报告准则。但实际情况是,仅有不到 30 家企业选择不予采用那 9 个段落,在 8 000 家欧洲上市公司中的占比还不到 1%,其余 99% 的上市公司都已全面采用国际财务报告准则。

此外,一个需要特别指出的事实是,全球正在以令人惊讶的速度采用国际财务报告准则。在美洲,几乎所有的拉丁美洲国家以及加拿大都加入了国际财务报告准则采用阵营。在亚太地区,澳大利亚、新西兰、韩国、中国香港以及新加坡都已经或即将全面采用国际财务报告准则。而南非和以色列也已采用国际财务报告准则。在欧洲,非欧盟成员国如土耳其和俄罗斯都已全面采用国际财务报告准则。G20 的大部分成员国也已施行国际财务报告准则。

关于国际财务报告准则的应用情况

有越来越多的批评认为,国际财务报告准则的应用不一致,使得财务报表的国际比较愈发困难。

这种说法有一定的道理,希腊主权债务的会计处理就是佐证。然而,多套会计准则共存也会产生同样的问题。如果只有唯一的一套财务报告语言,我们的工作就是努力提高应用的一致性。我们承诺将与证券监管机构以及会计职业界通力合作,提高国际财务报告准则在全球应用的一致性。这项工作费时费力,但必须要做。如果没有唯一的一套财务报告语言,那么,财务报告的国际一致性就依然是无法实现的幻想。

对美国来说,值得宽慰的是,即便采用了国际财务报告准则,美国证券交易委员会也仍然能够保有全面的实施控制权。所以,执行不同于美国公认会计准则的会计准则,并不会对美国造成任何损害。实际上,美国证券交易委员会所拥有的丰富经验和积极参与,对国际财务报告准则的施行大有裨益。

关于转换准备与实施成本问题

众多美国公司对因采用国际财务报告准则而产生的成本心存疑虑。既然这样,我们就不拐弯抹角,直奔主题,看看会发生哪些实际成本。

可以肯定的是,会计准则转换期会相对较长,对小型上市公司更是如此。与此同时,对上市公司来说,尽早采用国际财务报告准则是明智之举,因为事实证明,采用国际财务报告准则能够带来可观的净回报。

此外,转换的难度不应被夸大。会计准则趋同就是尽量弥补国际财务报告准则和美国公认会计原则之间的差异。美国已经储备了大量的国际财务报告准则知识。一直以来,美国证券交易委员会都致力于国际财务报告准则能力建设,对越来越多在美上市的外国企业发布的财务报表进行严密监管。通过遍布世界的子公司,许多大型跨国企业已经积累了丰富的国际财务报告准则应用经验。

美国特许金融分析师协会(CFA Institute)已经为所有参与特许金融分析师课程的学生开设了国际财务报告准则下的财务报表分析课程。从今年开始,美国注册会计师协会(AICPA)组织的注册会计师考试将会对国际财务报告准则知识进行测试。

一旦美国证券交易委员会决定实施国际财务报告准则,上述准备工作将确保美国可以从容应对。如果巴西和韩国可以在短时间内就能过渡到国际财务报告准则,那么,毫无疑问,美国也可以做到。

关于主权问题

另一个反对美国采用国际财务报告准则的理由是,此举会导致主权的丧失。美国证券交易委员会的职员报告也特别提到了这个问题。但毋庸置疑的是,无论美国是否采用国际财务报告准则,美国财务会计准则委员会和证券监督委员会都将继续肩负有关会计准则方面的最终职责。

显然，缔结任何国际协议，无论是世贸组织还是国际财务报告准则，都需要谈判和合作。美国将继续深度参与会计准则制定进程，而美国财务会计准则委员会所拥有的宝贵知识储备，也是国际会计准则理事会无法忽视的。

美国不会丧失对财务会计准则委员会的控制权，并仍将对国际会计准则理事会产生重要的影响。在国际会计准则理事会的15名理事会成员中，有4位美国人，毫无疑问，他们发挥着重要作用。

在这里，我想向我的同事帕特丽夏·麦克康纳（Patricia McConnell）表示祝贺，她连续16年成为美国会计分析领域的首席专家，并入选《机构投资者》杂志全美研究团队名人堂"。帕特丽夏丰富的从业经验以及与美国财务分析界的良好关系是国际会计准则理事会珍视的宝贵财富。

如果美国证券交易委员会借鉴其他国家和地区已实施的认可机制，美国的主权也能够得到切实的保护。一旦国际会计准则理事会制定的会计准则触及美国的基础利益，类似的认可机制就会启动"断路开关"，终止采用进程。此外，认可程序还能确保美国财务会计准则委员会的主导地位。即便趋同项目完成，国际会计准则理事会也仍应继续与美国财务会计准则委员会以及其他会计准则制定机构紧密合作，这一点至关重要。

关于国际会计准则理事会的独立性

最后一个议题，我想谈谈国际会计准则理事会为了成为全球会计准则制定机构而做了哪些准备工作。某些评论家将这一过程理解为国际会计准则理事会遵守的应循程序，担心国际财务报告准则的工作程序过于政治化。

在2001年国际会计准则理事会成立之初，其准则制定程序在很大程度上借鉴了美国财务会计准则委员会的做法。从那时候起，两个机构不断完善各自的应循程序。

对国际会计准则理事会这一方而言，我们对重要准则引入了效果分析以及实施后评估，极大地提升了会计准则制定和咨询活动的深度和透明度。

在我就职过的各个组织中，国际会计准则理事会的工作透明度最高，会商范围最广。

至于政治压力，我承认确实存在，但这并非国际会计准则理事会所独有。在金融危机最为严重的时候，利益相关方对国际会计准则理事会和美国财务会计准则委员会施加压力，要求放宽规定。当时的情况险象环生，两大组织承受了巨大的压力。我们的工作会直接影响商业利益，而商业利益背后隐匿的是各式各样的政客。但我认为，随着国际会计准则理事会的不断成长与多样化,特定利益集团想要对国际会计准则理事会施加影响绝非易事,难度越来越大。

就我个人而言,我不会在离开政坛之后仍将会计准则政治化;相反,我会运用我的政治智慧,竭尽所能,使会计准则远离政治的纠缠。

结束语

演讲一开始,我就从投资者保护的角度,阐述了透明度的重要性。关于这个话题,我的同事哈维·古尔德斯米德(Harvey Goldschmid)会进一步阐述。我认为,在国际财务报告政策制定方面,美国证券交易委员会应继续扮演先导者和领头羊的角色,这对保护美国以及全球投资者的利益至关重要。

很难想象,在历经十年的趋同努力后,美国会否决国际财务报告准则,在财务报告这类重要问题上有意放弃国际领导权。

国际财务报告准则仍在不断完善。美国承诺维持现有的国际财务报告准则趋同水平,这就要求美国财务会计准则委员会将绝大部分时间和精力用在消除新的差异之上。莫非这是美国财务会计准则委员会的那些专业人才、专业技术以及国际知识的最佳用武之地?如果美国选择放弃趋同,那么,所有的趋同工作成果将会化为泡影,前功尽弃。在金融危机中苦苦挣扎的各国决策者们,并不希望看到这样的结果。

综上所述,我对美国证券交易委员会采用国际财务报告准则的前景保持乐观。

我相信,国际财务报告准则必将成为全球财务报告语言的唯一选择,前途一片光明,发展势不可挡,成功的彼岸就在眼前。

女士们,先生们,感谢您的出席,祝愿本次大会圆满成功!

---

[1] http://www.sec.gov/comments/4-600/4600-39.pdf.
[2] US Committee on Capital Markets Regulation, see www.capmktsreg.org/competitiveness/index.html.
[3] http://www.sec.gov/comments/4-600/4600-137.pdf.
[4] American Accounting Association Financial Accounting Standards Committee, 2008.-Karim Jamal.

(张晓泉 翻译;张翔 校对;乔元芳 审定)

美国全面采用国际财务报告准则是保护投资者利益的绝佳选择

2011年12月6日,美国注册会计师协会大会在美国首都华盛顿召开,会议主题是"美国证券交易委员会与美国公众公司会计监督委员会(PCAOB)进展现状"。汉斯·胡格沃斯特出席会议并发表演讲。本文为演讲全文,标题为译者所加。

引 语

自2011年7月担任国际会计准则理事会主席以来,本次会议是我出席过的最大规模的会计职业界盛会。与会人数以及通过视频观看的人数众多,这从一个侧面说明美国对可靠财务报告期望甚高。

首先,请允许我花几分钟的时间作一个自我介绍,谈谈我担任国际会计准则理事会主席这一重要职务的前后经过。

在我的职业生涯中,大部分时间是为公众利益服务。在担任荷兰卫生部长和财政部长期间,我的主要工作是对荷兰福利体系进行精简,改变其臃肿状态。为此,我和我的同事们付出了很多努力。如今,荷兰政府是欧洲为数不多仍保留3A评级的国家之一。

2007年,我离开政坛,开始担任荷兰金融市场管理局(the Authority for the Financial Markets,相当于美国的证券交易委员会)主席。我本以为,从此我便进入相对"理性"的金融领域。

前路如何,我无法想象!在政坛摸爬滚打十年之后,我对金融界几乎一无所知,很快我就迷失了方向。

金融危机爆发后不久,我便受邀与哈维·高兹奇米德(Harvey Goldschmid)共同执掌金融危机咨询小组(Financial Crisis Advisory Group)。哈维曾在美国证券交易委员会担任委员,盛名在外。

金融危机咨询小组负责向国际会计准则理事会和美国财务会计准则委员会提供咨询服务,帮助它们共同应对金融危机。这次金融危机的惨痛经历,让我前所未有地意识到:对投资者进行保护,最好的方式莫过于确保透明度。事实上,没有透明度,就没有持久的稳定繁荣。

正是基于这些原因,能担任国际会计准则理事会主席,让我倍感荣幸,同时也给予我莫大的激励。

我的职业经历和背景,促使我为实现国际会计准则理事会的目标倾注了极大的热情,这些目标包括:谋求发展与维持稳定;投资者至上;建立一套单一的、全球公认的、高质量会计准则体系。这样一套会计准则必须独立制定、一致运用和强制实施。

这些目标耳熟能详,因为它们与美国财务会计准则委员会的目标非常接近。2001年国际会计准则理事会成立之际,其结构和治理方式很大程度上参照了美国财务会计准则委员会的模式。

国际会计准则理事会是一家独立的私营机构,其使命非常明确,一切皆以投资者为核心。国际会计准则理事会的治理结构共分为三个层次,全面、透明的应循程序是我们工作的核心。这些原则也被财务会计基金会(FAF)和美国财务会计准则委员会奉为主旨,深深地根植于我们的流程和标准之中。

在国际会计准则理事会的运行过程中,美国扮演了重要角色,这是事实而非夸大其词。2001年,在创立国际会计准则理事会框架的过程中,美国证券交易委员会发挥了关键作用。此外,美国人保罗·沃尔克(Paul Volcker)还出任国际会计准则理事会受托人委员会第一任主席。

2002年,国际会计准则理事会与美国财务会计准则委员会签订了《诺沃克协议》,双方承诺致力于会计准则趋同。国际会计准则理事会的成员鲍勃·赫兹(Bob Herz)成为美国财务会计准则委员会主席。

在国际会计准则理事会中,有4名理事会成员和5名受托人委员会委员代表美国利益。国际会计准则理事会下属的监督委员会由5个公共资本市场监管机构组成,玛丽·夏皮罗(Mary Schapiro)代表的是美国证券交易委员会。

在当选国际会计准则理事会主席之际,我曾表示,将为投资者保护而不懈追求,把它融入我的DNA。显然,对于国际会计准则理事会而言,美国也是国际会计准则理事会 DNA 链条上的一环,有着重要的作用。

全球会计准则

为确保透明度和资本市场有效运作,高质量的财务报告准则必不可少。

1973 年美国财务会计准则委员会成立时的资本市场状况与今日大不相同。当时,市场参与者大多位于同一司法管辖区,投资者和财务报告编制者采用相同的财务报告语言。

从那时起,尤其是在过去 20 年时间里,全球资本市场开始融合渗透,市场依存度不断加深;美国投资者放眼全球资本市场,寻求投资机会,分散投资风险;美国公司寻求在世界各地的资本市场上融资,而美国资本市场则寻求吸引海外企业到本土上市。

由于金融市场彼此关联和交织融合,因而建立一套全球统一的会计准则势在必行。投资者需要来自世界各地的财务报告具有可比性和可靠性。要保护全球投资者,统一的全球会计语言必不可少。

这就解释了为什么美国证券交易委员会需要不断考量美国现有会计体系是否需要进一步完善来应对资本市场新变化。现在的情况也是如此。

其他许多国家也提出了同样的问题,并几乎得出相同的结论:采用国际财务报告准则符合本国利益,是保护投资者利益的最佳方式。当前,世界上 100 多个国家(包括 G20 的大部分成员国)要求或允许本国企业采用国际财务报告准则,而实现这一成果仅仅花了不到十年的时间。

国际财务报告准则的使用范围已不再局限于欧洲。在过去五年时间里,我们看到国际财务报告准则得以广泛采用,扩围速度惊人。在美洲,几乎所有的拉丁美洲国家都加入了国际财务报告准则大家庭;北边的加拿大和南边的墨西哥亦是如此,后者于 2012 年开始采用国际财务报告准则。南非和以色列实现了国际财务报告准则的全面采用。在亚太地区,澳大利亚、中国香港、韩国、新西兰和新加坡也实现了国际财务报告准则的全面采用。日本已经允许部分公司使用整套国际财务报告准则编报财务报告,并将于明年决定是否强制要求企业全面过渡到国际财务报告准则。

在新兴市场,国际财务报告准则已成为事实上的财务报告准则。这些市场吸引了大量的外来投资,美国基金经理在其中寻求新的投资机会,以使其投资组合更具活力。在"金砖四国"中,巴西已经全面采用国际财务报告准则,俄罗斯即将实现全面采用,而中国正在向这个目标日益迈进。

当然，在全面采用国际财务报告准则的道路上，一些国家还必须采取进一步的举措，完成最后的步骤，为此，它们密切关注着美国的动向。

美国的决定

我认识到，美国证券交易委员会在是否采用国际财务报告准则的问题上面临诸多挑战和巨大压力。由于美国拥有世界上规模最大、流动性最强的资本市场，因此，处理国际财务报告准则过渡问题当然必须慎之又慎。美国证券交易委员会应该坚信，向国际财务报告准则过渡对美国而言是一项正确的决定。站在投资者保护和资本构成的角度，我相信的确如此。

美国投资者已经而且应该在全球范围内寻求投资回报机会。例如，在提交给美国证券交易委员会的材料中，加利福尼亚州公务员养老基金（CalPERS，美国最大的公共养老基金）披露，目前，该基金在全球47个市场中进行投资。如果美国证券交易委员会要在这种国际环境下保护 CalPERS，那么，它就必须积极参与到国际财务报告准则的制定和全球实施工作中。要做到这一点，美国证券交易委员会需要投身其中。

今年早些时候，在波士顿召开的国际财务报告准则会议上，福特汽车公司的财务主管向与会者解释了福特公司支持美国采用国际财务报告准则的原因。

通过视频演示，他清楚地阐释了福特公司支持单一高质量的会计准则，而且国际财务报告准则是实现这一目标的最有效手段。

福特公司并非个案。最近，阿彻丹尼尔斯米德兰公司（Archer-Daniel-Midland）、纽约梅隆银行（Bank of New York Mellon）、凯洛格公司（Kellogg）、克莱斯勒公司（Chrysler）和福特汽车信贷公司（Ford Motor Credit）也与福特一样加入支持国际财务报告准则的阵营，联名向美国证券交易委员会提交了一封公开信（http://www.sec.gov/comments/4-600/4600-39.pdf），呼吁美国公司采用国际财务报告准则。

在合并财务报表和协调公司内部的国际财务报告方面，这些公司已处于领先地位。我认为，美国应该赋予这类公司选择权，允许它们采用国际财务报告准则编报美国合并财务报告，虽然参与公司的数量有限，但却能够为国际财务报告准则应用提供很好的实测机会。

我知道，在美国市场上同时采用两套公认会计原则，不可避免地会引发一些担忧。但是，如果这些公司的主要竞争对手都采用国际财务报告准则，则其财务报告的可比性将得以增强。如果竞争对手属于在美国上市的外国发行人，已经纳入美国证券交易委员会的审查范围，那么，财务报告的可比性将进一步得到保证。

从全球视角来看，尽管美国是在有限的范围内为部分公司提供预先采用国际财务报告准则的选择权，也能够向世界发出一个明确的信号，那就是美国承诺将向国际财务报告准则过渡。

现在，我的理解是，对于引进国际财务报告准则，美国还存在一些立法上的顾虑，这也合乎情理。其中一个顾虑就是准则应用的一致性问题。最近，美国证券交易委员会的工作人员调查并公布了财富500强企业的国际财务报告准则应用情况，研究结果反映了上述顾虑。

研究显示，虽然财务报表基本上按照国际财务报告准则进行编制，但存在一些不一致的情况，这主要是因为缺乏会计政策披露以及单项准则应用情况的披露。

这些应用不一致的情况也许在世界范围内普遍存在，但是，我们不能因此而忽视这些顾虑。会计准则制定机构和证券监管机构都认识到，必须竭尽所能提高会计准则应用的一致性。

国家及地区性准则制定机构、参加证券委员会国际组织（IOSCO）的证券监管机构以及会计职业界的密切合作，有助于提高准则应用的一致性。

然而，需要重点指出的是，只有在单一会计语言的情况下，我们才谈得上提高准则应用的一致性。如果不存在全球统一的会计准则，那一致性将成为镜花水月，可望不可即。

顺便说一下，即便国际财务报告准则在美国境内得以采用，美国证券交易委员会也仍将保留其拥有的所有权利（包括执法权），这一点毋庸置疑。将国际财务报告准则引进美国，施行不同的会计准则，绝对不会给美国带来任何危险。相反，如果美国能够实施国际财务报告准则，这将有助于国际标准的提升。

下面，让我们从国际会计准则理事会视角出发，谈谈美国财务会计准则委员会所发挥的作用。美国证券交易委员会职员报告准确地切中了主权问题，强调美国财务会计准则委员会在认可国际财务报告准则在美国境内应用过程中所担当的角色。

在世界大多数地方，认可模式普遍存在，其中就包括澳大利亚、巴西、加拿大、欧洲和韩国。

美国全面采用国际财务报告准则是保护投资者利益的绝佳选择

通过认可机制,美国财务会计准则委员会和美国证券交易委员会可以保留对美国会计准则的最终责任和控制权。此外,认可机制还确保美国财务会计准则委员会在全球会计准则体系中拥有重要的地位。如果国际会计准则理事会不与美国财务会计准则委员会进行深度合作,那显而易见,国际会计准则理事会将面临会计准则不被认可的严重风险。

与此同时,要让认可模式顺利实施,其中的关键就是要为"不予认可"设定一个合理且较高的门槛,确保基本上不会出现"不予认可"的情况。如果国际财务报告准则得到不到认可,为迎合各方需求而反复改动,那国际财务报告准则应用就没有任何成效可言。

国际会计准则理事会全面遵守应循程序,确保与国家准则制定机构进行充分协调,确保这类偏离国际财务报告准则的现象不会呈泛滥之势。

要减少诱惑,防止偏离,确保国际财务报告准则得以全面采用,方法之一就是国际会计准则理事会在工作的各个阶段,加强与国家及地区性准则制定机构的合作,这其中就包括美国财务会计准则委员会。

最近,美国财务会计基金会针对2011年11月发布的《美国证券交易委员会员工报告:探索可能的融合之路》,向美国证券交易委员会递交了一封意见函,此举引发了国家准则制定机构的角色定位问题。如何与准则制定机构进行合作,美国证券交易委员会的员工报告树立了很好的榜样。国家及地区性准则制定机构必须成为国际会计准则理事会的眼睛和耳朵,而国际会计准则理事会必须与它们进行密切的协商合作。

此外,我越来越确信,我们之间未来的合作将超越单纯的意见咨询关系。要让国家及地区性会计准则制定机构更积极地参与进来,我们需要一个更加制度化的安排。财务会计基金会意见函提供了几个选项,值得我们思考。

最后,针对趋同工作,我想发表几点看法。

我们与美国财务会计准则委员会的趋同合作收获巨大,国际财务报告准则和美国公认会计原则都得到了极大的改进,两者的规定日益接近。

因此,就此止步、维持现状具有很大的诱惑力。但是,从长期来看,维持现状会导致会计准则制定的决策反复无常、不够稳定,不可避免地产生解决方案的分歧,或者产生次优的结果。

让我们以金融工具项目为例,谈一谈其中的"抵消处理"事项。起步阶段,我们与美国财务会计准则委员会保持一致,但最后,我们双方的规定却不尽相同。美国允许银行在其资产负债表上按净值列报衍生工具,而亚洲和欧洲的银行却需按照衍生工具总额进行列报。结果是,在投资者看来,美国许多银行的衍生工具金额都要小于其亚洲和欧洲同行。

我们希望通过附注披露尽量缩小差距,但我觉得美国或其他地区的投资者会认为这不是一个令人满意的结果。与此同时,我们自认为国际会计准则理事会的结论对于投资者而言才是正确的。我相信,莱斯利女士对美国财务会计准则委员会也秉持同样的看法。

这是一个简单明了的事实,当存在由独立思考的专业人士所组成的两个机构时,他们有时会很容易产生不同的结论。

同理,如果我把国际会计准则理事会一分为二,要求它们各自独立地考虑10个相同的项目,毫无疑问,两个部门不会在10个项目上形成相同的意见。

我敢肯定,美国证券交易委员会也意识到,它的决策结果不可能与其他机构的决策完全一致。显然,要作出何种决策,这完全取决于美国证券交易委员会自身的考量。但同样明显的是,国际会计准则理事会以及美国境内支持全球统一会计准则的利益相关者,期望美国证券交易委员会所作的决策能够清晰明确,具有积极意义。

结束语

演讲一开始,我就强调,透明度和可比性对于投资者具有重要意义。在经济全球化的大环境下,投资者需要全球统一的会计语言,国际财务报告准则是唯一选择。对于财务会计基金会在意见函中所倡导的方法,其基础理念就是逐步引进国际财务报告准则。

这封意见函的大部分内容与美国证券交易委员会2011年早些时候发布的《美国证券交易委员会员工报告:探索可能的国际财务报告准则融合之路》(2011年5月,http://www.sec.gov)相一致。事实上,正如我之前的提议,认可方法是切实可行的。

同时,需要着重指出的是,任何一种方法都须具备一些关键特性,以帮助我们实现共同目标——一套全球统一的、高质量的会计准则。

我们需要为首次"认可流程"设定一个明确的完成时间表。此外,我们还可以推定,在应循程序完全得以遵从,国家准则制定机构广泛参与的情况下,"不予认可"这种情形基本不太可能出现。一旦首次认可流程得以完成,美国公司可以对外宣称同时遵守了美国公认会计原则和国际财务报告准则。

最后,作为我个人的节日愿望,我希望美国证券交易委员会能认真考虑其中的利弊得失,允许部分美国公司尽早采用国际财务报告准则。

今天,我们齐聚一堂,无论你是会计准则制定者、财务报表编报者、财务报表完整性检验者还是商业企业业绩数据研究者,我们都为实现全球自由贸易和资本自由流动而尽一份绵薄之力。在这项共同事业中,国际会计准则理事会所有员工将全力以赴,肩负起自身使命。

无论是美国还是国际社会,都十分重视投资者保护。在决定财务报告政策方面,美国证券交易委员会地位突出,但也有力不能及之处。我们希望能与美国同舟共济,我们期待你们的承诺,同样,你们也可以信赖和依靠我们。

女士们、先生们,感谢你们拨冗出席,预祝本次会议圆满成功。

(张翔 翻译;张晓泉 校对;乔元芳 审定)

纵论收入确认、租赁和金融工具

2012年1月23日,安永会计师事务所(Ernst & Young)在俄罗斯首都莫斯科举办了一场国际财务报告准则研讨会。汉斯·胡格沃斯特(Hans Hoogervorst)出席会议并发表演讲。本文为演讲全文,标题为译者所加。

引 语

这是我的首次俄罗斯之行,俄罗斯的人民、历史和文化一直让我非常着迷。

作为世界第六大经济体,同时也是当前驱动全球经济增长的"金砖四国"成员之一,俄罗斯理应成为一个重要的金融中心,但目前的情况还不是如此。

许多大型的俄罗斯公司到伦敦或纽约融资,但鲜有国际公司到莫斯科联交所上市。据我所知,俄罗斯正寻求解决这一问题的途径,打造各种基础要件,为建设国际金融中心而积极筹备。

在所有基础要件中,最重要的一个就是俄罗斯承诺:从2012年起,全面采用国际财务报告准则。尤其重要的是,俄罗斯正以正确的方式向前迈进:未对国际财务报告准则作任何修订,未添加任何内容,同时,也未遗漏任何规定,全盘采纳了国际会计准则理事会所颁布的国际财务报告准则,并要求所有公众上市公司全面采用。这些举措给人留下了深刻的印象。俄罗斯全面、明确地践行了它对全球会计准则所作的承诺。对此,我们表示衷心祝贺。

承诺一旦得以遵守和实施,使用国际财务报告准则的国际公司就可以到俄罗斯融资,同时,国际投资者也能够完整透彻地了解俄罗斯的财务报表。

为响应俄罗斯的这一承诺,在会计准则制定的全过程中,国际会计准则理事会将与俄罗斯的利益相关者保持密切合作。

现在,我将转向今天的正题,尤其要谈谈我后续讨论将涉及的三个主题。

首先,我将简要介绍一下国际财务报告准则的工作项目——我们已经取得的成就,以及未来的构想。

其次,我将谈谈自己对于全球准则前景的展望。

最后,针对俄罗斯等新兴经济体在应用国际财务报告准则过程中所遭遇的具体挑战,我想谈谈为解决这一问题国际会计准则理事会正着手进行的工作。

国际财务报告准则路线图

首先,让我们看看当前的工作项目。当前,我们需要完成趋同协议的剩余项目,尽可能制定出高质量的准则。

2002年,国际会计准则理事会与美国财务会计准则委员会签署了《诺沃克协议》,共同设定了准则趋同路线图。2006年,为完善和协调国际财务报告准则和美国公认会计原则,双方签订了谅解备忘录,进一步完善了趋同计划。

会计准则制定机构因其快速的行动能力,而为外界所称道。在短短五年时间内,国际会计准则理事会和美国财务会计准则委员会已经完成了大部分趋同项目,谅解备忘录中仅剩下三个项目有待完成:金融工具、收入确认以及租赁,外加一个未列入谅解备忘录的项目——保险合同。

令人宽慰的是,我们显然在所有剩余项目上都取得一定的进展。

首先介绍一下收入确认项目。收入是损益表的首行数据,对于每个企业都十分重要。然而,更为重要的是,只有我们制定一项正确的会计准则,收入数据才能发挥应有的作用。这个主题非常重要,因此,我们在制定该准则时异常慎重。目前,我们已经发布了第二次征求意见稿,意见征询期为120天,截止到2012年3月。

外界普遍认为,现行的美国收入准则太过繁琐,而国际财务报告准则的相关规定又不够详细,新准则将取而代之。我们需要各方的建议和反馈,以确保我们正确处理了有关问题。

其次,就是租赁会计处理问题。尽管这个问题困难重重,但却亟需改进。

对于许多公司来说,在资产负债表表外融资中,租赁债务所占比重最大。

诸位尽管听到了各种传闻,但我们从来都无意利用会计准则来扼杀租赁行业。租赁业务为公司带来了许多重要的经济利益,这一点不会动摇。

国际会计准则理事会的所有要求,无非就是租赁交易的会计处理方法应使投资者获得清晰透明的信息。然而,让我感到奇怪的是,租赁的相关信息即使就在公司管理层手头上,投资者却也无法获知,而不得不对公司的租赁负债情况进行估计与猜测。这部分债务所涉及的金额可能非常巨大。

国际会计准则理事会和美国财务会计准则委员会再次修订了相关建议,我们期待不久之后能发布征求意见稿以征寻公众意见。在此,我再次强调,如果想得到高质量的成果,诸位的意见和建议至关重要。

谅解备忘录最后一个趋同项目就是金融工具。在该项目上,我们遭遇了重重困难。我们花费了十多年的时间来制定《国际会计准则第39号——金融工具:确认和计量》(IAS 39),即现行的金融工具准则。这个项目进展到一半的时候,全球遭遇了80年来最严重的金融危机,致使这项工作变得更加困难。

国际会计准则理事会和美国财务会计准则委员会已经各行其道。虽然我们双方都试图作出最好的回应,但是,实现趋同越来越具挑战性。

从金融工具的分类和计量开始,我们就面临一系列的困难抉择。

我们的目的是制定一个全新的准则,以取代国际会计准则第39号。

在不到一年的时间,我们就完成了第一阶段工作,并于2009年年末发布了《国际财务报告准则第9号——金融工具》。这是一个高质量的准则,它减少了国际会计准则第39号的复杂规定,解决了"自身信用"的会计处理问题。

我们对外进行宣传沟通,开展意见征集工作,并根据反馈意见对建议稿进行修订。上述工作获得了各方广泛好评。

与此同时,美国财务会计准则委员会也进一步完善了金融工具分类和计量方法。

他们根据征求意见稿所收集到的反馈意见,将全面公允价值计量模式改为混合计量模式。即便如此,我们双方的观点仍存在分歧,但并非差之千里、不可弥合。

同时,保险合同会计准则也取得进展。我们越来越清楚地意识到,该准则与国际财务报告准则第9号相互关联,有些问题还有待解决。我们逐步认识到,只要对国际财务报告准则第9号进行有限修订,就既可以使保险合同会计取得重大进展,又有助于推动会计准则趋同。目前,我们已经着手这项工作。

虽然我们仅打算进行有限的改革,但毫无疑问,在实务中可能面临进行更大范围调整的压力。不管如何,潜在收益显而易见。我们将慎重处理,继续前行,将修订限制在最小范围内,只作绝对必要的更改。

至于资产减值项目,国际会计准则理事会和美国财务会计准则委员会在研究提出几个备选方法后,最终形成了一个可行模型。最近,我们双方同意将预期贷款损失分为三类,国际会计准则理事会的工作人员分别称之为"良性账户"、"问题账户"和"恶性账户"。

我希望我们双方能尽快推进到征求意见稿阶段。但即便如此,也需要正确处理,不能操之过急。

如果一切进展顺利的话,那么,国际会计准则理事会和美国财务会计准则委员会将在今年年底前结束该阶段的工作。

关于套期保值会计,我们提出了一个通用模型,获得了各方的认可。我们即将在网站上发布该模型的职员草案,确保一切问题都得到完全恰当的处理。

同时,我们也给予美国财务会计准则委员会更多的时间,仔细考量我们所提出的建议。我们深信,该套期保值模型能够直击现代商业实践的经济实质,为投资者提供更可靠的视角。通过纠正会计不匹配问题,该模型为投资者提供了一个更好的视角,可以清楚地了解公司是如何对冲其经济风险的。此外,这项工作还将建立起宏观套期保值会计的基础原则,这部分内容将形成一个单独的征求意见稿。

最后,我们来谈一谈保险合同项目,这是另一项棘手的领域。

2001年,国际会计准则理事会开始运作时,就认识到保险行业亟需会计指引,但国际会计准则理事会制定新准则需要花费一定的时间。因此,国际会计准则理事会建议保险交易继续沿用当地的会计实务进行处理。

此举所导致的结果就是,保险公司在报告经营数据时,会计处理多种多样,而且异常复杂。

投资者常常认为保险会计处理就是"暗箱操作"。由于缺乏透明度,保险公司就可以在其他金融服务领域以比竞争对手更低的价格进行交易。

世界各地已经形成了不同的保险会计实务,从而使保险合同项目充满挑战。我们正与美国财务会计准则委员会合作,力图开发出一个模型,将保险合同的财务报告水平提升到通用和改善的高度。我们双方承诺加紧工作,尽快完成该项目。

以上向诸位介绍的就是我们当前工作的进展情况。

那么,下一步该怎么办?

2011年7月,我们发布了一份咨询文件,就趋同项目完成以后国际会计准则理事会的工作议程征询各方意见。我们所提的问题颇具开放性,诸如:哪些内容亟需修订? 如何最有效地利用可动用的有限资源?

在未来的工作议程中,部分项目处于备选地位,显然需要考虑。

所有人都希望我们能完成概念框架,因为概念框架是支撑国际会计准则理事会工作的哲学基础和方法论。对此,我们将会认真考虑。

此外,外界一致认为我们还应考虑绩效报告和其他综合收益问题,而且呼声一直很高。但是,该以何种方式开展这项工作,各方意见不一。

有人主张取消其他综合收益,也有人希望保留这个项目,但希望我们能为这个概念提供更坚实的支撑。

其他综合收益是否应该重分类计入损益,也是许多人要考虑的首要问题。

通过2011年7月的咨询活动,我们认识到,俄罗斯等许多新加入的司法管辖区都有各自的合理需求,其中包括外币折算、同一控制下的企业合并、农业和其他许多问题。为此,我们不得不谨慎选择,以防列入工作议程的项目超出我们的承受能力。

最普遍的要求就是希望会计准则在一段时间内保持稳定,在某些情况下甚至还要求"某个非常具体的项目"保持稳定。然而,世界不同地区对"非常具体的项目"有不同界定,因此,一旦"保持稳定"成为现实,我们必定面临艰难的选择。

然而,我想情况还不至于此。因为在经历了过去几年的狂热修订后,即便不是全部,也仍有绝大部分利益相关方希望放缓修订步伐,使会计准则保持相对稳定。

全球会计准则的前景

我要阐述的第二个主题是全球会计准则的前景。

我注意到,在过去的十年,我们已经取得了巨大进步。国际会计准则理事会成立之前,各个国家或机构各自为政、各行其事,财务报告在全球范围内基本不具可比性。

自国际会计准则理事会成立后,进步神速,成就引人瞩目。现在,世界上已有100多个国家或地区要求或允许企业采用国际财务报告准则。

推动建立全球统一会计准则,是全球金融改革议程的重要组成部分,借此有望提升透明度,并在此基础上建立一个更好、更具可塑性的全球金融基础架构。

目前,G20大部分成员国已要求企业使用国际财务报告准则。继巴西之后,俄罗斯开始全面采用国际财务报告准则。至此,"金砖四国"中已有半数成员加入国际财务报告准则大家庭。此外,中国和印度也正朝这个方向积极迈进。

中国在很短的时间内便取得了长足进步,如今,中国会计准则与国际财务报告准则越来越接近。

中国要全面实现与国际财务报告准则的趋同,仍需迈出几小步。但我深信,对于这个取得惊人成就的国家而言,要完成最后几小步并非难事。

印度当局对本地会计准则正在进行大刀阔斧的修订,但要全面采用国际财务报告准则,印度还有一些障碍需要克服。然而,通过上周对印度的访问,我深切感受到这个国家迫切希望加入国际财务报告准则的大家庭。

谈到日本,为实现国际财务报告准则与日本公认会计原则的趋同,多年以来,国际会计准则理事会与日本会计准则委员会(ASBJ)保持了良好的合作关系。

作为对趋同的认可,目前日本允许本国大型国际公司采用国际财务报告准则编制财务报告。

几家日本企业已经这么做了,我相信,有越来越多的日本企业将纷纷效仿。

此外,日本将在今年决定是否从目前的执行日本公认会计原则转为强制要求执行国际财务报告准则。如果是的话,那么,日本什么时候开始实施?一旦日本决定全面采用国际财务报告准则,对如何安排过渡期,外界也存在一些争论。但相对于是否转换,这个问题倒是次要的。

接下来谈谈美国的情况。

无论我走到哪里,人们问得最多的问题就是:美国是否采用国际财务报告准则?如果答案是肯定的,那么,何时采用?以何种方式采用?

对于美国证券交易委员会的内部决策,我没有任何发言权。然而,近日,美国证券交易委员会首席会计师在公开场合表示,美国证券交易委员会将在未来几个月内就是否采用国际财务报告准则作出决定。

作出这个决定绝非轻而易举。在过去几十年时间里,美国已经制定颁布了一套复杂的财务报告准则。因此,对于过渡问题,他们必须慎之又慎。

这就是我支持美国证券交易委员会职员工作计划所阐述的认可国际财务报告准则一般方法的原因。需要着重指出的是,美国承诺将支持全球会计准则,这不仅是美国证券交易委员会的政策,也是美国政府的态度和G20的政策,而在这个集团中,美国的作用至关重要。

美国证券交易委员会在作出决策的过程中,必然会面临许多实务上的挑战。我也不否认,这些挑战的确存在。然而,我以及美国财务会计准则委员会的同仁已经明确表示过,以其他名目继续趋同项目,是一种不可接受的推进方式。我坚信,美国最终会加入国际财务报告准则大家庭,理由很简单,我们彼此需要,唇齿相依。

大力支持新兴经济体实现会计准则趋同

我想论及的第三个也是最后一个话题是:对于俄罗斯等已经采用国际财务报告准则的新兴经济体,国际会计准则理事会所提供的帮助及所做的工作。

国际金融市场呈现出紧密融合之势,但发展并不平衡。美国、日本以及欧洲许多地方,资本市场高度成熟,流动性极高。而在世界其他地方(如俄罗斯),当地资本市场正以惊人的速度发展,但起点要低很多。如果采用以市场为基础的定价,那么,这些国家将面临挑战。不论金融市场属于什么类型,也不管是发达经济体还是新兴经济体,单一的全球统一会计准则都必须能够得到一致应用。

我们已经采取了一系列举措,以确保在制定会计准则的过程中考虑新兴经济体的需求,这与G20的要求保持一致。

首先,我们建立了"新兴经济体工作组"(EEG),俄罗斯是发起成员之一。

新兴经济体工作组由国际会计准则理事会领导,并由中国财政部提供秘书长人选。该小组已召开两次会议,其发展前景令人鼓舞。

其次,我们还修改了国际财务报告准则基金会章程,考虑了更多类型、来自更多地区的利益相关者的广泛诉求。如此一来,新兴经济体就有机会在受托人委员会、理事会及其下属的各类咨询机构中更好地主张自己的权益。

再次,在伦敦、纽约和东京这三个成熟的金融中心以外,我们显著加强了对外推广和接触的力度。

本次会议得到了国际财务报告准则基金会的支持,这为我们的宣传推广工作提供了一个很好的范例。国际会计准则理事会国际活动总监韦恩·阿普顿(Wayne Upton)继续将新兴经济体推广作为重点工作,在过去的一年中,他先后走访了16个国家和地区。

最后,我们还就国际财务报告准则政策事宜咨询新兴经济体的意见。2011年6月,国际财务报告准则基金会在印度尼西亚举办了第二届国际财务报告准则国际政策论坛,来自会计准则制定机构、中央银行、监管机构以及20多个国家政府的代表出席了此次盛会。

结束语

女士们、先生们,非常感谢诸位能出席本次研讨会。目前,我们还有很多工作需要完成。一方面,我们要完成剩余的趋同项目,制定出高质量的准则;与此同时,我们还需认真考虑将来的工作议程,密切关注俄罗斯等新成员的需求。

在"国际财务报告准则"向"全球统一财务报告准则"转换的征程中,我们又前进了一步。

你们已经作出将全面采用国际财务报告准则的承诺。在此,我也要向你们承诺:在国际财务报告准则前行的道路上,我们将伴你左右,提供所需支持。

感谢各位拨冗参加本次研讨会。预祝大会取得圆满成功。

(张翔 翻译;张晓泉 校对;乔元芳 审定)

把国际会计准则理事会建设得更为强大

2012年3月7日,墨西哥财务报告准则研究会在首都墨西哥城举办大会。汉斯·胡格沃斯特出席会议并发表演讲。本文为演讲全文,标题为译者所加。

引　语

担任国际会计准则理事会主席的一大"福利",就是我有机会出访一些美丽奇妙的地方,墨西哥便是其中之一。

当年攻读硕士学位时,我的主修专业就是拉丁美洲研究。因此,对我而言,访问墨西哥一直是愉快之旅,从未觉得是件苦差事。

当然,墨西哥并不仅仅是一处旅游胜地。它与40多个国家和地区签订了自由贸易协定,成为全世界国际贸易领域最开放的国家之一。墨西哥的经济以出口为导向,全球化让这个国家受益匪浅。墨西哥拥有良好的商业环境以及技术高度娴熟的劳动力,从而成为跨国企业投资的首选地之一。

墨西哥决定从2012年起要求上市公司全面采用国际财务报告准则(IFRS),在本土经济全面融入全球经济的背景下,这一决定具有非同寻常的意义。从行业标准的经验可以看出,采用公认的行业标准,大大促进了商业经营的效率,对于财务报告来讲亦是如此。在墨西哥毫无修订、全面采用国际财务报告准则之后,它将与100多个国家和地区(其中包括G20 2/3 的成员国)使用共同的财务报告标准。

从今年开始,国际投资者将会看到相当"面熟"的墨西哥财务报表。

能取得这些成就,大部分功劳应该归属于墨西哥财务报告准则研究会(CINIF)。墨西哥财务报告准则研究会是国际会计准则理事会的重要合作伙伴,非常感谢你们长期以来持续不断地支持。

接下来,让我们进入今日的主题。

众所周知,国际会计准则理事会与美国财务会计准则委员会(FASB)的会计准则趋同项目已接近尾声。趋同征程,漫漫十年,一路走来,我们已经取得了骄人的成绩。目前,还有四个趋同项目尚未完成,我希望双方将来可以在比较短的时间段内完成这项工作。稍后,我的朋友、国际会计准则理事会理事阿马罗·戈麦斯(Amaro Gomes)将向大家介绍这些项目的最新进展。

那么,趋同之后,国际会计准则理事会该做些什么呢?未来几年,国际会计准则理事会将呈现出什么样的面貌?我们的工作重点将是什么?又应该如何利用可动用的有限资源?

在过去一年左右的时间里,国际会计准则理事会及其受托人对上述问题进行了认真思考。

最近,受托人完成了战略评估工作,国际会计准则理事会也对自己的未来工作计划进行了第一轮全面评估,评估工作即将完成。

如果您想了解国际财务报告的未来发展趋势,最好的途径莫过于关注这两项评估工作。在接下来的时间里,我将对其中最重要的元素进行解读。

工作日程咨询工作

首先,让我们谈谈工作日程的公众意见咨询工作。

国际会计准则理事会前任主席戴维·泰迪(David Tweedie)爵士过去常说,国际会计准则理事会对其工作日程没有多大的掌控权。

回首过往,情况的确如此。国际会计准则理事会在成立后的头五年时间里,主要致力于及时改进国际财务报告准则,推进欧洲及其他国家采用。随后的五年,又忙于与美国财务会计准则委员会开展会计准则趋同项目。

虽说这两项安排取得了重大成果,极大地提高了财务报告质量,但它们却限制了国际会计准则理事会的工作计划。

现在,这些工作大部分已经结束。自成立以来,国际会计准则理事会第一次可以相对自由地制定新的工作安排。

之所以说"相对自由",是因为根据章程规定,国际会计准则理事会在每项新国际财务报告准则或现有准则进行重大修订实施两年后,必须完成实施情况评估工作。要恰当、及时地开展这些评估工作,国际会计准则理事会必须花费一定的时间,耗费一定的资源。

除此之外的其他事项都还有待进一步敲定。为此,国际会计准则理事会针对未来的工作日程开展了彻底、全面的咨询工作。2011年,我们发布了一份咨询文件,提出了若干想法征求公众意见,更重要的是为工作日程寻求反馈意见。与此同时,理事会和工作人员还举办了多次会议、圆桌讨论、网络广播和其他推介活动。比如,下周五,我们将在墨西哥城的墨西哥公共会计师公会举办一场论坛。

为广泛征求全球投资界的意见,我们付出了艰苦卓绝的努力。

我们都知道,要鼓励投资者对某项会计准则的特定内容发表评论十分困难,尤其是该准则可能在五年后才会生效。

但我们毫不气馁,与世界各地的买卖双方分析师、研究机构负责人和基金经理进行了多次会晤。我们还举办了国际性网络广播,开展在线调查,调查投资者代表团体的意见,比如特许金融分析师协会等。

我很高兴地看到,上述努力得到了直接的回报,我们的工作日程征询工作收到了许多投资者的反馈意见。截至目前,我们收到的反馈意见比国际会计准则理事会其他任何征询活动都多。

这项意见征询工作仍在进行之中。目前我不想对咨询结果妄下定论,但是我们很容易地梳理出反馈意见所围绕的几项常见主题。

常见的反馈意见就是要求设置一个稳定期,对此我十分理解。十年前,世界主要经济体都没有采用国际财务报告准则。而现在,世界上100多个国家和地区已经采用国际财务报告准则。此外,很多准则都已重新修订。十年间,发生了翻天覆地的变化。所以,全球各地国际财务报告准则的拥护者都希望国际财务报告准则保持一段时间的稳定,静待喧嚣之后尘埃落定,这个要求并不过分。

由于世界大部分国家和地区都加入了国际财务报告准则大家庭,现在哪怕对一项准则稍加修订,也将影响成千上万的财务报告编制者,就像在平静的湖水中投入了一颗石子,激起层层涟漪。投资者必须熟悉这些新规则,审计师必须学会如何进行审计,而监管机构也需要强化实施。

而且,并不只是最终准则才需要进行消化。我们以讨论稿、征求意见稿等形式针对每项提议征求公众意见,都需要利益相关者认真考虑并在多数情况下给予回应。

这是我们承担而且必须严肃对待的一项职责。因此,我们在制定工作日程时，一定要对最需要改革的领域、最重要的领域进行认真挑选。做最需要做的事情，修订最需要修订的准则，而不是其他。

在完成趋同工作后，我们需要开展哪些工作？事实上，许多工作领域都是从咨询工作得到的反馈意见中总结出来的。

首先，几乎所有反馈者都一致要求我们完成概念框架的修订，因为概念框架是国际会计准则理事会的决策基础。当我们面对众多选项，无法作出非此即彼的选择时，概念框架有助于国际会计准则理事会作出使会计准则相互协调一致的决策。

此外，概念框架也是公司实施以原则为导向的会计准则时可供参考的重要依据。

现行概念框架合理有效地发挥了自身功能。然而，咨询工作得到的反馈意见却表明，我们应该优先完成概念框架修订工作。比如，计量等领域就十分重要，不容忽视。

其次，我们越来越清晰地认识到，我们正在遭受披露超载之痛。但是，披露超载并不能完全归咎于财务报告。显而易见的事实是，商业活动变得越来越复杂。财务报告的职责是对这些复杂的业务进行描述，而不是加以掩盖。

此外，并不是所有的披露内容都能为投资者提供有用信息。按标准模板进行的披露，无非机械地勾选项目，不能帮助投资者真正了解企业的业务实质。这个问题需要财务报告编制者、审计师、监管机构和准则制定机构多方联手，共同解决。

按照国际会计准则理事会的设想，我们需要确保披露要求恰如其分。自下而上，从局部到整体，确保首次采用会计准则时，每一项披露要求都确有必要，都能使投资者获得所必需的信息。

然而，从自上而下的视角来看，披露内容到底从整体上改善了财务报告的清晰度，抑或让财务报告使用者更加不明就里，更加难以了解企业的实际运营状况呢？

我认为，不存在简单、快速的解决方法。众口难调，同样的披露信息对于某些投资者而言可能凌乱拥塞、杂而无用，而对其他投资者而言却很可能价值千金、珍贵无比。把已经存在的信息从财务报告中删除，并不是一件轻而易举的事情。但是，从工作日程咨询工作收集到的反馈信息来看，众多反馈者，尤其是规模较小的上市公司，都把披露作为一个重要问题，它们认为自己所承担的披露负担过重,超出了承受能力。

然而,值得庆幸的是,我们并非毫无准备,一切从零开始;相反,我们在该领域已经出色地完成了一些准备工作。

苏格兰和新西兰会计机构、法国会计标准局、欧洲财务报告咨询小组(EFRAG)、英国财务报告委员会(FRC)和美国财务会计准则委员会针对当前的披露要求,各自开展了独立的研究。国际会计准则理事会将继续与这些机构及其他同行紧密合作,共同制定出全新的国际财务报告准则披露框架。

接下来,我们必须解决与"其他综合收益"(OCI)相关的问题。

当某些收益不具备特定的性质时,越来越多的企业将它们统统塞入其他综合收益。企业将收益作为其他综合收益进行报告,往往意味着企业经营出现这样或那样的问题,而投资者却往往忽略其他综合收益中蕴含的风险。

通过更加清晰地界定其他综合收益,不仅能够解决对收益波动及财务报告的无休止争论,也能够解决"转回"这个棘手的问题。尽管没有手到擒来、泾渭分明的答案,但我对其他综合收益这个项目非常期待,热情投入,希望能有所作为。

最后,理事会还需要考虑几个挑战性不太大的其他项目,包括农业、同一控制下的企业合并、恶性通货膨胀和价格管制的会计处理。

我们虽计划就此进一步展开圆桌讨论,但坦率地讲,前进的方向已经明晰。

当然,我也不排除考虑其他项目的可能性,但是,如果要使国际财务报告准则保持相对稳定,我们就必须对项目进行艰难的选择。

战略审核

接下来,我介绍一下受托人的战略审核工作。

众所周知,国际财务报告准则受托人近期对国际会计准则理事会的战略和愿景进行了全面、深入的审核。

国际财务报告准则基金会下属的监督委员会负责监督受托人的工作,它也同时独立地审核了国际会计准则理事会的治理结构。两份审核工作报告很值得一读。

受托人报告提出了一系列很好的建设性意见。

这些建设性意见包括:改进国际会计准则理事会应循程序的监督工作,

建立一个专门的研究部门。

然而,我认为其中最重要的建议,是要求国际会计准则理事会加强与国家会计准则制定机构、监管机构和会计职业组织的相互联系,并将这种关系正式确定下来。

制定国际财务报告准则,离不开国家及地区性准则制定机构的密切合作。准则一旦发布,就会在世界各地的司法管辖区中得到认可和实施。审计师需要遵从新发布的准则,而证券监管机构需要监督新准则的实施情况。

到现在为止,通过与会计准则供应链上其他参与者的非正式对话,我们已经取得了巨大成就。然而,现在是结束这种松散合作关系的时候了,我们需要加强相互联系,建立正式关系,打造一个更加有机统一的财务报告供应链。

一个有机统一的财务报告供应链意味着我们能够更好地确保会计准则质量。

我认为这项工作有两大益处。

首先,将国家及地区性准则制定机构与国际会计准则理事会更紧密地融合起来,强化合作,形成一个正式的联络网,可以让它们在准则制定的早期阶段就参与进来,这对我们开展全球准则制定大有裨益。

通过这种形式,国际会计准则理事会可以更加包容的方式开展工作,可与国家会计准则制定机构一道共同承担研究、实地测试和宣传活动这些"繁重任务"。此外,在考虑棘手问题时,国际会计准则理事会还可以召集更多的人才,集思广益。同样,这种方式还能建立一个更加正式的机制,为我们的准则制定工作吸纳更多的建议,集众家之所长。

这种网络化的工作机制具备相当潜力,可以提高会计准则质量,减少国际会计准则理事会及其他准则制定机构之间的重复劳动,降低某项特定准则不被认可的风险。

这就是拉美会计准则制定集团(GLASS)的成立对国际会计准则理事会具有重要意义的原因。因为它有望提供一个区域性论坛平台,通过这个平台,国家主管部门可相互交流意见与看法。我们非常期望这项举措能获得成功,取得实效。

其次,这种网络化工作机制还将为财务报告供应链上的所有参与者提供一种合作机制,促进国际财务报告准则得到更加连贯一致的运用。

统一的全球会计准则,只是提供了一个基准,这套会计准则更加需要在全球范围内一致地得到认可、实施、审计及执行。这种网络化工作机制将为证券及审计监管机构、会计职业界以及国际会计准则理事会提供一个论坛,讨论提升一致性的方式方法,解决分歧与矛盾。

无论从哪方面来看,这种网络化工作机制都是全球会计准则拼图中缺失的一块图片。

但是,组建这个网络同样充满挑战。

成员的吸收标准是什么?当提及"国家会计准则制定机构"时,大部分人明白我们意之所指。

然而,不同国家对"国家会计准则制定机构"的设置差异颇大。像美国财务会计准则委员会或墨西哥财务报告准则研究会,它们是完全独立的机构,而另外一些国家的会计准则制定机构却隶属于财政部或中央银行。

对于从墨西哥财务报告准则研究会这类国家准则制定机构,以及从拉美会计准则制定集团等区域性准则制定机构获取的不同意见,我们应该如何进行平衡?此外,像欧洲财务报告咨询小组这类机构,它们虽然不是准则制定机构,但在认可国际财务报告准则上发挥着显著作用,对于它们的意见,我们又该如何处理?

这个网络与国际会计准则理事会之间应该如何互动交流?它是否应该采取技术咨询委员会的形式,与现有的国际财务报告准则咨询委员会采用相似的结构形式,还是应该创建其他机制?

这些都是我们面临的挑战,需要在未来几个月内着手解决。但是,我确信,要实现全球统一财务报告准则目标,建立这样一个有机统一的财务报告供应链必不可少。

结束语

女士们、先生们,非常感谢您认真的倾听。我们尚有很多重要工作需要完成,而墨西哥作为G20的轮值主席国,你们的支持对我们而言非常重要。

未来几年,国际会计准则理事会最重要的目标和挑战是什么?今天,我在这里与你们分享了我的个人观点。我们未来的工作安排日渐清晰。我们衷心地期望,财务报告供应链各方参与者之间能建立更加紧密、更加牢固的联系,帮助我们开发出高质量的、全球范围内一致实施的财务报告准则。

感谢各位拨冗出席,衷心预祝本次大会圆满成功。

(张翔 翻译;曹宇红 校对;乔元芳 审定)

国际会计准则理事会未来展望

2012年4月4日,韩国会计准则委员会(KASB)和韩国会计学院在韩国首尔联合举办研讨会。汉斯·胡格沃斯特出席会议并发表演讲。本文为演讲全文,标题为译者所加。

引　语

女士们、先生们,尊敬的各位来宾,能有机会出席本次论坛,与在座业内杰出人士进行交流,我倍感荣幸。

我要感谢国际财务报告准则基金会受托人委员会委员郑德龟以及韩国注册会计师协会主席OuHyung Kwon,两位的开场致辞令人鼓舞。

同时,我还想感谢国际会计准则理事会新任理事钟吾苏先生的建设性意见。今后,钟吾苏先生将与我们共同工作,这也是国际会计准则理事会的一大幸事。

自九个月前出任国际会计准则理事会主席以来,这是我第二次访问韩国,也是我的第五次亚洲之行。在过去的六个月中,我访问亚洲的次数超过包括美国在内的其他任何地区。我相信,对于大多数国际会计准则理事会理事和高级工作人员而言,情况也是如此。

这种状况并不令人惊讶。国际会计准则理事会正在坚定前行,力求成为全球会计准则制定机构,这就意味着我们要确保不偏不倚地倾听世界各地的意见。全世界经济增长最快的国家多位于亚洲,我们需确保所制定的准则能满足亚洲国家之所需。

我们可以通过多种方式开展这项工作。

首先，在国家层面，我们与当地机构，如韩国会计准则委员会以及韩国注册会计师协会，保持了非常紧密的合作关系。在钟吾苏先生就任国际会计准则理事会理事后，这一合作关系将得到进一步的加强。

其次，在地区层面，我们与亚洲—大洋洲准则制定机构组（AOSSG）开展合作，了解这个地区的总体意见和想法。亚洲—大洋洲准则制定机构组已经成立并运行数年，成为国际会计准则理事会非常得力的宣传推广者。今年晚些时候，国际会计准则理事会将在伦敦以外开设首家海外办事处。该办事处位于日本东京，各部门员工已全部到位，能够满足整个亚洲—大洋洲地区的服务需求。

最后，我们建立了新兴经济体工作组（EEG），韩国是创始成员之一。

新兴经济体工作组由国际会计准则理事会国际活动总监韦恩·阿普顿（Wayne Upton）领导，他今天也一并出席了本次论坛。新兴经济体工作组是一个非常重要的组织，它提供了绝佳的论坛平台，帮助我们了解在实施国际财务报告准则的特定要求（如公允价值计量）时新兴经济体所面临的挑战。总体来看，通过上述途径，韩国的利益在我们各级组织中都得到了很好的体现和表达。

现在，让我们切入今天的主题。众所周知，国际会计准则理事会与美国财务会计准则委员会的会计准则趋同项目即将完成。趋同征程，漫漫十年，一路走来，我们双方取得巨大成就。目前，我们还有四个趋同项目有待完成，分别是租赁、收入确认、金融工具和保险会计处理。

我希望双方可以在比较短的时间内完成这项工作。但我也明白，对于会计事务而言，即便希望"短时间"完成，其实也可能需要较长的时间才能结束。

我认为，如果美国证券交易委员会能就美国采用国际财务报告准则问题作出及时肯定的决策，那么，剩余的趋同项目将得以快速推进。毋庸置疑，我非常期待那一时刻的到来。

那么，接下来该做什么呢？未来几年，国际会计准则理事会将面临什么样的局面？我们的工作重点将是什么？我们应该如何使用可动用的有限资源？

在过去一年多时间里，国际会计准则理事会及国际财务报告准则基金会受托人委员会对上述问题进行了认真思考。

最近，受托人委员会完成了战略评估工作，国际会计准则理事会也针对未来工作计划开展了第一轮公众意见征询活动,该项工作即将完成。

今天,我想重点谈一谈意见征询工作可能得到的成果。

国际会计准则理事会的未来工作日程

2011年,我们发布了一份征询意见文件,提出了若干想法征求公众意见,但更重要的是为国际会计准则理事会的未来工作日程征求各方意见。

与此同时,国际会计准则理事会及其职员还为此举办了多次会议、圆桌讨论、网络广播和其他宣传活动。尽管意见征询工作尚未结束,但我们发现,反馈意见主要集中在几个共同的主题。

最常见的反馈意见就是要求国际财务报告准则在一段时间内保持相对稳定。虽然我认为这不太可能实现,但我还是能够理解这种要求和呼声。十年前,世界主要经济体几乎都没有采用国际财务报告准则。而现在,世界上100多个国家和地区已经采用国际财务报告准则,同时,很多准则都进行了重新修订。十年的时间,发生了如此翻天覆地的变化。所以,全球会计界人士都希望会计准则能相对稳定,一切悬而未决的问题都能尘埃落定,这个要求并不过分。

这就是我们在确定工作日程时,为什么一定要对需要改革的最重要的领域进行认真筛选。我们需要集中精力,专心做那些最需要做的事情,修订最需要修订的内容。

在完成趋同项目后,我们需要开展哪些工作?从咨询工作收集到的反馈意见中,我们自然而然地总结出不少未来需要开展工作的领域。

首先,几乎所有反馈者都要求我们完成概念框架的修订工作。这个框架是国际会计准则理事会的决策基础。当我们面对众多选项,不能作出非此即彼的抉择时,该框架有助于国际会计准则理事会作出决断,保持各项准则相互协调一致。此外,该框架也是公司实施以原则为导向的会计准则时的重要参考。

现有的概念框架合理有效地发挥了自身功能。但是,客观地讲,"计量"等领域仍然不够完善。我想大家很容易理解其中的原因,毕竟,计量是会计核算中主观判断性最强、最难以处理,也是政治色彩最浓的部分。

我们要使会计计量更加严格规范、清晰明确,但这将是一项极其艰巨的任务,需要集思广益、勇敢开拓。

其次,不少成员抱怨披露负担过重。然而,这些负担并不能完全归咎于财务报告。

　　显而易见的事实是，商业活动越来越复杂，财务报告的职责就是描述这些复杂性，而不是掩盖它们。

　　当然，也不是所有披露都能为投资者提供有用信息。按标准模板进行的披露，无非机械地勾选项目，不能帮助投资者真正了解企业的业务实质。这个问题需要财务报告编制者、审计师、监管机构和准则制定机构多方联手，共同解决。

　　按照国际会计准则理事会的愿望，我们需要确保披露要求恰如其分。自下而上，从局部到整体，确保首次采用会计准则时，每一项披露要求都确有必要，都能使投资者获得所必需的信息。然而，从自上而下的视角来看，披露内容到底从整体上改善了财务报告的清晰度，抑或是让财务报告使用者更加不明就里，更加难以了解企业的实际运营状况？

　　国际会计准则理事会咨询委员会最近一次会议取得了丰硕的成果，与会各方就披露事项惊人地达成了共识，大家一致认为处理披露问题不可能一蹴而就。

　　众口难调，同样的披露信息对于某些投资者而言可能凌乱拥塞、杂而无用，而对其他投资者而言却很可能价值千金、珍贵无比。把已经存在的信息从财务报告中删除，并不是一件轻而易举的事。但是，从工作日程咨询工作收集到的反馈信息来看，众多反馈者，尤其是规模较小的上市公司，都把披露作为一个重要问题，它们认为自己所承担的披露负担过重，超出了承受能力。

　　然而，值得庆幸的是，我们并非毫无准备，一切从零开始；相反，全球各地的一些会计准则制定机构已经出色地完成了部分准备工作，这有助于我们评估和反思现有披露方式。

　　接下来，我们必须解决"其他综合收益"（OCI）问题。几乎所有人都要求我们更加明确地阐释：什么是其他综合收益？其他综合收益包括哪些项目？它与损益是什么关系？已经计入其他综合收益的项目是否允许转回，再计入损益？

　　过去一年，各方围绕其他综合收益展开了激烈的讨论。然而，让我吃惊的是，追求高额损益的企业往往希望将尽可能多的项目纳入其他综合收益。

　　当然，前提条件必须是计入其他综合收益的项目能够及时转回，再计入损益。今天，我无法预计这些提议将带来什么样的结果，我只能说，损益和其他综合收益并存，往往可能产生适得其反的结果。

我认为，尽管与损益相比，其他综合收益具有较大的不确定性，但我们不应当把其他综合收益视为无关紧要的数字，隐藏在附注之中。

其他综合收益并不是没有存在的意义。尤其对于金融机构而言，它们的资产负债表构成复杂、数额巨大，其他综合收益能够承载非常重要的信息，是反映资产负债表质量的重要指标。

对投资者来说，即使利得或损失尚未实现，了解资产负债表中的利得或损失也非常重要。其他综合收益能够提供资产和负债之间的期限错配信息，也是利率波动的敏感信号。

由于控制资产负债表的波动是金融机构管理层的核心任务，因此，其他综合收益可以作为一项非常重要的业绩指标。

我们必须更加明确地界定"其他综合收益"，同时，还需解决"转回"这个棘手的问题。在世界各地，许多机构都支持计入其他综合收益的项目"转回"计入损益，主要理由就是，通过转回可以确保损益总额最终与现金流量总额相等。

这是一个非常具有说服力的论据。尽管如此，国际会计准则理事会从未倾向于将其他综合收益转回计入损益，主要原因之一就是，企业可以控制利得和损失的实现时间，从而为盈余管理留下空间。正是因为如此，在允许转回时，投资者通常需要分析研究转回前的损益情况。因为投资者明白，转回能够掩饰主体的真实业绩。

我相信，在未来几年内，我们还会就这个问题展开有趣而激烈的讨论。

我对这个议题兴趣十足，并十分期待能尽快开展这项工作。如果我们能为其他综合收益提供更坚实的理论基础，我确信，其他综合收益作为一项绩效指标，对投资者的有用性将得以提高。

除了这些重大项目外，我们可能还将考虑一些重要性稍次的项目，比如农业、同一控制下的企业合并、恶性通货膨胀和价格管制行业。

我们必须限定工作内容。过去几年的经验表明，在同一时间尝试开展过多工作，往往得不偿失。与此同时，对于世界不同地区所面对的问题，我们不可能将其束之高阁，推迟三年再处理。比如，我清楚地意识到，韩国非常希望国际会计准则理事会能修订外币折算准则。

这就是为什么我们决定在国际会计准则理事会技术活动高级总监艾伦·特谢拉（Alan Teixeira）的领导下，为我们的工作计划增加一个"研究阶段"的原因所在。研究阶段指的是项目的初选阶段,只有通过研究阶段的项目才能列为国际会计准则理事会工作计划的待选项目。

然而,对于在伦敦堪农街30号设立国际财务报告准则大学一事,我们没有任何计划,既没措施,也无设想。我们能做的就是界定研究工作的标准,邀请其他会计准则制定机构与我们合作,共同开展研究,公布研究发现。

外币折算就是一个很好的例子,它有可能列入国际会计准则理事会的研究计划。针对这个议题,韩国会计准则委员会和国际会计准则理事会紧急问题工作小组已经开展了大量卓有成效的研究工作。然而,我意识到,关于应该如何推进这个项目,各方观点尚未统一。

我们将参考韩国会计准则委员会和其他机构的研究成果,并在国际会计准则理事会研究计划的指导下,进一步深化该项研究。事实上,我们可能要求韩国会计准则委员会承担繁重的改进工作,这些改进工作通常发生在准则制定工作的讨论稿阶段。这将帮助我们在准则制定过程中,尽早了解有关国家及行业的观点。

有了研究阶段,一旦某个项目列入国际会计准则理事会的工作计划,既能缩减国际财务报告准则新准则的开发时间,同时也不会增加国际会计准则理事会的工作负担。

在研究阶段,其他会计准则制定机构可在国际会计准则理事会设定的标准范围内参与调研工作。我们在工作流程中引入该阶段,就是一个很好的例子,表明我们期望能与韩国会计准则委员会等机构建立正式关系,加强合作。

结束语

女士们、先生们,非常感谢诸位的认真倾听。我们有重要的工作需要完成,而你们的支持对我们非常重要。

感谢各位拨冗出席,衷心祝愿大会取得圆满成功。

(张翔 翻译;张晓泉 校对;乔元芳 审定)

纵论会计透明度与金融稳定

2012年6月4日，欧洲央行(ECB)第三次会议在德国法兰克福举行，会议主题是"中央银行的会计、财务报告和公司治理"。汉斯·胡格沃斯特出席会议并发表演讲。本文为演讲全文，标题为译者所加。

在会计问题论战中，有一个十分特别的问题持续升温，引发各界激烈争论，这个问题就是：财务报告的主要目的到底是保证透明度，还是服务和服从稳定性目标？

在这场辩论中，人们往往将透明度和稳定性并列提出，似乎这是两个相互冲突的目标。但我认为，从本质上而言，这一矛盾并不存在，将二者对立起来将会适得其反。在我看来，透明度是实现稳定必不可少的前提条件，这一点显而易见。事实上，信用危机的爆发，在很大程度上可以归因于透明度的缺失。在投资者毫不知情的情况下，资产负债表表内和表外业务都积聚了巨大的风险。如果没有充分的透明度，就不能很好地了解风险的大小，那么最终维护稳定将成为一句空谈。

简而言之，稳定性不等同于透明度，但是没有透明度就没有持久的稳定可言。因此，通过提升透明度，会计准则和财务报告才能为稳定作出贡献。在介绍国际会计准则理事会的工作计划之前，我想先明确阐明国际会计准则理事会在哪些领域无能为力。

稳定性应该是高度透明的产物，但是它不应该成为会计准则制定机构的主要目标。维护稳定不属于我们的职责范围，而且我们也缺乏必要的手段来促进稳定。例如，我们不能为银行业设置资本金要求。这项职能属于以谨慎著称的监管机构和中央银行，因为维护稳定是它们的主要任务。

除此之外，会计准则制定机构制定的准则不能粉饰太平，让人误以为不具备稳定性的项目具有稳定性。坦率地讲，我们有时候甚至怀疑，外界要求我们为某些工具提供稳定性假象，而实际上这些工具的价值存在内在波动。当不存在不稳定性的时候，会计准则不应该制造出不稳定性；但是当不稳定性确实存在时，会计准则当然也不能掩饰这些不稳定性。

外界认为，国际会计准则理事会可以通过很多方式为提升金融行业透明度作出贡献，比如，与巴塞尔委员会、金融稳定委员会等非常谨慎的组织和监管机构进行密切磋商。

首先，会计准则制定机构已经改进了合并财务报表要求，防止出现不良的表外融资，美国公认会计原则尤其加强了对这方面的要求。在金融危机期间，国际财务报告准则的合并原则因明确清晰而表现不俗，但在美国，通过特殊目的载体和回购交易产生的表外融资却引发了严重的问题。通过提高合并财务报表的相关要求和加强披露，我们有理由相信上述问题将成为历史。

在会计准则制定机构与谨慎监管机构和中央银行之间，公允价值会计一直是双方争论的最大焦点。反对者认为，不论经济是上行还是下行，一旦采用公允价值会计处理，对市场价格的过度依赖将进一步加剧经济周期波动。这些批评者认为，公允价值会计将加剧"顺周期效应"，造成人为波动，从而威胁到稳定性。

受金融危机影响，有效市场假说受到了严重的质疑，这一事实似乎有力地印证了反对者的推理。欧洲央行和巴塞尔委员会要求我们限制公允价值的使用，以解决"顺周期效应"问题。

我之前担任过财政部长，也履行过监管者职责，我对市场有效假说一直持怀疑态度。我曾多次亲眼目睹市场在短期内变得疯狂异常。不过，既然要在市场环境下运营，那么，我们最好做好准备以应对市场的诡谲多变。然而，银行家作为市场的主要参与者甚至做市商，却告诉我市场信息不可信，这让我大为震惊！

此外，对于金融业这类易受市场波动影响的行业，很难想象状况又是如何。银行的资产和负债都易受市场影响。资产（不管是衍生产品还是房产抵押贷款）对经济周期都十分敏感。即使是镀金的3A级政府债券，也可能在很短时间内变得一文不值，爱尔兰就是一个很好的例子。

银行业的负债也易受市场波动影响，这点众所周知。只要轻点鼠标，刹那间，不管是大规模获得的融资，还是零星获得的融资，都可能蒸发殆尽。但这个风险似乎还不足为惧，监管部门居然还允许银行业以极其微薄的资本开展业务。20世纪，银行业的缓冲资本标准大幅下降。就在金融危机爆发之前，许多银行的有形普通股权益资本已经微不足道，仅占资产总额的1％～3％，有时甚至更低。

总之，近期市场波动源于金融业的商业模式本身。如果非要说会计处理在其中起到了一定的作用，那么这个作用也是很小的。事实上，许多独立研究发现，在这场金融动荡中，公允价值会计起到的作用非常小。这个结论也仅仅是预计，无法得以验证，因为绝大多数银行传统资产（如贷款）仍然按照摊余成本计量。

在《国际财务报告准则第9号——金融工具》（IFRS 9）中，国际会计准则理事会决定继续采用混合计量模式。国际财务报告准则第9号规定，金融工具如果具备贷款的基本特征，并以合同约定收益的方式进行管理，那么，这类工具需按照摊余成本计量。对于此类工具而言，相较于短期市场波动，摊余成本能够提供更可靠的信息。

目前，国际会计准则理事会正重新考量国际财务报告准则第9号的某些内容。

最近，针对既以收取合同约定现金流量为目标，又以出售资产为目标而进行管理的那些债务工具，我们决定重建一个金融资产分类，对该类金融资产将以公允价值计量，但相应的公允价值变动计入其他综合收益。以流动性管理为目的而持有的资产也可以采用这种计量方法。如果资产仅仅以收取合同约定现金流量为目的（其中包括传统债务工具），将继续按照摊余成本计量，这与我们之前的建议没有根本的区别。

今天，我想讨论的最后一个与透明度有关的话题就是"资产减值"。摊余成本计量方法想要可靠、可信，一个完善且运行良好的减值模型非常重要。我们现有的减值模型是以"已发生损失"为基础的，金融危机爆发之后，该模型遭受不少批评，认为其提取的减值准备不够充分，而且计提时点过晚。

我们认为，这些批评只有部分能站得住脚。事实上，许多银行的市值远低于其账面价值，这表明市场参与者不相信银行现有的拨备水平能够反映它们的经济现状。

我之所以说这些批评只有部分合理，是因为我确信，在过去几年里，已发生损失模型原本可以得到更有效的实施。我认为,在目前环境下,银行之所以没有核销某些资产,并不是因为缺乏触发机制,而是因为相关机构犹豫不决,或者受到了政治压力。

希腊政府债券没有得到及时减记的例子就很能说明问题。尽管希腊债券市场严重混乱,债券评级不断下调,贴现率急剧攀升,但是大多数银行仍未采取任何行动,直到重组决策出台后才开始计提减值准备。即便如此,一些银行还认为21%的计提比例已经足够充分。总而言之,我们相信,即使根据当前的减值规定,银行也能采取比这更果断的措施。

然而,国际会计准则理事会和美国财务会计准则委员会都认为我们应该采用更具前瞻性的减值模型。事实上,我们正在开发预期损失模型,且进展良好。

预期损失模式的基本原则如下:对所有新增金融资产,从购入的第一天开始,就应该根据未来12个月的预期损失,为其设立减值准备。如果随后信用质量恶化,合同约定的现金流量无法收回变得"合理可能"时,就应该确认整个寿命周期内的损失。但是,我们不会尝试对什么是"合理可能"进行严格定义,它主要是指当一项资产恶化时,现金短缺可能性开始以某一加速度上升时所达到的"拐点"。

从某种程度上说,预期损失模型需要依靠判断,因为我们不可能精确预测违约概率何时开始加速攀升。在进行判断时,市场指标可以而且也应该作为重要的参考。所以,即使资产按照摊余成本计量,公允价值指标也能为其提供非常重要的信息。

我们以主权债务证券举例说明。如果一项主权债务面临明显的可持续问题,级别降低至投资级以下,而且市场贴现率高达两位数,那么很明显,这项主权债务很可能不能收回全部的合同约定现金流。即便这个问题证券仍然有效,我们也应该确认整个寿命周期内的损失。参考当前的市场环境,我们就能意识到,预期损失模型比现有模型能更加及时地确认损失。

据我所知,许多谨慎的监管机构希望预期损失模型能够平缓信贷的激增或萎缩。他们常将西班牙银行在金融危机爆发前采用的动态拨备模型作为例子展示。虽然动态拨备模型包含了预期损失模型的某些要素,但显然它不能起到很好的反周期作用。

我认为,我们对会计规则在"反经济周期"方面的作用的期望必须切合实际,这是因为:首先,会计准则不是经济政策工具,会计的任务是尽可能如实地反映财务和经济状况。抑制经济周期,既不是我们的工作任务,也不是我们的专业范围。

其次,正如我之前所说的,预期损失模型也依赖于一定程度的判断。在本次经济危机爆发之前,许多银行及其监管者显然无法精准地预测风险之所在。信贷狂欢持续发酵,对它的警示不断见诸报端,但是,因信贷而引发的严重问题始终未被预见。

纵观经济发展历程,信贷泡沫和经济萧条贯穿其中。有鉴于此,我们无法保证银行家在未来能比现在更好地预测风险。所以,经济繁荣时期累积的风险不太可能全部被及时地识别。即使运用预期损失模型,许多损失也只有在经济下行时方能显现出来。

一旦信贷危机爆发,风险将大规模地显现出来,西班牙目前面临的状况就是一个很好的例子。自金融危机爆发以来,西班牙银行已核销的资产金额约为其国内生产总值(GDP)的18%。有些人认为,该比例还可能进一步上升。西班牙银行的动态拨备体系被巨额损失彻底摧毁。

这个教训告诉我们:经济的周期性波动太过强劲,单靠会计难以有效抗衡。不过,我相信预期损失模型的引进将极大地改善这种状况。

首先,预期损失模型能够更及时、更切合实际地提取准备金,让金融业的风险意识更具前瞻性。其次,对银行体系进行及时的清理,有利于将资源释放出来集中到经济的可行领域,而不是浪费在毫无生机的公司身上。

第三,也许也是最重要的一点,谈及对金融行业信誉的破坏性,首当其冲的便是对问题资产真正严重性的持续低估。只确认一部分不可避免的损失,在短期内也许能争取到一些时间,但最终将导致一轮接一轮的"具有决定意义的"救援方案,并逐渐侵蚀市场信心。

显而易见,银行要严格、充分地应用预期损失模型,前提条件就是保证适当的资本化水平。最近,巴塞尔协议对资本要求进行了改革,但这是否能满足资本保障需求,尚存争议。

在金融危机爆发前,银行通过调低风险比重,提高杠杆比例,将巴塞尔资本充足率玩弄于鼓掌之间,这一点有据可查。银行似乎很好地满足了10%的一级资本充足率要求,但其实际杠杆可能高达40、50甚至60倍!巴塞尔资本充足率原为提高银行透明度,结果却被滥用成为银行掩饰实际杠杆的工具。

巴塞尔协议Ⅲ无疑将是一个很大的进步,因为它从"质"和"量"两方面提高了资本要求。此外,它还引入杠杆比率,能够更清楚地洞悉银行真实的资产负债情况。然而,巴塞尔协议Ⅲ仍然允许银行利用高达 33 倍的杠杆。虽然我不是一个审慎监管者,但我好奇如果一家银行仅仅利用 20 倍杠杆,是否会引发类似西班牙或爱尔兰的危机。

此外,资产的风险权重系统仍然危机重重,它允许银行假定主权债务没有或基本没有风险,现在我们应该很清楚这种假定是非常不可靠的。尽管西班牙和爱尔兰的公共债务水平非常低,但几乎是在一夜之间,它们便失去了 3A 评级。

不仅仅是风险权重问题,而且由于高评级主权缺乏大规模曝光,致使银行受到极大驱动,承载了过多的主权风险。一旦某个主权步入危险区域,拨备需求就可能急剧增长。当然,这不是一个会计问题,而是一个实实在在的审慎监管问题。通过预期损失模型,审慎监管的漏洞能比现在更快地暴露出来。预期损失模型本身是一个好东西,但银行监管机构最好还是未雨绸缪。

总之,我相信随着预期损失模型的引入,损失能够比现在更及时地得到确认。已发生损失模型为损失确认提供了太多拖延余地,因此必须予以取代。但是,我们不要期望预期损失模型本身能够极大地削弱信贷周期的"顺周期性"。

除非银行家及其监管者能够更好地遏制信贷扩张和相关风险,否则,信用崩溃和巨额亏损将会定期发生。即使这样,预期损失模型还是优于已发生损失模型。但预期损失模型要想得到严格的应用,必不可少的前提就是银行要有充足的资本保障。若非如此,即使向来遵纪守法的银行监管机构也可能抵挡不住诱惑,纵容银行规避会计规定,拖延解决问题的时间。显然,我们应该消除这种诱惑。

(张翔 翻译;张晓泉 校对;乔元芳 审定)

非精确的会计世界

2012年6月20日,国际会计教育与研究协会(IAAER)在荷兰首都阿姆斯特丹举办大会。汉斯·胡格沃斯特出席会议并发表了题为《非精确的会计世界》的演讲。本文为演讲全文。

对决策制定者而言,会计问题是他们最需要直接处理的主题之一。会计主要是描述过去,如实地反映已发生的交易或事项。会计是一项枯燥乏味的工作,就像一个"数豆人"。难道"数豆"也能引发诸多问题吗?

多年来,众多的证券监管机构发现,会计政策是最难处理、最富争议的议题之一,他们向我谈及此事时表示颇感意外。不过,只要问一下日本金融厅(FSA)、美国证券交易委员会(SEC)或欧盟委员会,我们就会发现全球情况大多如此。

那么,到底是什么让会计成为如此热议的话题?

当然,原因是多方面的。国际会计准则理事会前任主席戴维·泰迪(David Tweedie)爵士过去常说,会计的责任就是让资本主义恪守诚信。由此,会计准则制定机构面临如此大的压力也就不足为奇了!缺乏透明度,使得某些商业模式可以大行其道。各位回想一下金融危机爆发之前,银行业的"特殊目的载体"(Special Purpose Vehicles)就是如此。

会计为何如此具有争议的第二个原因就是会计方法不可避免地会涉及职业判断和主观成分,而这又很容易产生诸多分歧。

去年7月出任国际会计准则理事会主席之际,我充分意识到,我所面对的不是一个按照科学铁律来行事的世界。我当时就认识到,会计和经济学面临着同样的问题:开展会计或者经济工作,我们需要运用数学工具,但是千万别指望计算得出的结果分毫不差、精确无比。总而言之,我对会计问题毫无头绪。

一年时间过去了,经过努力学习,迅速累积会计知识后,现在,我必须承认之前我对会计的理解太过肤浅。是什么打开了我的视野,让我举例一二吧。

首先,国际财务报告准则和美国公认会计原则都规定了复杂多样的计量技术,从历史成本、使用价值到公允价值都有,另外还有许多介于历史成本与公允价值之间的计量技术,这让我大为诧异。在历史成本或现值的基础上,国际财务报告准则先后使用了20多种计量技术。一般情况下,这些计量技术差异微小,所以,数量之多也不足为奇,无需过度纠结。

但是,计量技术种类繁多,导致会计准则制定者在回答如何对某项资产或者负债进行估值时,往往很难找到一个明确的答案。

需要注意的是,在不同的商业模式下,会计准则针对同一资产也可能产生不同的计量结果。例如,一项债务证券,当作为交易性金融资产持有时,要求按照市场价格进行计量;而当它作为持有至到期资产时,需按照历史成本列报。在这种情况下,运用商业模式法的确提供了貌似合理的答案。然而,人们也发现,持有至到期的政府债券,其估值可能高于交易性资产组合中的同类债券,后者可能存在折价,这与人们的直觉矛盾、有违常理。依据严谨的科学精神,对于同种债券出现双重计量结果,显然令人无法接受。

计量工作所面临的最大困境之一是无形资产的计量。众所周知,无形资产虽然不具备实物形态,但确实存在。Facebook 的商业理念价值巨大(虽然同上月相比,下降了 25%),与之相比,其有形资产的价值却相对较小。

同样,药品专利的盈利潜力往往相当巨大。但是,商业理念和专利这两类无形资产的价值,却无法在资产负债表上得到反映(或虽得到反映,但列报价值低于真实价值)。《国际会计准则第 38 号——无形资产》(IAS 38)设定了一系列严格的条件,只有在符合条件的前提下,才允许将无形资产开发支出予以有限资本化。但我们知道,该项准则尚不完善,它以历史成本为基础,无法反映无形资产的真实价值。

事实上,确定或计量无形资产的价值相当困难。高企的股价净值比充分表明,无形资产不仅存在,而且价值不菲。但是,在互联网泡沫破灭以后,企业都无意将无形资产计入资产负债表,个中缘由可以理解。

虽然国际财务报告准则不允许企业确认内部形成的商誉,但要求企业将企业合并时所支付的溢价确认为商誉。商誉是一个混合体,既包括被收购企业内部形成的商誉,也包括通过企业合并而可能产生的协同效应。商誉中的大多数元素具有高度的不确定性及主观性,最后往往南柯一梦。

对于通过收购获取的商誉,企业必须每年进行减值测试。但在实际操作中,很多企业似乎并没有严格进行减值测试。通常情况下,在企业将减值状况记录到资产负债表之前,股票价格就已提前反映了这一情况。换句话讲,减值测试过于滞后。总而言之,一个不错的想法就是,我们应根据《国际财务报告准则第3号——企业合并》(IFRS 3)实施后的评估情况,重新审视商誉。

不仅是资产负债表充满不精确和不确定性,在定义和计量收益时,我们也同样遇到了不少问题。我们报告收益时,会涉及三项主要内容:传统意义上的损益或净收益、其他综合收益以及综合收益总额。综合收益总额最简单,它是净利润和其他综合收益的合计数。因此,尽管综合收益总额这个指标值得关注,但似乎没有多少人注意到它。

净收益和其他综合收益之间的区别,还缺乏一个明确严谨的定义基础。损益是传统的经营绩效指标,在此基础上,企业再确定薪酬和分红方案,但其他综合收益的意义却不清晰。最初,其他综合收益只是一个"载体",企业将某些外币折算损益从净利润中剥离出来纳入其中。逐渐地,其他综合收益发展成为一个"容纳器",企业为避免资产负债表波动过大,将某些特定的利得或损失统统确认为其他综合收益。其他综合收益归集未实现利得或损失,但这是一个模糊的概念,没有清楚地指明设置这个项目的目的,以及它的具体含义。

但是,这并不意味着其他综合收益百无一用。尤其对于金融机构而言,它们的资产负债表内容庞大,其他综合收益可以包含非常重要的信息,反映资产负债表质量。对于投资者而言,很重要的是,他们需要弄清楚资产负债表中利得或损失的内容,即便这些利得或损失尚未实现,也同样重要。

将来,其他综合收益必将成为了解保险合同的重要信息来源。几周之前,美国财务会计准则委员会和国际会计准则理事会建议,将折现率波动所引起的保险负债变动额计入其他综合收益。国际会计准则理事会的许多利益相关者也希望我们作出如此规定。

财务报告编制者和使用者都不希望承保成果被资产负债表的波动所掩盖。因此,其他综合收益将变得越来越大,包含更多有用信息,例如作为反映资产、负债期限错配的指标。

要作出采用其他综合收益的决定,并不容易。国际会计准则理事会理事斯蒂芬·库珀(Stephen Cooper)在演讲中,向我们展示了一项直白、明确的分析——如果把净收益与其他综合收益相互阻断,而不联系起来进行解读,就极有可能产生令人迷惑不解的信息。我们将通过改善列报方法,努力解决其中的部分问题。但是,毫无疑问,只有考量构成综合收益总额的所有因素,才能掌握保险公司的经营业绩全貌。对此,我们将在新保险合同准则的"结论基础"中明确地指出这一点。

在即将开展的概念框架修订工作中,我们将从更基础的地方着手,探讨净收益和其他综合收益的区别。国际会计准则理事会的所有利益相关方都希望我们能为其他综合收益的含义提供一个坚实的理论基础,为此我们将全力以赴。目前,虽然我们可能还不完全清楚其他综合收益的实际重要性,但我们可以确信,净收益也不是一个非常精确的绩效指标。净收益和其他综合收益都需要判断,金融行业尤其如此。

会计为什么会出现这种模棱两可、缺乏精确的情形呢?很大程度上,这可以简单地归结为会计的本质使然。我们充分认识到,会计计价不仅是一门科学,也是一门艺术。国际财务报告准则概念框架指出:"通用目的财务报告并不企图揭示报告主体的价值,而是通过提供信息,来帮助使用者估计报告主体的价值。"价值是外部人士最为关注的指标。对于"哪种计量技术能最有效地计量价值",我们往往没有泾渭分明的明确答案。

会计的这种不完美,不应成为怀疑国际财务报告准则重要性的理由。恰恰相反,我深信,国际财务报告准则是市场经济信任基石中不可或缺的要素。在一个由众多参与者管理其他参与者资财的经济体系中,高质量的会计准则能够使市场保持透明,因而具有极其重要的作用。

作为一套全球性准则,国际财务报告准则为全球投资者带了巨大收益,而在此之前,财务报告之间缺乏可比性。一些学术研究发现,国际财务报告准则有助于降低资本成本。

此外,财务报告不是非得追求数学的严格精确才有用,它只是一项工具,帮助投资者作出决策。众所周知,沃伦·巴菲特(Warren Buffett)将财务报告作为简易的、粗略的判断清单:只要在财务报告中发现存在5~6个问题,他就会放弃投资。

只要看看保险行业,我们就清楚,恰当的会计准则是多么重要。目前,国际财务报告准则体系中尚缺乏成熟的保险会计准则,致使该行业的财务报告采用了许多公认会计原则中没有规定的计量方法,严重缺乏可比性。

正是因为保险行业财务报告缺乏严谨、统一的会计基础,从而为弥补透明度缺失带来的风险,投资者通常要求更高的资本回报。

由于没有理论支撑,缺乏良好财务报告应该具有的透明度,公共部门会计也呈现出初级无序状态。虽然国际公共部门会计准则理事会(IPSASB)基于国际财务报告准则为公共部门制定了健全的准则,但这套准则并未得到有效的实施。世界各国政府都不能为其所承担的金额巨大、没有资金支持的社会保障债务提供完整的信息。如果私营部门的高管们也像各国财政部长这般作为,那么,他们将面临牢狱之灾。

所以,国际财务报告准则的相关性和重要性毋庸置疑。会计趋同项目接近尾声,国际会计准则理事会准备开展新的工作,将精力主要集中在进一步提高准则质量上。虽然前面提到的不精确和模糊性无法完全避免,但我们有责任尽可能地减少会计灰色地带。

那么,我们应该如何着手呢?我认为,我们应该遵循以下三个原则:原则导向、务实主义和坚持不懈。

原则导向:由于会计不是一门精确科学,因此,原则导向的会计准则制定方法将是发展的正确方向。如果必须使用判断,那么这种判断应该以明确清晰的原则为指导,而不能依靠详尽繁琐、貌似精确的规则。

我们将完成概念框架的审核工作,处理计量、绩效指标、其他综合收益、重分类等一系列棘手问题,以强化和巩固基本原则。

虽然我不会天真地认为,新的概念框架将解决所有问题,但我认为新框架将为我们提供更坚实的基础。完整的概念框架虽然不能提供精确的答案,但它应该在资产和负债的确认、计量技术和绩效指标等方面为我们提供指引。

务实主义:我们知道,不是每个问题都存在非此即彼的精确答案,会计准则制定工作就应该本着务实主义的态度,按人所共知的常识行事。凯恩斯(Keynes)曾经说过,与精确的错误相比,大致的正确更重要。我们不要试图迫使企业追求片面的精确,而放弃了最基本的准确。

此外,务实主义还意味着,对可能出现的任何对会计准则的不恰当应用,我们都需要进行仔细的观察和分析。面临高度的不确定性,无论何时我们都应该极其谨慎地进行处理。刚才,我以无形资产为例进行了说明。我们都知道无形资产的确存在,但要计量它却是一大难题。如果国际财务报告准则为无形资产确认预留太大的空间,错误或滥用的可能性也就大为增加。

在这种情况下,国际财务报告准则最好是要求更多地运用定性报告,而不是貌似精确的定量报告。

我想顺便说一句，不少人建议，国际会计准则理事会制定会计准则时，应立足于防范会计准则被滥用。我认为，这毫无道理。如果一项会计准则留下了太多的滥用空间，那我们最好是采取措施来改变这种滥用状态。要知道，滥用空间过大，那就为创造性会计留下太多的诱惑和刺激。

务实主义非常重要，但不能把它与机会主义混为一谈，这也是要同时强调"坚持不懈"的原因。我们在工作中一直持续不断地面临种种压力，对于会计准则制定机构而言，坚持不懈、持之以恒是一种难能可贵的品质。会计准则制定工作，一方面应该敏锐地回应并充分考虑合法的商业诉求，想其所想；另一方面，当面对特殊的利益诉求时，也要保持坚定和独立的立场，做我所做。末日宿命论者曾多次放言，如果采用国际财务报告准则，商业将走入死胡同。我们却同时看到，有问题的行业在采用我们的准则后，似乎能够奇迹般地起死回生。我们的确需要广泛听取各方意见与建议，但与此同时，我们还是必须有自己的原则和决断。

如果投资者的意见和观点能够比目前得到更广泛地倾听、更清晰地表述，那么，国际会计准则理事会无疑将获益匪浅，坚定步伐、稳步前行。虽然投资者是国际会计准则理事会的主要服务对象，但很多时候，他们的声音被喧嚣的商业利益诉求所淹没。未来几年，我们将进一步加大投入，密切与投资者的关系，确保开展公众意见征询工作时，我们不会偏听偏信，能够获取更客观公正、不偏不倚的反馈意见。此外，我们尤其希望与所谓的"最终用户"加强联系。

所谓"最终用户"，我是指那些"真正投资者"，他们是实际拥有自有资产的人或机构，比如机构投资者。如能获得投资界的支持，相信我们的前路会更加畅通、平坦。

国际会计准则理事会将在今后新的工作日程中坚持原则导向、务实主义和坚持不懈。未来几年，我们将加强基础原则的建设，尽可能提高准则定量内容的比重。如果定量不太可行，那么我们将说明情况，并将更多的精力放在定性信息上。

"大道至简，知易行难。"国际会计准则理事会及其工作人员将积极主动地迎接挑战。无论如何，我可以确定，未来几年绝对不会"平淡无奇"。

（张翔 翻译；张晓泉 校对；乔元芳 审定）

审慎：消亡抑或生存？

2012年9月18日，欧洲会计师联合会(FEE)在比利时首都布鲁塞尔举办大会，主题为"公司报告的未来"。汉斯·胡格沃斯特出席会议并发表题为《审慎：消亡抑或生存？》的演讲。本文为演讲全文。

女士们，先生们，我非常感谢欧洲会计师联合会给我这个机会，让我有幸参加今天的会议。众所周知，自2005年起，欧洲和其他国家就开始采用国际财务报告准则，欧洲率先启动迈向全球会计准则。欧洲的会计职业界在这个过程中扮演了至关重要的角色。对于欧洲会计师联合会及各位成员在这项重大工作中起到的引领作用，我和国际会计准则理事会的同仁表示衷心感谢。

今天会议的主题是"公司报告的未来"，现在正是研究这个主题的绝佳时机。过去的十年间，我们看到财务报告不乏革新之举。十年前，还没有一个企业采用国际准则，而今天已有100多个国家的企业采用国际准则，其中包括3/4的G20成员国。相对于其他措施，这已经是一个前所未有的成就了。

那么，变革之后将会发生什么？公司报告的未来是什么呢？对这个问题的研究，目前存在多种倡议，重点之一是对公司报告有个更为全盘的视角，这样的报告称为综合报告。综合报告的目标是整合众多报告要求，包括可持续性、环境保护、社会问题，当然也包括财务报告。这些主题正变得越来越相互依赖，很多投资者都想了解它们之间的相互作用。我也认为，投资者要准确地理解财务报告，的确需要非财务性关键业绩指标。比如，一家企业可能会决定大幅度削减对雇员在培训和教育上的支出。这个决定或许会令下一季度的报表看上去增色不少，但它对企业的长期盈利能力会造成无法估量的损失。基于这些原因,我支持这个重要的倡议,我对自己能够成为国际综合报告委员会的理事会成员而感到高兴。

尽管财务报告比综合报告发展得更为深入,但我们却还在纠结一些非常基础的问题。国际会计准则理事会的概念框架里对资产和负债下了定义,但我们仍然发现这些定义还不能完全令人满意。

当你期望每一个会计师都能够明确区分"我的"和"你的"的时候,我们仍然不能十分确定如何区分所有者权益和负债。计量一个主体的业绩同样很困难。我们要计量净收益,但是还有其他综合收益,尽管其金额一直在增加,但我们对到底何为其他综合收益却还没有把握。

下一阶段概念框架修订工作中所要解决的问题都很棘手。我们正计划就会计要素、计量和列报编写新章目,当然还包括一个坚实的披露框架。这也许是我们能够着手做的最重要的工作。基础概念正确了,准则制定工作就可以有一个合理的、前后一致的参照。

这项工作的重要性是基于这样一个事实,即时至今日现行概念框架仍是个具有激烈争议的主题。这里我专门讨论一下"审慎"。当国际会计准则理事会于2010年9月修订概念框架第一章时,用"中立"取代了"审慎"。从那时开始,国际财务报告准则经常遭到所谓"事实上不审慎"的抨击,据称由此导致了虚报利润和(或)低报负债。例如,批评者把对不良贷款损失的低计归咎于已发生损失模型,把不适当地确认未实现利润归咎于使用了公允价值计量。

对于这些批评,我们必须严肃对待。我在以前的发言中说过,财务报告远不是一门精密科学,它高度依赖于判断。如果这些判断出现倾向乐观的系统性错误,投资者所获得的信息显然就会非常糟糕,因为夸大利润不可避免地会导致对投资的估价过高。

但是,在我审视国际财务报告准则是否导致了财务报告不够审慎之前,首先让我们设法确定"审慎"的确切含义。原来的概念框架把"审慎"列为可靠性(现在框架称为"忠实陈报")的一个特征,并认为审慎是在不确定情况下进行判断时,必须包含一定程度的谨慎,以便不高估资产或收益,不低报负债或费用。

你也许非常想知道,"审慎"的这个定义到底有什么问题?我的回答是:绝对没有错。这个定义的意思是,如果你对一项资产或者一项负债的价值持有怀疑,最好是保持谨慎,这也是我们应该努力运用到日常生活中去的一个显而易见的普通常识。

尽管谨慎是过度乐观假设的对立面,但原"审慎"定义也含有一个明确的警示,就是反对建立秘密准备和过度准备。这一警示的初衷就是预防甜饼会计和收益平滑。对此,我再次表示百分之百地赞成。

过度的稳健主义会产生两个问题。首先,在经济回升时期,利润被人为地压低,投资者或许会错失一个好的投资机会。但最大的问题在经济衰退周期中才会爆发,因为在这种情况下,秘密准备将用于人为地调高主体的盈余。利润被夸大,从而掩盖了主体业绩的恶化。更进一步的后果是破坏透明度,因为投资者可能被误导,诱使其更长时间地持有投资。

通常来讲,甜饼会计动摇了对财务报告可靠性的信心。1993年,德国戴姆勒克莱斯勒再次获得在美国上市的机会。在转为执行美国公认会计原则以后,戴姆勒财务报表中的大量秘密准备显露无遗。虽然戴姆勒的财务状况比之前报告的情况好很多,但这一情况引发很多人的疑虑,那就是德国公认会计原则如此缺乏透明度,对其他德国公司到底会有怎样的影响?人们当然知道,那些秘密准备也能方便地变成秘密损失。

既然原来的"审慎"定义既强调谨慎又反对甜饼会计,我也认为完全正确,那为什么还要删除它呢?

一个原因是国际财务报告准则要与美国公认会计原则实现趋同,而美国公认会计原则并没有定义何为"审慎"。通常而言,人们认为审慎性在实务中常被用来作为甜饼会计的挡箭牌。在这一方面,认识到盈余管理动力无穷非常重要,因为无论是报酬还是声誉,都在很大程度上依赖于盈余数字的稳定增长。因此,管理层高度奖掖会计人员平滑盈余的能力。

甚至分析师也经常有意或无意地对某些允许盈余管理的会计技术表示赞同,因为分析师依靠预测盈余来生存,盈余的过度波动会使预测变得异常困难!鉴于存在这些诱惑,国际会计准则理事会和美国财务会计准则委员会都觉得有必要通过删除"审慎"概念来强调财务报告的中立性。在这样的背景之下,我感到这是一个能够站得住脚的决定。

对于我而言,修改后的概念框架也不难接受,因为原来的审慎就是指"倘若存疑,即须谨慎",而这一观念在我们的准则里依然根深蒂固。现在我给各位举几个例子:

——尽管公允价值常被视作过于激进,但在国际财务报告准则第13号中,当使用模型评估技术来计量公允价值时,实际上我们要求进行风险调整。

——尽管担保或保证事项尚未发生,但国际财务报告准则仍要求把它们记录为负债。

——存货按成本与可变现净值孰低入账,又是一个运用谨慎的主要例证。

——要求减值测试以确保财务状况表中资产的账面金额不高于可收回金额。

——国际财务报告准则也有严格的规则来规范资产负债表列报,表外融资的空间很小。

——众所周知,国际财务报告准则严格限制衍生金融工具的净额列报。按照美国公认会计原则,不同主体所报告的衍生金融工具,其差别可能高达资产负债表的 30% 或 40%。我们深信,衍生金融工具如此重要,净仓位又大幅波动,绝不能把它降格到财务报表附注中去。

——即将出台的租赁会计准则是使资产负债表表外融资更为透明的另一项努力。全世界的分析师通常都因租赁业务而调整资产负债表,因为他们认为租赁是资产负债表表外融资项目。这一做法相当审慎,我们将把这一做法融入国际财务报告准则。

——同样,国际财务报告准则基于控制原则的合并规则非常严格。至于哪个公司需要合并进来,我们采用的是定性原则,而不是选择一条明线,即使所拥有的一个公司的权益低于 50% 也是如此。

鉴于上述例子,对英国政府最近所说"不同意国际财务报告准则导致审慎缺失"就不足为奇了,因为"审慎的概念继续渗透在会计准则之中"。我认为这是一个恰如其分的结论。

尽管如此,我认为还是必须意识到,利用原来的审慎概念来改进国际财务报告准则还有进一步的空间。我在以前的演讲中提到过与无形资产相关的风险,这些风险的存在毋庸置疑,但要计量它们却面临巨大挑战。

在这方面,我特别关注因企业合并而产生的商誉。商誉是一个混合体,含有许多内容,包括被兼并公司的自创商誉和因企业合并而预期产生的协同效应。它们通常具有实际价值,但却没人知道它们的精确价值。商誉的很多因素具有高度不确定性和主观性,它们往往虚假不实。

正是由于其主观性,对商誉的会计处理极易操纵资产负债表和损益表。在正常情况下,你会期望至少部分商誉将被逐渐摊销,因为就预期协同效应而支付的那部分商誉已经实现。但在实务中,主体也许对商誉减值难下决心,以免给人以作出了不良投资决策的印象。另一方面,新任首席执行官却有强烈的动机确认其前任在并购上的巨额减值。基础干净而坚实了,他们就能或多或少地确保未来的稳定收益流。问题是对于这些决策,现行规则是否足够严格。

对这些问题,没有简单的解决方案。在即将进行的对《国际财务报告准则第 3 号——企业合并》重新评估期间,也许值得花点时间重新审视减值规则。但我也坦承,这的确面临重大挑战,这也是我首次承认这一点。

前已述及,对公允价值会计的常见批评是说它将导致不恰当地确认未实现利润。我认为,这样的批评多半没有事实根据。应该引起注意的是,相比摊余成本,公允价值计量通常能够更快地捕捉经济衰退迹象,就像近期所见到的就希腊债务所作的资产减值那样。然而,我也确信,在概念框架的"计量"那一章中,我们未来工作的一个重要问题就是如何处理未实现盈余和已实现盈余。

国际财务报告准则致力于构筑充分谨慎的最新例证是我们在金融工具预期损失模型方面的工作。金融危机爆发之后,基于已发生损失的现行减值模型,因其过于微乎其微且为时过晚而备受指责。国际会计准则理事会和美国财务会计准则委员会都得出结论,认为减值模型的确需要着眼未来。在过去的 18 个月里,我们致力于得出一个趋同解决方案。

大家知道,美国财务会计准则委员会就模型开发形成了另外一种理念,尽管我们共同参与了开发,但目前看起来不太可能形成趋同方案。无论最终结果如何,这两种方法都是基于预期损失,而且与现行模型相比,两种方法对信用的预期变化均能作出更快反应。

两个模型都存在任何预期损失模型的主要缺陷,即主观性增强,因为估计预期损失要比计量已发生损失需要更多的判断,可靠性将成为一个现实问题。

国际会计准则理事会认为,至为重要的是,预期损失模型必须满足两个条件:第一,它应该尽可能如实地反映经济现实;第二,它应该尽可能缩小盈余管理空间。现在我对上面两个问题作一点详细说明。

要使预期损失模型反映经济现实状况,初始日确认的损失越小越好。因为显而易见,在按市场条件进行贷款时,初始日并不会遭受损失。如果在初始日就确认整个寿命期间的损失,将使贷款的账面价值显著低于其经济价值。给予中小型企业的贷款中,未达到投资级别的情况相当普遍,初始日确认的这些损失相当可观,投资者无疑对这些数字疑虑重重。

全面确认初始日预期损失,也会产生严重且无法预计的后果。当银行盈利降低时，银行做高利润最简便易行的方法，就是减少新增贷款，从而避免初始日损失。相比当前情形，银行贷款的顺周期效应更为突出。

此外，基于整个预期寿命期初始日损失的模型，即使是基于历史统计，也必定高度主观。这些统计数据其实非常不可靠，正像美国和西班牙抵押贷款市场所表现的那样。只要稍微调整一下寿命期的预期损失，就会给收益造成巨大影响。盈余管理的诱惑将很难抗拒。

此外，初始日大量提取准备或许是稳健的，但随后也可能用它来掩盖恶化的业绩。正因如此，金融危机咨询组在2009年6月发布的最终报告称，尽管预期损失模型看上去比已发生损失模型更为审慎，但公司董事会必须小心翼翼地规避盈余管理，因为盈余管理可降低透明度。由于我也是金融危机咨询组的联合主席，因而我全力支持这个结论，各位应该不足为奇。

基于这些原因，国际会计准则理事会的模型要求，只有在贷款恶化之后，才能确认寿命周期内的全部损失。我们的建议用会计术语来说就是：当一笔贷款产生恶化且无法全部收回合同现金流量成为合理可能时，贷款即发生减值。这个分界线比现行的已发生损失模型要低很多，但它避免了初始日确认寿命期内全部损失的陷阱。我们承认，国际会计准则理事会的模型也要求运用判断，不会完全摆脱主观性。我们正致力于制定恰当的应用指南，尽可能将主观性而产生的空间控制在有限范围之内。

现在来归纳一下我的结论。我想刚才的发言已经阐述得很清楚，按照国际财务报告准则提供的信息尽可能中立绝对至为重要。倾向稳健主义的系统性偏差，削弱了收益作为业绩指标的价值。对于将"审慎"从概念框架中删除这一事实，国际会计准则理事会认为有必要完全清楚地加以说明，我今天的发言也阐述了我的个人理解。

我也通过举例说明，"审慎"的基本宗旨对国际会计准则理事会的工作依然至关重要。事实上，谨慎的运用散见在许多国际财务报告准则之中，而且在制定新的国际财务报告准则时仍然是一个重要问题。因此，人们或许会得出这样的结论——原有的概念不仅没有消亡，而且还生机勃勃。各位从本人刚才的发言中可知，我对此没有丝毫怀疑，这一点非常明确。正如旧约所言："于我而言，旧信条已经足够。"

女士们，先生们，谢谢各位。祝大会取得圆满成功！

（乔元芳 翻译并审校）

会计协调和全球经济后果

2012年11月6日,汉斯·胡格沃斯特在伦敦经济学院发表题为《会计协调和全球经济后果》的长篇公开演讲。本文为演讲全文。

引 语

今晚能够站在这里向各位介绍国际会计准则理事会的工作,我感到非常荣幸。我希望在结束演讲时,各位已经确信,制定国际会计准则对全球经济意义重大。我们的工作非常重要且充满挑战,甚至可以说非常有趣。

如果各位对我的职业生涯有所了解就会明白,为什么于我而言会计颇具挑战,因为我不是一名受过专业训练的会计师。事实上,我是在阿姆斯特丹大学读的历史,之后在美国的约翰霍普金斯大学研究国际关系。在美国的银行工作了一段时间以后,灵光一现我又投身公益去了。回到荷兰以后,我进入政界当了议员,之后历任财政部长、社会事务部长和卫生部长。在此期间,我和我的同事们致力于改革荷兰的福利状况,收效颇佳,各位可以看到荷兰经济已恢复了先前的实力。

离开政界后,我担任金融市场管理局主席有几个年头。金融市场管理局是荷兰的金融监管部门,全面负责商业行为监管,相当于英国的金融监管局。我的职责就是确保金融业的透明以及公平地对待客户。由于我上任时刚刚爆发金融危机,因此,这项任务极富挑战。

金融市场管理局也负责监管财务报告,这是我第一次接触财务报告,然而我吃惊地发现这个领域令人着迷。随着金融危机的逐步加剧,金融界开始责怪现行会计规则,认为是它导致了国际金融体系的动荡。我认为,这样的责难根本经不起推敲，这就好像人们经常将怒气发在带来坏消息的人身上一样。

我的一个小失误在于我发表了几次演讲来阐述这个主题。

结果是那几次演讲引起了国际会计准则理事会的注意，他们希望我一起来领导一个咨询小组，向国际会计准则理事会和美国财务会计准则委员会共同应对金融危机提供咨询。几年后，我被提请担任国际会计准则理事会主席，于是我在2011年7月走马上任。

从这件事情里可以得到什么教训呢？那就是"小心祸从口出"！

可是，既然我不是一名专业会计师，为什么还有兴趣担任国际会计准则理事会主席一职呢？请相信我，自我被提名的那年起，特别是在整整五天的理事会会议期间，要讨论保险负债实际利息的八种备选方法，或者其他什么高精尖的会计玩艺儿，我都一直就此反躬自问。

玩笑归玩笑，事实上会计的确颇为重要。我的前任戴维·泰迪就说过，会计的使命就是让资本主义保持诚实可信。

这一点我非常赞同。在公开资本市场中，大部分所运作的都是其他人的金钱。

投资者与被投资者之间通常互不熟知，因此他们之间的关系高度依赖于对经济规范、市场和机构的信任。

金融危机已证明了公开资本市场的制约机制有多么不堪一击。银行系统仅靠或隐或显的政府支持就可以孤注一掷。我们正处在有史以来最大的信用泡沫当中，甚至在金融危机爆发五年之后，一场全球性的经济灾难仍极有可能发生。

很多公司畸高的薪酬也证明，公开资本市场保护投资者利益的方法极差。由于高管的薪酬往往与盈余挂钩，因此，允许以有利的方式列报盈余的会计规则，对公司管理层来说有巨大的利益。会计的许多突破，是艰难战胜既得利益的成果，我在之后的演讲中会提及许多活生生的例子。

各位应该明白了，为什么就连会计也充满政治火药味，又为什么会让一个前政客来领导国际会计准则理事会。形象地说，就是让小偷抓小偷。

高质量的财务信息是市场经济的血液。一个病人如果血液供应不足，器官就会衰竭，病人随之死亡。财务报告也是如此。如果数据无法使投资者信服，金融市场即停止运转。对于市场经济而言，这真是糟糕透顶。因为在市场经济条件下，财务报告是必不可少的公共商品。

财务报告、市场经济以及全球化

我现在要转为谈论世界经济全球化与纷纷采用国际会计准则之间的关系。在过去十年间,财务报告领域里最为惊人的发展,是由我供职的国际会计准则理事会所制定的国际财务报告准则,已被世界上绝大多数发达国家和新兴经济体所接纳。

这其中的原因有许多,但最主要的一点就是当今金融市场的全球互联性。资本不再具有国界,投资者在全球范围内进行多样化经营和寻求投资机会。跨国公司希望全球业务活动均采用同一套会计记录,监管机构和政策制定者也都希望为财务报告提供一个公正公平的平台。

在这样一个全球化的大背景下,再保留国家会计准则,就显得荒唐无理。

因为各国采用不同的会计准则,将引致全球金融市场摩擦,既使投资者感到迷惑,也给公司增加不必要的成本。为此,G20 在其发布的新闻公报中一再对国际会计准则理事会的工作表示支持,并呼吁迅速推进会计准则的全球化。

令人欣慰的是,在过去十年里,我们已取得了令人瞩目的进展。自 2001 年以来,已有 100 多个国家采用了国际财务报告准则,其中包括超过 2/3 的 G20 成员国。半数世界 500 强企业采用国际财务报告准则编制财务报告。

看看欧洲就能理解这一成就是多么巨大。2002 年,欧盟决定自 2005 年起采用国际财务报告准则。那时的 25 个成员国只有不到三年的准备时间。而到了 2005 年 1 月 1 日,约 8 000 个公司同时从 20 多个不同国家会计准则转而一致采用国际财务报告准则。这的确是一个了不起的成就。

在欧盟的引领下,其他国家纷纷效仿。看一下国际财务报告准则的版图,包括了所有南美洲国家、北美的墨西哥和加拿大、整个加勒比地区、澳大利亚、新西兰及附近南太平洋诸岛,亚洲和非洲的大部分地区,当然还有欧洲,也包括一些非欧盟国家,比如俄罗斯和土耳其。

一些发展中经济体,如中国、韩国和巴西,对我们的工作也都非常支持。它们把采用国际财务报告准则视作一个契机,以确保其在全球顶尖财务报告中占有一席之地。比如说中国就为国际会计准则理事会的新兴经济体工作小组提供了秘书处。我们已认识到亚太地区新兴经济体的重要性,下周就将在这一地区开设第一个地区办事处,地点位于东京。

十年多一点的时间就能取得如此成就,的确进步惊人。在我看来,国际财务报告准则成为全球标准,势不可挡。

当然,我们也不能忽视这样一个事实,就是美国至今还没有决定是否和如何采用国际财务报告准则。

作为世界最大的经济体,我们非常希望美国成为国际财务报告准则大家庭的真正一员。美国证券交易委员会(SEC)长期支持我们的工作,也承认国际财务报告准则的高质量,并允许在美国上市的非本土公司使用国际财务报告准则。据估算,目前大约有500多家在美上市公司采用国际财务报告准则,多数来自欧洲。

美国证券交易委员会原本要在2011年就国际财务报告准则作出决定,但却在2011年7月宣布推迟决定。我们真切希望在2013年听到好消息。为了维持信用体系,G20呼吁全球使用统一的会计准则,尽快取得进展显得尤为重要。

国际会计准则理事会也已为自己在世界经济治理的舞台上争得了一席之地。

国际会计准则理事会作为金融稳定理事会成员,正同在全球金融体系中负有责任的其他国际组织密切合作。在这方面,我们有机会协助确立全球监管改革议程。

为什么财务报告如此具有争议

我要讲的第二个问题是,为什么财务报告如此具有争议,其中的原因很多。合理地说,我们并不总是能自圆其说。很多人认为,美国的公认会计原则和国际财务报告准则中过多、过细的披露要求需要修改。的确,有时候我们的准则似乎并无道理。比如说,因银行自身的债务价值下降而允许已饱受评级下降诟病的银行确认利得,客气地讲是"有悖常理"。针对这些案例,我们已经或者正在解决这些问题,但这并不能帮助我们从困境中脱身。

而在另一些领域里之所以出现争议,是因为我们试图给金融体系的某些阴暗角落带去一丝光亮。历史上的案例包括股票期权的费用化以及将养老金负债确认进入资产负债表,而是否将租赁业务确认进入资产负债表的论争,则成为最新的案例。

多年以前,国际会计准则理事会和美国财务会计准则委员会共同向既得利益集团宣战,以便将公司授予的股票期权计入费用。之前,公司授予股票期权并不计入费用,看起来似乎并无成本,但这些期权显然稀释了现有股东的股权。当时的游说活动规模巨大,部分是由科技行业领导的,目的就是为了维持现状。但游说人员始终无法回答一个问题:如果股票期权确实没有任何成本,为什么不把股票期权授予全体员工？甚至美国传奇投资家沃伦·巴菲特也卷入了这场激烈的论战。他在伯克希尔哈撒韦公司1998年的年报[1]中写到:"近年来,心情沮丧的首席执行官和审计师与美国财务会计准则委员会展开了激烈的斗争,因为美国财务会计准则委员会试图揭开期权幻觉的面纱,但事实上没有人站出来支持美国财务会计准则委员会。它的对手甚至将国会也拉进来,声称被夸大的费用攸关国家利益。"

用于游说美国国会以及其他政策制定者的费用超过7 000万美元[2],但最后的结果是,会计准则制定者取得最终胜利。在这个过程中,国际会计准则理事会作为开路先锋,为美国财务会计准则委员会铺平了道路。

差不多十年之后,很少再有人质疑将股票期权确认为费用的合理性,这已经成为一个众所周知的商业惯例。

养老金以及其他退休后福利也有类似境遇。许多年前,这些负债都不记入资产负债表。

不加计量自然无法管理,结果是在股东毫不知情的情况下,很多公司管理层就按名义金额放弃公司资产。

那时候,将退休金负债纳入资产负债表争议巨大。在某种程度上,现在也依然如此。但是,类似的负债目前通常是董事会和投资者讨论的议题。特别是当很多公司的养老金计划麻烦不断,如果继续向坏的方向发展就会使公司陷入窘境时更是如此。

当前,我们在租赁会计问题上面临着同样的论争与较量。尽管租赁合同通常包含很重的融资成分,但绝大多数租赁合同并不纳入资产负债表。像航空公司、铁路公司等很多公司,表外融资的金额相当可观。

更为严重的是,提供融资的却往往不是银行或银行的附属机构。如果公司为购买资产而以贷款的形式进行融资,贷款就会被记录入账。而称其为租赁后,它就在账簿上奇迹般地消失了。依我之见,如果这个东西看起来像只鸭子,像鸭子一样游泳,叫起来也像只鸭子,那这应该就是一只鸭子。租赁或其他负债的情况也是如此。

如今,大多数分析师只能根据公司披露的基本信息,凭经验来猜测被隐藏的租赁真实杠杆率。这事非常奇怪,信息明明就在管理层的手边,还要让分析师去猜测与租赁相关的负债。这就是国际会计准则理事会急于创设新的租赁会计准则的原因,事实上也是我们与美国财务准则委员会紧密合作正在进行的工作。

公司偏好表外融资,是因为表外融资可以掩盖其真实的杠杆率,而为此目的过度使用租赁业务的公司,财务状况并不好。

租赁业本身也在全力抗争,被游说重重包围的美国国会的议员们,正在草拟一封写给美国财务会计准则委员会的信。据美国一份最新的报告显示,如果国际会计准则理事会与美国财务会计准则委员会将租赁记入资产负债表的努力成为现实的话,仅在美国就将失去190 000个工作机会。可是,如果我没记错的话,当时国际会计准则理事会和美国财务会计准则委员会共同努力将股票期权费用化的时候,他们也提出过同样的责难。

此类游说并不出人意料,美国证券交易委员会对此早有先见之明。2005年6月,美国证券交易委员会就表外安排向国会提交了一份报告[3],就变革租赁会计方法据理力争。报告中这样写道:

"事实上,基于会计指南的租赁架构已如此大行其道,对租赁指南的重大调整将遭遇强大的阻力。这些阻力既来自于已经习惯于通过设计租赁业务来达到各种不同目的的财务报告编报者,也来自于服务于财务报告编报者的第三方。"

这些文字被证明相当有预见性。由于畸高的杠杆率导致了金融危机的发生,我们把隐性杠杆率透明化的努力,理应受到全世界的欢迎。而事实却是,我们面对的仍是一场艰难的论战。我们必须争取一切可能的支持,以免被游说击败。我们需要国家会计准则制定者、类似于美国证券交易委员会的监管者、投资者和其他方方面面坚定信念,支持我们把格外亟需的透明性引入这一重要领域。我们需要掷地有声的明确支持,以反击资金充足且资源丰沛的游说活动。

会计作为一门经济科学

至此,我已经向诸位阐明了会计的公共利益所在以及会计为何如此具有争议。我认为会计之所以有趣的第三个原因,是因为它挑战智慧,充满乐趣。基本而言,会计就是一门经济科学。

这样说意味着,与经济学一样,会计与其说是科学,还不如说是艺术,我这样说绝无冒犯之意。像其他经济学科一样,编制财务报告也经常需要进行判断。会计学也存在经济学家族其他成员同样的问题：工作时需要运用数学，但你不能指望会有数学运算那样精确的结果。

例如，即使是一项相同的资产或负债，商业模式不同，会计也会有多种不同的方法来计量。像无形资产的计量就困难重重，比如：收购了一家公司，如何计量其品牌价值？

财务报告的本质特征就是专业判断的应用。然而，我们不应忘记，在许多情况下，专业判断不过就是推理推测而已。

我们之所以花大量时间修订概念框架，是因为概念框架是会计准则的理论基石。

概念框架解决的是最基本的问题，诸如什么是资产，负债与所有者权益如何区分，如何计量收入。这些问题似乎非常简单，但我相信要得到正确的答案绝非易事！

及时修订概念框架，几乎得到普遍一致的支持。概念框架是国际会计准则理事会决策的参照标准。在选择不够明晰的时候，概念框架的作用就是促进国际会计准则理事会作出使各项会计准则保持一致的决策。在企业运用原则导向的会计准则时，概念框架也是重要的参考。

国际会计准则理事会的现有概念框架很好地发挥了作用，但某些领域（如计量）仍稍有欠缺。这也不难理解，因为计量是会计最具主观臆断、最难处理且最具政治化的领域。在这个领域，我们需要的是更加严谨和明确，这将是一项极为艰巨的任务，需要大量的智力投入，也需要极大的勇气。

无论结果如何，都不太会得到全体一致的拥护。试设想，一群全球顶尖经济学家坐在一起制定宏观经济学概念框架，唯一必然的成果就是唇枪舌战、颜面尽失、一事无成！诺贝尔经济学奖就自动授予那个唯一生存下来的经济学家。会计师都谦逊富有教养，我肯定我们都会彬彬有礼，但就永远轮不上举世盛誉了。

结束语

女士们，先生们，非常荣幸今天能够和大家分享我的一些看法。总之，我深信国际财务报告准则必将成为全球标准，我也深信会计准则制定者们一定会继续保持低调，因为哪怕是向好的方向变革，变革也不受欢迎，这是由于有太多的人可以从保持现状中获益。

感谢各位在百忙之中聆听我的演讲。我想，既然这里是伦敦经济学院，我非常期待有一些具有挑战性的提问。相信各位一定不会让我失望吧!

---

[1] Berkshire Hathaway Inc.1998 Annual Report. www.berkshirehathaway.com.
[2] Warren McGregor.IASB 十年点滴.澳大利亚会计回顾,2012 年 9 月.
[3] Report and Recommendations Pursuant to Section 401(c) of the Sarbanes-Oxley Act of 2002 On Arrangements with Off-Balance Sheet Implications, Special Purpose Entities, and Transparency of Filings by Issuers, June 2005. www.sec.gov.

(乔元芳 翻译并审校)

消除对国际财务报告准则
的偏见与误解

2012年11月15日,国际会计准则理事会亚洲—大洋洲办事处成立,汉斯·胡格沃斯特出席成立大会并发表题为《消除对国际财务报告准则的偏见与误解》的开幕致辞。本文为演讲全文。

中冢部长、萩原主席以及各位尊敬的嘉宾:

今天,国际会计准则理事会(IASB)在伦敦之外的首家海外办事处正式成立了,能够代表国际会计准则理事会出席本次盛会,我深感荣幸。首家海外办事处之所以选址亚洲—大洋洲地区,是因为该地区是不二之选,这也是我能够怀着愉快的心情来到这里的原因所在。在此,十分感谢日本财务会计准则基金会(JFASF)为设立办事处所提供的支持和帮助,我坚信亚洲—大洋洲地区办事处将会获得巨大的成功,这一点毋庸置疑。

首先,亚洲—大洋洲地区是当今世界最具活力的经济区域。该地区有如此多的国家、地区以及公司愿意使用我们所制定的会计语言与世界各地的投资者进行沟通,对国际会计准则理事会来说这是一种巨大的荣誉。因此,国际会计准则理事会需要在本地区筹建办事机构,以确保我们制定的财务报告准则能够全面满足这一重要地区的需求。

其次,在财务报告领域,亚洲—大洋洲地区拥有许多知识渊博、经验丰富的业内专家。站在国际会计准则理事会的立场,我们一直都很期待收到来自该地区的反馈意见以及其他评论。这些意见和评论对我们制定高质量的会计准则、拓展工作思路有着极为重要的参考价值。我们希望通过建立这个办事处,能够更好地倾听来自该地区的声音。

整个亚洲—大洋洲地区共有25个发展程度各异、经济水平参差不齐的国家和地区，各自的想法和诉求差异很大。亚洲—大洋洲会计准则制定机构组（Asia-Oceania Standard-Setters Group）的主要工作就是汇总这些国家和地区的意见和观点，尽可能地统筹协调，向国际会计准则理事会传递亚洲—大洋洲地区的统一心声。我们真诚地希望该办事处能够有助于进一步深化该地区的合作与沟通交流。此外，设立办事处的另一个目的是为了确保亚洲能够融入国际会计准则理事会的日常工作。

亚洲—大洋洲地区办事处的成立，也有助于国际会计准则理事会加深对这一地区的了解。作为一个成立时间不长、相对年轻的组织，国际会计准则理事会仍有许多工作要做。我经常穿梭于世界各地，注意到仍然有一些关于国际会计准则理事会的误解尚待消除。借此机会，请允许我予以澄清。

对国际会计准则理事会的一个长期误解，是认为国际会计准则理事会只对公允价值感兴趣（或许暗地里）。而事实上，我们一直都是混合计量模式的支持者。虽然美国财务会计准则委员会的同行们曾对金融工具提出了完全以公允价值计量的模式，但国际会计准则理事会却始终认为，混合计量模式更加合适。我们完全同意，对交易活跃的金融工具使用公允价值计量，具有很好的相关性。但是，对一家制造业公司来说，用公允价值来计量其不动产、厂房以及设备则毫无道理，没有任何意义。

目前，我们正在重新审视"概念框架"中"计量"那一章的内容。我们将针对在何种特定环境下应使用哪种计量模式制定明确的原则。当然，"计量"一直是一个难点，因此我们的工作面临着重重困难，最终结果尚无法预料。然而，即便此项工作刚刚起步，我亦可大胆预言，最终绝不会把公允价值作为唯一的计量技术。因此，有关公允价值的的误解和争论可以休矣。

对国际会计准则理事会的第二个误解是，国际会计准则理事会只关注资产负债表，并以综合收益取代净收益。与第一个误解一样，我找不到可以支持这种偏见的任何证据。我们不会将资产负债表或损益表中的某一类信息，认定为财务报告的主要关注点。实际上，资产负债表与损益表是互补的，我们同样将净收益视为一项重要的业绩指标。但是，综合收益也包括了许多不同的项目，可供财务报表使用者单独分析。

尽管如此，但我们也意识到，确实需要厘清以不同方式列报不同利得和损失应遵循的基本原则。其他综合收益已经成为一个被广泛讨论的敏感会计问题，然而实际情况却是，没有人知道其他综合收益的真正含义是什么。厘清净收益与其他综合收益之间的关系，使收益列报变得更有意义，是国际会计准则理事会应有的责任。在重新审视概念框架的过程中,我们将努力实现上述目标,希望我们能够成功!

与此同时,请各位放心,我们没有将损益从业绩计量指标中剔除的想法,也不会将综合收益作为衡量业绩的唯一指标。这再次说明,事实不等同于流言。

由于对国际会计准则理事会存在的前两个误解,导致了第三个长期存在、持续不断的误解,那就是国际财务报告准则只是伦敦和华尔街金融才俊的掌上玩物。这个误解认为,国际财务报告准则与那些有着浓厚制造业传统国家的文化是不相容的。在这里我再次声明,这种想法并不正确。放眼世界,绝大多数使用国际财务报告准则的公司,其业务均涉及制造业、零售业以及服务业等常规经济业务。自2007年全球金融危机爆发之日起,媒体就国际财务报告准则对于金融机构的意义进行了连篇累牍地报道。但媒体报道与现实大相径庭,"实体经济"中的企业每天都在使用国际财务报告准则。

我想谈的第四个也是最后一个误解就是国际会计准则理事会被认为是由远在伦敦的英国人所掌控的象牙塔。幸运的是,得益于我们加强与世界各地利益相关方的沟通,这种批评声似乎有所减弱。

事实上,国际会计准则理事会并不是一个隶属于某个国家的组织,而是一个真正的国际化组织。我们的工作人员和理事来自于世界各地,他们都致力于为公众利益而努力工作。我们的使命只有一个,那就是制定高质量的会计准则,更好地为世界各地的利益相关方提供服务。在制定会计准则时,我们十分重视来自世界各地的专业意见。通过建立会计准则咨询论坛(ASAF),我们将进一步加深与诸如亚洲—大洋洲会计准则制定机构组(AOSSG)等国际和地区性会计准则制定机构之间的互动关系。

亚洲—大洋洲办事处的设立是一个有着重大象征意义的时刻,表达了国际会计准则理事会致力成为一个真正的全球性组织的承诺。

我们将信守承诺,继续为亚洲—大洋洲地区及其利益相关方提供优质的服务,不辜负你们的信任。最后,我想再次对日本政府和日本财务会计准则基金会表示感谢,正是你们的努力,亚洲—大洋洲地区办事处才能顺利成立,谢谢!

(郭尧 翻译;张晓泉 校对;乔元芳 审定)

致力实现财务报告的一致性

2013年1月17日,汉斯·胡格沃斯特接受安永会计师事务所邀请,在伦敦城市大学卡斯商学院发表了题为《致力实现财务报告的一致性》的演讲。本文为演讲全文。

各位,下午好,很高兴受邀参加本次会议。众所周知,国际会计准则理事会一直致力于发展自身的研究能力,并为此付出了相当多的努力。这项工作的思路之一,就是鼓励开展独立研究,以作为国际会计准则理事会活动的有效补充。因此,在了解蒲柏教授及其团队所开展的研究之后,我大受鼓舞。

这项研究深入透彻、系统全面,令人印象深刻。研究报告的主要结论是:在资产减值披露方面,欧洲各国差异很大;国际财务报告准则的应用水平参差不齐。虽然准则是否得到一致的应用,并不是国际会计准则理事会的主要职责,但我们对这些研究发现倍感兴趣。

2005年,欧洲决定全面采用国际财务报告准则时,面对的是一个未知的前景,有着太多的不确定因素。

在这之前,没有一个机构尝试过在这样一个经济、文化呈多元化的地区中采用同一套会计准则,并一字不差地予以实施。世界其他国家和地区密切关注着欧洲的实施效果。

国际财务报告准则实施一年后,欧洲委员会[1]发起的一项研究发现,尽管采用国际财务报告准则颇具挑战性,但最终获得了成功。该项研究得出结论:"各方已经形成普遍共识,认为国际财务报告准则让各国之间、同行业竞争者之间以及各行业之间的财务报表比较变得更加容易"。

然而,要获得最大限度的可比性,就必须保证准则得到一致的应用、审计及执行。对于欧盟而言，27个成员国差异巨大，不仅执行方式和风格各不相同，而且经济规模差异颇大，最大经济体的经济总量是最小经济体经济总量的400多倍。在这种情况下，要保证国际财务报告准则一致实施和执行是一项不小的挑战。

今天展示的研究报告显示，国际财务报告准则在欧盟各成员国的采用和执行程度有所差异，监管环境更严格的成员国更有可能生成高质量的报告。对此，我并不感到惊讶。

但是，即使存在强有力的监管环境，也不能确保准则得到一致的应用。近期，美国证券交易委员会（SEC）针对国际财务报告准则应用情况发布的职员报告[2]指出，2010年，美国证券交易委员会对大约4 500家发行人的财务报告进行了审核，结果发现约15%的财务报告需要进行重述。这表明在美国这样一个复杂的经济体中，即使公认会计原则（GAAP）早已得到广泛深入的实施，会计准则的一致应用仍然是一项挑战。

国际财务报告准则的批评者认为，既然国际财务报告准则在全球范围内未得到一致的应用和执行，那么就没有必要采用国际财务报告准则。当然，这种观点纯属无稽之谈。事实上，相对于那些数量众多、各不相同而且也同样没有得到一致应用的国家会计准则，即使未得到一致应用，全球性准则所提供的报告可比性也会更高。

如果没有一个全球性准则，就绝对不可能实现全球财务报告之间的可比性。通过提高国际财务报告准则在全球的一致应用，将极大地增强财务报告的可比性。

采用统一的会计语言后，我们能够更容易地发现准则应用的不一致之处，并加以改进。如果欧洲没有采用单一的会计语言，那么这份研究报告就不可能出炉。正是因为有了国际财务报告准则，该报告才能清楚地识别出特定司法管辖区在应用国际财务报告准则方面存在的问题。我相信，欧洲证券与市场管理局（ESMA）将会利用这些研究发现，鼓励各成员国进一步提高国际财务报告准则应用的一致性。

在保障国际财务报告准则一致性应用的道路上，监管机构和审计师应该肩负重任，带头应对挑战。但是，我们也认识到，在这一过程中，国际会计准则理事会也需要发挥重要作用。接下来的几分钟，我将向各位介绍一下由国际会计准则理事会牵头，在以下五个领域中所开展的工作情况。

第一，作为会计准则制定者，我们最显著的贡献就是制定出以原则为导向,能够在全球范围内得到一致实施、审核和执行的会计准则。

在过去的几年里,我们加强了新准则制定工作的质量控制。

我们深化了与亚洲—大洋洲会计准则制定机构小组(AOSSG)、欧洲财务报告咨询小组(EFRAG)等国家及地区准则制定机构的合作,并宣布建立一个新平台——会计准则咨询论坛(ASAF),以加强准则制定机构之间的合作与互动。

未来几个月,会计准则咨询论坛就将启动并运转。就像汽车制造商在不同的地形条件下测试其新开发车型一样,会计准则咨询论坛也将协助我们对新准则进行"路测",以了解和掌握新准则在欧盟这种多元化的地区中是如何发挥作用的。

第二,作为改进应循程序的成果,目前我们已经完成了一项重要会计准则和解释实施两年后评估的工作。

会计准则实施的后评估,为我们提供了重要的安全防护网,能够识别并纠正一致性应用等方面不可预见的难题,因为这些问题只有在实务应用中才能暴露出来。

目前,我们即将完成"分部报告"准则的评估工作,这是我们开展的第一项实施情况评估工作,接下来我们还将开展"企业合并"准则的评估工作。

第三,最近,我们完成了对国际财务报告准则解释委员会的审核工作,为期两年。通过此次审核,准则解释委员会将拥有更多的手段,用以解决实践中的多样性问题,并能够对解决问题的请求进行更有效的回应。

准则解释委员会负责诠释准则,帮助国际会计准则理事会对会计准则进行小幅改进。

第四,我们正加紧制作教育培训材料。去年12月,我们发布了"公允价值计量"培训指南。目前,我们正在为"合营安排"编制类似的指导材料。

第五,我们显著加强了与证券监管机构的合作。例如,在国际层面,证券委员会国际组织(IOSCO)给予我们大力支持;在地区层面,则有欧洲证券与市场管理局的密切合作。

我本人和国际会计准则理事会受托人主席米歇尔·普拉达(Michel Prada)过去都曾在证券监管机构任职,这充分证明国际会计准则理事会与证券监管机构之间存在天然的密切关系。

我们与各个组织之间的对话务实有效,我们正寻求通过更多的方式拓展这种合作关系,也许可以采用某种形式的谅解备忘录或其他正式协议。

总而言之，为应对准则一致性应用挑战，我们作出了许多努力，包括使准则的措辞更加严谨清晰、提供更多的支持、对请求解释与回答的问题给予更及时的回应，以及与其他各方合作强化准则的执行。

与此同时，我们不应该忘记已经取得的成就。大约十年前，同一项交易在欧盟境内就有 25 种完全不同的会计处理方法。而如今，欧盟已经实现了会计准则统一，相同的交易均按相同的方法处理。对此项成就，欧洲应该引以为荣。

我前面已经提及，要解决准则应用的一致性问题，需要准则制定机构、审计师、监管机构和其他各方的通力协作，而大型会计师事务所更应该在这方面发挥重要作用。

大型会计师事务所具有其他机构所不具备的优势，它们的触角遍及全球，在欧盟境内（从最大国家到最小国家）以及在全球各地都设有分支机构。

本项研究由安永发起并赞助。在共同解决财务报告一直存在的一致性挑战方面，我非常希望听到安永自身的行动计划。

女士们、先生们，感谢你们拨冗出席。

---

[1] 欧盟委员会．欧盟关于实施国际财务报告准则和公允价值的指令.www.icaew.com．

[2] 美国证券交易委员会考虑将国际财务报告准则纳入美国发行人财务报告体系的工作计划，2012 年 7 月，第 31 页.www.sec.gov．

（张翔 翻译；张晓泉 校对；乔元芳 审定）

会计与长期投资:"买入并持有"并非"买入并期待"

2013年4月9日,英格兰和威尔士特许会计师协会与国际财务报告准则基金会受托人在英国伦敦联合举办大会,汉斯·胡格沃斯特出席并发表《会计与长期投资:"买入并持有"并非"买入并期待"》的演讲。本文为演讲全文。

作为一名前政客,我对短期主义的弊病了如指掌。哈罗德·威尔逊(Harold Wilson)曾说过一句名言:"在政治领域,一周就称得上是漫长了。"当然,他作此评价时,互联网和24小时不间断新闻的时代尚未到来。但遗憾的是,短期主义仍是当今经济中的一大问题。有两大因素导致了短期主义:一是在现代市场经济中,人们管理他人资金的广度和深度前所未有;二是随着经济复杂性的日益加剧,投资者和被投资者之间的距离急剧拉大。

一直以来,公司治理与监管机构都在加快步伐,努力与日益复杂的金融中介机构以及诸多诱惑保持同步。投资者将资金托付给了经理人,却没有多少投资者能够实时掌握经理人的动态。此外,投资者与经理人之间的利益冲突也成为常态。投资公司本应以管理投资人的资金为己任,但与此同时,他们也在管理着自己的退休基金。如此一来,投资经理将会遭受怎样的指责?

所有的这一切,都是短期主义梦寐以求的"后门"。在巨大的利益驱使下,基金经理会作出"动量驱动型"(momentum-driven)的投资决策。事实上,近期的研究显示,这的确是一种获利颇丰的操作模式[1]。在短期内,无论大趋势是否合理,跟随大趋势通常是最保险的方式。只要一切运行正常,基金经理就不会听到责备的声音,一旦情况发生变化、曲终人散,他也可以把责任推给市场。

除此之外,当前的宏观经济政策也对秉持长期投资理念的投资者不利。

世界各国央行为了确保经济发展的持续性，纷纷采用积极扩张的政策。这些政策对未来的影响尚未可知，但是很有可能结局惨烈。

众多观察人士都担心金融市场的短视行为会对长期投资和经济增长产生危害。近期，针对这个问题，金融稳定理事会(FSB)、30国集团和欧盟委员会(EC)纷纷发布研究报告[2]。虽然会计准则不是该议题的核心，但是这些报告还是对准则提出了一些建议，认为会计准则应该为实行长线投资的投资者提供更多的帮助。

那么，为推动建立健康的长期投资环境，国际会计准则理事会应发挥怎样的作用呢？我认为，这是我们工作中至关重要、不可或缺的组成部分。我的前任戴维·泰迪爵士(David Tweedie)反复强调，会计准则的主要职责就是使资本主义诚实可信。管理层的固有职责是高效地运用公司资源并获得最佳的经营成果，而财务报告就是要迫使管理层披露他们的履职情况，这就是受托责任(stewardship)的基本原则，从本质上，它意味着"问责"(accountability)。

几年前，我们将"受托责任"一词从概念框架中删除，一些批评人士对此表示遗憾。更有甚者，认为这一举动表明国际会计准则理事会不再对长期投资者的利益予以重视。面对指责，我们通常的回答是，删除"受托责任"仅仅是因为很难把它翻译成其他语言。此外，我们认为，修订后的概念框架仍然贯穿"受托责任"这项基本原则的实质。如果你仔细地研读过概念框架，就会发现情况确实如此。当然，我也知道，你要找到对"受托责任"原则本质的明确描述，的确有点困难。

财务报告非常重要的一项职能就是促使管理层披露受托责任履行情况，这一点毋庸置疑。管理层有义务告知投资者：公司拥有哪些资源，为何获取这些资源，以及如何使用所获得的资源。同时，管理层还应该告知投资者：公司在经营过程中产生哪些债务或其他义务，为什么会有这些债务，以及如何偿付这些债务。这些信息不仅能帮助投资者作出买入、持有或卖出的投资决策，而且也有助于他们对管理层的管理活动进行投票表决。如果"受托责任"一词很难翻译，或许我们可以用更合适的单词来取代它，比如"问责"(accountability)。

毫无疑问，不管如何称呼"受托责任"，都不会影响其成为财务报告的核心目标。除了基本原则以外，会计准则还有其他方法对长期投资者产生影响吗？现在有一种观点十分流行，认为由于国际财务报告准则过度依赖公允价值和其他现值计量方法，从而抑制了长期投资。据称，过度使用公允价值，刺激了有目的的财务行为设计和短期利益的豪取。

那么，事实又是如何呢？实际情况是，除金融行业外，绝大多数公司都很少使用公允价值会计，它们的大部分资产和负债还是以历史成本计量。如果诸位一直关注国际会计准则理事会的概念框架讨论，就应该知道这种情况不会改变。即便是在金融业，摊余成本仍然是重要的计量基础。无论是现在还是将来，大多数银行的传统资产（如贷款等）都是按照摊余成本来计量。因此，很多学术研究都得出"在金融危机期间，公允价值并不是经济波动的主要动因"的结论，就不足为奇了。

当然，相较于其他行业，目前的计量方法对金融业的影响要更大一些。很多金融工具在流动性充分的活跃市场上24小时不间断地被交易，所以，市场价格能够传递最具相关性的信息。在金融危机期间，公允价值就充分发挥了作用，能够更加及时地提供已注入市场的有害金融工具的相关信息。相对无视公允价值的人，那些关注公允价值信号的财务报告编制者和投资者所遭受的损失要小很多。金融业所使用的现行价格计量方法将会在我们随后出台的保险合同会计准则中得到更多的使用。各位可能知道，国际会计准则理事会即将完成保险合同会计准则征求意见稿的拟定工作。由于目前许多保险公司都采用历史成本计量方法，拟出台的保险准则将规定以现行价格来计量保险负债。在就保险合同会计准则征询公众意见过程中，也会部分地涉及长期投资和短期主义的相关讨论。

保险界业内人士对新准则的影响表示忧虑。他们认为新准则将制造更大的收益波动，既妨碍他们进行长期投资，也无法提供具有稳定收益的保险产品。那么，哪些是事实，哪些是臆想呢？我首先需要指出的是，保险业是体量庞大的非常重要的投资者。仅仅在欧洲，保险业就拥有价值5.4万亿欧元的投资组合。寿险业务是一项长期负债业务，所以，保险业潜意识里更偏好稳健的长期投资。

遗憾的是，目前的货币政策让保险业度日如年。近期，作为欧洲保险业的监管机构，欧洲保险和职业养老金管理局（EIOPA）因长期持续低利率对保险业所造成的影响而敲响了警钟。从负债角度，低利率将增加保险公司债务的现值，同时资产回报也在缩水。换句话说，如果低利率政策持续，保险商的资产所产生的现金流将不足以支付投保人的索赔申请。

欧洲保险和职业养老金管理局担心，相当数量的保险商将不能满足其资本要求。欧洲保险和职业养老金管理局分析认为，日本的部分保险公司就曾因为持续低利率而破产，其他保险商不得不下调对客户承诺的投资回报率[3]。如果说保险业是金融危机的受害者,那么,它绝对是一名沉默的受害者。保险业未能成为新闻头条的部分原因,是因为缺少恰当的会计准则,从而使存在的问题无法暴露出来。

在许多司法管辖区,保险公司以历史成本来计量保险负债,尽管呈报的结果看上去挺合理,但是这种结果基于完全过时的利率,甚至采用的是 10 年前的利率。欧洲保险和职业养老金管理局认为:"虽然低利率的影响并未马上显现在资产负债表里,但这并不意味着问题不存在,这些隐含的问题将累积成真正的风险。"

新的保险合同会计准则将要求保险公司使用现行利率计量负债,从而使隐藏的问题暴露在光天化日之下,帮助投资者更好地了解保险行业的真实业绩。与此同时,市场也将获得更多关于保险公司负债与资产有效匹配方面的信息。批评者认为,利率和其他市场波动因素无处不在,而新准则将导致不必要的短期波动。

我们不会对这些批评视而不见。实际上,保险合同准则征求意见稿将包含很多减少会计波动的建议。但是,我们坚决抵制通过人为方式来平抑波动的建议。某些保险商提出的建议,在前述 30 国集团报告中也有所提及。其中一个建议是,保险负债的计量应该基于保险公司所持有资产的预期收益。部分保险业内人士对此建议欢欣鼓舞,但是我们对此顾虑重重。我们称之为"充满希望和愿景"的会计方法。我们认为,将负债的计量建立在不确定的资产收益上的做法并不谨慎,"买入并持有"不能变为"买入并期待"。

30 国集团报告的附录包含了更加激进的消除短期波动的方法,被称为"目标日会计法"。该方法的主要建议是:要求保险公司将其多元化权益证券投资组合纳入"目标日基金"并承诺将长期持有;为平滑短期波动,该基金将以成本和市场价格的时间加权平均数进行估值。

这个建议也同样存在问题。如果公司的会计记录是基于平均数而不是报告日的市场价值,那将严重危及对财务报告的信任。市场参与者最为简单的应对策略,就是直接将目标日基金的价值再转换为市场价值。我认为,国际会计准则理事会可以使市场参与者免受这种调整的麻烦。我们始终认为,现行价值计量能够最好地反映出保险公司的财务状况,新的会计准则也将进行重大改进。如果它导致财务数据的波动,那可能正好反映了真实的经济风险。只有拥有充足的资本,才能抵御这种风险,而会计准则不应该试图去掩盖风险。

最后,我想强调的是,即便是长期投资者,也不应该回避短期波动,因为你根本不知道短期到底有多"短"。各国的中央银行均认为,目前的利率水平是

"异常的低"。事实上,日本采用超低利率政策已经长达15年了!西方国家采用低利率也已超过5年了,没有人知道利率何时能够恢复到正常水平。

据估计,从伦敦飞往纽约的航班,只有10%的时间是在正确的航向上飞行。飞机的飞行方向不单纯取决于飞行员,还有很多外部因素,比如风速和风向。

为了能够实现安全飞抵纽约这一长期目标,飞行员需要不断地进行短期微调。做生意也是一样。瑞士著名的长期投资家布尔杰·恩科霍姆(Boerje Ekholm)最近表示,他的公司总是有一个长期目标,"但是我们会像猎犬一样,甄别你的短期经营能力"。他强调,为了达到长期目标,管理者应该每天进行评估[4]。如果你没有及时地调整经营方向,那么,事态的发展将迫使你花费成倍的努力来拨乱反正。

因此,对那些告诉你他们只关心长期、不想受市场价值打扰的人,你要多加小心。身为一家放眼未来的公司,应该有能力承受不可避免的市场短期波动。真正的问题在于,我们在经济系统中积累了史无前例的高杠杆,而极端杠杆化的结果是将把金融业中的绝大部分公司推向危险的边缘。即便在《巴塞尔协议Ⅲ》出台之后,银行依然能够通过负债来筹措97%的资产。如此之高的负债水平对长期增长有着怎样的影响,我无从知晓。现在,连保险业也开始涉足高风险领域。它们进入了债券市场,不是出于会计原因,而是因为它们没有足够的资本来承受股权投资的风险。

对于这些风险,国际会计准则理事会要出台相应的对策,不能视而不见,假装它们并不存在。正如飞机已经偏离了航线,而飞行员却被告知正在飞往纽约一样,如果我们制定的准则没有起到矫正作用,那么这些准则就一无所用。那些关注长期投资的人也应该知道他们投资活动的现状。国际会计准则理事会的工作,就是尽可能地为短期和长期活动提供最大的透明度。我们会竭尽所能,随时为长期投资者提供他们所需要的信息。

---

[1]持续活跃的市场战略.金融时报,2013—03—08.

[2]金融稳定委员会.影响长期投资有效性的金融监管因素,2009—02—08;G30.长期融资和经济增长.欧盟.欧洲经济的长期融资,2013—03—25.http://www.ft.com/cms/s/0/077de35e-93bc-11e2-b528-00144feabdc0.html#axzz2OUkkNNrf.

[3]EIOPA.长期低利率环境下的监管响应,2013—02—28.

[4]斯堪的纳维亚半岛:模式化管理.金融时报,2013—03—21.

(曹宇红 翻译;张晓泉 校对;乔元芳 审定)

国际财务报告准则与印度尼西亚会计准则:2013 及未来展望

2013 年 3 月 6 日,印度尼西亚会计师协会(IAI)和东盟会计师联合会(AFA)联合在印度尼西亚首都雅加达举办了名为"2013 年及未来的国际财务报告准则动态:对印度尼西亚的影响"的国际研讨会。汉斯·胡格沃斯特出席会议并发表题为《国际财务报告准则与印度尼西亚会计准则:2013 及未来展望》的演讲。本文为演讲全文。

尊敬的女士们、先生们:

这并不是我的首次印度尼西亚之行。20 世纪 90 年代后期,在担任荷兰政府社会事务部副部长期间,我第一次访问了印度尼西亚,深刻地感受到了这个国家的魅力以及雅加达这座城市的活力,这个国家所展现出来的巨大潜力给我留下了深刻的印象。印度尼西亚是世界第四大人口大国,拥有富庶的天然资源。我清楚地意识到在未来数十年的时间里,这些自然资源优势将助推印度尼西亚经济的强劲增长。

但是,在我首次访问时,印度尼西亚的经济形势并不乐观。实际上,这个国家当时深受亚洲金融危机的影响。与周边许多国家一样,印度尼西亚经历了一段相当困难的时期:低迷的经济以及动荡的政治格局。

2007 年,我作为一名普通的观光者再次访问了印度尼西亚。这一次访问,我充分体验了美丽如画的风景并结识了善良友好的人民。作为一名荷兰人,我在很小的时候就曾接触过印度尼西亚的文化(和美食),我很高兴能有此机会进一步认识和了解这个国家。遗憾的是,那次旅行的时间太短暂,但是这并不妨碍我见证这个国家已经发生的变化:印度尼西亚正一步步走出亚洲金融危机的泥潭,金融系统得以重建,经济开始复苏。

这次是我的第三次印度尼西亚之行，所见所感又大有不同。虽然严重的金融和经济危机再次爆发，但是这次危机始发于西方国家而不是亚洲。亚洲国家已经从20世纪90年代的经济危机中吸取了教训，因此在应对这次危机时更显从容不迫。

而这次，西方国家显然忘记了它们曾教给亚洲的应对方法，这就好比医生给病人开具了处方，自己却没有遵照执行，现在只能自尝苦果。在这次经济危机中，西方国家的银行系统崩溃，公共财政陷入混乱。至今，这些工业化国家还在为经济复苏和增长而苦苦挣扎。

而这一次，国际货币基金组织（IMF）又会给印度尼西亚什么样的评分呢？在这里，请允许我引用一份2012年度报告的评价："在过去的十年里，印度尼西亚对其政策框架进行了根本性的改革，虽然全球经济自2007年以来表现疲软，但印度尼西亚经济还能独善其身。"此外，报告还指出："强有力的政策框架帮助印度尼西亚更快地摆脱了2008年全球金融危机的影响，比其他亚洲国家表现更好。"15年前，当IMF强迫印度尼西亚签署紧缩支出方案以换取紧急贷款时，它是否能够预见到这个国家今日所取得的成效？

当前，印度尼西亚正释放着自己的潜能，一路前行。2005年，高盛（GoldmanSachs）罗列了11个能充当全球经济发展引擎的"下一代经济体"，印度尼西亚名列其中。高盛预测印度尼西亚经济增长将高于全球平均水平，到2050年，其经济规模将有望超过德国甚至英国。

当然，没有人能准确预测40年后的世界格局。但是不可否认的是，印度尼西亚拥有实现上述目标的潜力。说到这里，回到今天的主题，我可以肯定地告诉大家，国际财务报告准则作为一项重要工具，可以帮助印度尼西亚充分释放自己的潜能。我也相信全面采用国际财务报告准则将有助于印度尼西亚保持其良好的经济发展态势。

在解释国际财务报告准则将如何让印度尼西亚受益之前，请允许我先向在座各位介绍一下国际财务报告准则是如何发展成为全球统一的财务报告语言的。

十年前，世界上只有极少数国家采用国际财务报告准则，但现在，已经有100多个国家要求或者允许使用国际财务报告准则，G20成员国中已有3/4的国家加入国际财务报告准则阵营。在美洲，几乎所有的拉丁美洲国家以及加拿大已经采用国际财务报告准则。美国虽然还没有作出最终决定，但是允许500多家在美上市的外国发行人使用国际财务报告准则。在欧洲，所有国家都已采用国际财务报告准则。在亚洲—大洋洲地区，韩国、马来西亚、澳大利亚、新西兰以及中国香港实现了国际财务报告准则的全面采用，许多国家正朝这个方向努力着。中国所采用的会计准则与国际财务报告准则在很大程度上实现了趋同，而在日本，预计采用国际财务报告准则的公司数量将显著增加。全球500强企业中，已经有一半的企业采用国际财务报告准则编制财务报告。每年都有新的国家或地区加入国际财务报告准则阵营，最近俄罗斯和中国台湾就作出了采用国际财务报告准则的决定。

这些进展缘何在短时期内就得以实现？为什么如此多的国家和地区，不管是大国还是小地区，都放弃了自己熟悉的当地会计准则转而采用国际财务报告准则？当然，每个国家或地区都有各自的原因。

欧洲着手建立一个共同经济体，为此，它需要一套通用的财务报告语言。本世纪初，欧盟成员国采用不同的会计语言，数量众多。比如，德国的会计制度与其税务制度结合得非常紧密，而与之相反，英国的会计制度则与美国的会计制度没有多大差别。会计语言的多样化导致了理解和沟通的障碍。

2002年，欧盟决定采用国际财务报告准则，并在短短三年的时间内实现了这一目标。2005年，欧盟25个成员国境内超过7 000家公司同时转换采用国际财务报告准则。多项调研报告均认为，欧盟采用国际财务报告准则这一举措取得了巨大的成功，增加了透明度并提高了可比性。投资者一方面要求数据能更加真实可靠，另一方面还期望降低资金成本。欧盟成功采用国际财务报告准则，正应验了一句老话："有志者，事竟成"。

如果说采用国际财务报告准则为欧洲国家带来了经济收益，那么一旦新兴经济体采用国际财务报告准则，它们将获得什么样的收益呢？事实上，20世纪90年代亚洲发生的经济危机可以说是一个重要的推动因素，促进了国际财务报告准则在该地区的发展和传播。许许多多的投资者刚有机会试水国际市场投资，亚洲经济危机就给了他们当头一棒。投资者希望接触到的财务报表能与国内财务报表保持一致。国际财务报告准则响应投资者需求，提供了一种全球性的会计语言，增加资本市场的可信度，同时降低资金成本。

对于许多新兴经济体而言，采用国际财务报告准则成为一个重要宣言——向全世界展示自己的雄心壮志，并承诺遵守最高标准的财务报告准则。比如，一名伦敦、纽约或是香港的投资者可以阅读韩国公司按国际财务报告准则编制的财务报表,充分了解和熟悉该公司的财务状况。

一些国家,比如韩国,之前国际投资者因不熟悉韩国自身会计规则会对韩国公司的评估打所谓的"韩国折扣",在采用国际财务报告准则后这种情况将有所缓解。今天,这些国际投资者可以将韩国公司与其分布在世界100多个国家的国际同行进行比较和对比。

需要提请大家注意的是,只有完全采用国际财务报告准则才能充分享受到"国际财务报告准则品牌"所带来的全部收益。对于外国投资者而言,很难将细微差别与显著差异区分开来。如果一个国家或地区不能确保全面采用国际财务报告准则,那么投资者就有可能认为当地准则与国际财务报告准则之间的差异比实际差异更大。如果一个国家或者地区排除了所有的困难,已经采用了95%的国际财务报告准则,那么,请确保采用剩下的5%吧。否则,这个国家或地区就会陷入尴尬的境地:经历了所有的准则过渡之痛,却没有获得国际社会的全面认同。

几乎所有的国家或地区在采纳国际财务报告准则之初,在将国内会计实务向国际财务报告准则转换时都会面临一些挑战,这些都在预料之中。多数情况下,这些问题都能得以解决;但有些时候,这些问题却相当复杂,比如印度尼西亚的土地所有权问题。

大部分国家和地区认为,全面采用国际财务报告准则提高了可信度,相较于为了解决本土问题而不断地修订本土准则而言,前者的益处更大。其他国家或地区也会面临同样的问题,这为我们提供了机会,可以通过集思广益、通过统一处理的方式来更好地解决问题。如此一来,国际财务报告准则采用者都可以从这些改进中获益。

我非常高兴地看到,印度尼西亚的国际财务报告准则采用工作已经步入正轨,其财务会计准则委员会(DSAK)在主席罗西塔·乌利·西纳加(Rosita Uli Sinaga)的有力带领下取得了长足的进步。但是,全面采用国际财务报告准则的征途尚未结束。要让国际投资者相信印度尼西亚为释放自身潜力正全力以赴,那么,完成准则转换将是至关重要的一步。

今天我要告诉大家,我和我所在的组织将为印度尼西亚的准则转换工作提供全力的支持。我们将协助你们完成最后的一小步,以收获全面采用国际财务报告准则的丰硕果实。我完全相信印度尼西亚能克服这些仅存的障碍,实现国际财务报告准则的全面采用。

国际会计准则理事会与印度尼西亚财务会计准则委员会之间已经结成

了牢固的合作关系,双方工作代表精诚合作。我相信双方的合作空间还可以进一步加深。

亚洲—大洋洲是世界经济的重要组成部分,国际会计准则理事会已经投入了大量的资源以支持该地区的经济发展。为更好地服务于印度尼西亚及该地区其他重要经济体,最近,我们在日本东京设立了亚洲—大洋洲办事处。主任光弘竹村(Mitsuhiro Takemura)是我的好友兼同事,他也出席了今天的会议,目的就是为了更好地了解印度尼西亚的国际财务报告准则实施计划,并提供更好的协助。

与此同时,为了更好地了解资本市场欠发达国家或地区在采用国际财务报告准则时所面对的挑战,我们还设立了新兴经济体工作组,由国际财务报告准则解释委员会主席韦恩·阿普顿(Wayne Upton)领导。看到印度尼西亚积极响应新兴经济体工作组的工作,我感到非常高兴。

除此之外,我们继续与亚洲—大洋洲准则制定机构组(AOSSG)保持密切的合作关系,亚洲—大洋洲准则制定机构组为这个多样化地区提供了一个重要机制,可以协调各方观点。印度尼西亚会计准则委员会主席罗西塔也是亚洲—大洋洲准则制定机构组成员之一,他非常有效地利用这一机制,对印度尼西亚事务进行了强有力的表达。为加强与世界各地准则制定机构的合作,我们特意创办了"会计准则咨询论坛"(ASAF),而亚洲—大洋洲准则制定机构组很可能获得该论坛的代表席位。

这些举措为印度尼西亚提供了大好的机会,以更积极地参与财务报告准则的相关工作。大门已经开启,印度尼西亚可以像其他国家或地区一样,通过多种方式充分利用这个机遇。

比如,你们可以帮助我们完成会计领域的调研工作,尤其是那些印度尼西亚具备丰富经验的领域。同时,我还鼓励你们继续在亚洲—大洋洲准则制定机构组中积极表达自己的意见。在我们举行的讨论中,欧洲、美国和其他潜在的ASAF成员通常非常积极,畅所欲言。亚洲—大洋洲准则制定机构组需要向外界传递清晰、统一的声音,这一点尤为重要。

接下来,我将介绍我们目前开展的工作以及未来的工作计划。

当前开展的工作

我们的主要工作就是完成美国财务会计准则委员会趋同项目的剩余任务,当前尚有四个重大项目有待完成。首先,我先讲讲与美国完全实现趋同的两项会计准则。

收入确认准则

第一个项目便是收入确认。收入是最重要的数据，对每个企业都意义重大，它也是实务操作中存在分歧最多的领域。因此，该准则是我们工作的重中之重。

2011年11月，我们发布了经修订的征求意见稿，并计划在今年上半年发布完整准则。新准则既不会像美国准则那样过于详细繁杂，也不会像国际准则那样过于简单笼统。

针对国际财务报告准则所采用的"完工百分比"会计方法，修订后的收入确认准则应该能解决与之相关的几个问题。我们认识到，这一直是印度尼西亚商业房地产和建筑行业格外关注的问题。

历史上，各个公司在确认住宅房地产建造所产生的利润时，处理方法存在一些差异。因此，国际财务报告准则解释委员会于2007年发布了《国际财务报告解释公告第15号——房地产建造协议》(IFRIC 15)。但是，在实际操作中，却很难理解并应用该解释公告。国际会计准则理事会尝试在新的收入确认准则中解决这些问题。

新准则将设定一个清晰的原则，即应该在商品或服务交付给客户时确认收入。新准则还将提供支持性指引，为如何确认住宅房地产建筑合同所产生的收入提供更清晰的指导。我们认为，新准则将能够解决印度尼西亚现存的大部分准则解释问题。

正如我前面提到的，对每个企业而言，收入是一个关键的绩效指标，因此，我认为这个项目是趋同工作所取得的巨大成就之一。

租赁

第二项准则就是租赁，这是一个非常复杂的领域，同时也是一个亟需改进的领域。虽然租赁合同通常涉及非常重大的融资交易，但绝大部分租赁合同在资产负债表上得不到反映。许多公司，如航空公司和铁路公司，其表外融资金额可能非常庞大。

更为重要的是，提供融资服务的公司大部分都不是银行或者银行分支机构。如果以贷款的形式购买资产，那么这项融资服务可以在财务报表中得以反映。但是如果通过租赁形式，这项业务会奇迹般地在账簿中消失了。

你可能看到一些报道，声称如果会计规则发生变化将导致租赁行业全军覆没，这有些言过其实。租赁为公司带来了许多重要的经济收益，这一点不会发生改变。我们所追求的目标是通过一种方式,将这些租赁交易纳入报表,让投资者知悉。

当前,大部分分析师通过公司披露的基本信息,再根据自己的经验,对公司真实的、隐而未露的租赁杠杆进行技术性猜测。一方面,公司管理层手里掌握着现成的租赁信息;另一方面,分析师却需要对租赁相关的负债情况进行估计猜测,这种现象非常奇怪。

所以,国际会计准则理事会急需建立新的租赁准则。当前,我们与美国财务会计准则委员会密切合作,正在积极推进这项工作。双方的建议稿修订工作即将完成,我们计划尽快发布最终版的征求意见稿。来自印度尼西亚的反馈意见非常重要,有助于我们发布高质量的准则。

金融工具

第一阶段:分类和计量

正如你们所了解的,我们对金融工具会计规则的改革分为几个阶段进行,第一阶段就是金融工具的分类和计量。在起步阶段,国际会计准则理事会和美国财务会计准则委员会双方持有完全不同的观点:美国财务会计准则委员会最初倾向于"完全公允价值计量法",而国际会计准则理事会则选择了"混合计量法"。但双方设法让计量方法逐步趋同,我认为这也是一个成就。

2012年初,国际会计准则理事会和美国财务会计准则委员会达成一致,同意对各自的计量模式进行修订。《国际财务报告准则第9号——金融工具》进一步澄清了摊余成本业务模式,并引入了一个新的计量类别——以公允价值计量且其变动计入其他综合收益。与此同时,美国财务会计准则委员会采纳了混合计量方法,该方法与国际会计准则理事会方法非常相似。2012年11月,我们发布了建议稿,欢迎大家积极提供意见和建议。

第二阶段:减值

在对《国际会计准则第39号——金融工具:确认和计量》(IAS 39)进行修订的时候,所面临的最大挑战就是减值问题。当前,国际财务报告准则和美国公认会计原则(US GAAP)都采用"已发生损失减值模型"。许多人对此表示担忧,认为该模型可能导致贷款损失得不到及时、足额的确认。国际会计准则理事会和美国财务会计准则委员会认为必须用"预计损失模型"取代现有的"已发生损失模型"。

在经历了几次失败的尝试后,我们将于近日发布第三版,也可能是最后一版意见征求稿。我们相信,新的"预计损失模型"将有利于更加及时地确认贷款损失。根据新准则,银行需要预估所有贷款在 12 个月内发生违约的概率,并在此基础上建立损失准备。如果一项贷款的信用质量已经显著恶化,银行必须全额确认寿命期间的预计损失。

我们曾与美国财务会计准则委员会合作开发了"预计信用损失模型",而新模型是该方法的简化版本。去年 7 月,美国财务会计准则委员会决定开发自己的模型,要求企业在初始确认相关资产时就全额确认寿命期间的预计损失。

在接下来的几个月里,两个委员会将整理各自模型所收集到的反馈意见。在意见征求期内,我们将保持沟通渠道的畅通,并计划在 2013 年对收到的反馈意见进行再次审议。我希望双方能够形成更加一致的解决方案,但目前下定论还为时尚早。

第三阶段:套期会计

根据国际会计准则理事会收到的反馈意见,公众认为《国际会计准则第 39 号——金融工具:确认和计量》规定的套期会计要求随意性、规则性太强,不能满足风险管理需要。因此,为更好地反映风险管理活动,我们提议对套期会计规定进行基础性的修订。同时,我们希望套期会计规定能更容易被非金融机构理解和接受。这项工作基本接近尾声,发布最终准则指日可待,我们相信新准则能极大地改进现有的实务操作。

保险

在剩下的趋同项目中,保险是一个令人头疼的问题,让我彻夜难眠。当前,国际财务报告准则中没有合适的保险准则,而且美国准则也需要进行更新。因此,保险公司根据国际财务报告准则编制财务报表时存在极大的差异并且相当复杂。投资者时常认为保险的会计处理就犹如"暗箱操作",缺乏必要的透明度,导致风险溢价相应提高,最终造成保险公司的股票价格低于金融服务行业其他领域公司的股票价格。

这个项目非常具有挑战性,因为当前世界各地对保险的会计处理已经形成了不同的财务报告模式。许多保险公司在进行计量时所采用的会计假设都已经非常过时,因此,在当前低利率的市场环境下,保险公司很有可能遭受损失,这一点让人尤其担忧。没有一个合适的准则可以参考,投资者也无法正确地判断金融风险的大小程度。

为了开发一个合适的模型,将保险合同财务报告提升至正常水平,我们与美国财务会计准则委员会进行了通力合作。虽然我们双方的准则不太可能完全趋同,但是它们都以当前计量为基础,因此能够极大地提高保险行业的透明度。我们计划在今年上半年发布征求意见稿。

未来工作安排

很显然,为完成所有这些项目,我们还有非常重要的工作需要做,但我们已经取得了一些长足的进步,正朝着目标稳步前行。上述项目都将接近尾声,为此,我们为自己制订了新的工作计划和安排。

实施和维护工作

国际会计准则理事会负责制定可执行的会计准则,并将工作重点放在解决准则的实施问题上。去年,国际会计准则理事会就工作安排征询公众意见时,许多反馈者建议我们应该更加注重国际财务报告准则现有准则的维护工作,而不是一味追求新规范。我们的维护工作包括对准则进行解释、小范围的改进(包括年度改进)以及教育推广工作。

反馈者提出了很好的建议。曾有一段时间,我们将主要精力放在国际会计准则理事会与其他准则的联合趋同项目上,而现在,对于国际会计准则理事会及其解释委员会而言,应该更多地关注和解决国际财务报告准则的实际应用问题。

概念框架

2012年5月,我们决定重新启动概念框架项目。这或许是我们所承担的最重要项目,它获得了成员们的广泛支持。我们知道,如果能建立起正确的基础概念,那么,我们未来的准则制定工作将获得良好、一致的参考依据。

当前,我们的框架包括了各类资产和负债的定义,但是这些定义至今仍未令人完全满意。公众相信会计师们能清楚地界定"你的(资产或负债)"还是"我的(资产或负债)",但是,我们至今对如何区分"权益"与"负债"仍没有完全的把握。

对一家实体的业绩进行计量也不是一件容易的事情。我们计量"净收益",但是还存在"其他综合收益",而且后者还呈不断增长的态势,但我们尚不能完全清楚这些收益的含义。在对概念框架进行下一步修订的时候,我们还需要解决这些棘手的问题。

我们希望能尽快地建立起这个重要框架,为我们未来的工作提供指导。为此,我们设定了一个大胆的目标,计划在2015年9月之前完成概念框架新内容。我们期待能在 2013 年 6 月之前实现第一个重要里程碑，即发布概念框架讨论稿。

准则层面的项目

在对工作日程进行意见征集后，我们发现大部分反馈意见都呼吁设置静默期。这一要求并不让人意外，因为在过去的十年里我们经历了太多、太迅速的变化。虽然设置绝对静默期是不太可能的，但为了响应公众呼吁，我们还是制订了计划，只对小部分准则议题开展工作。

这些议题包括"农业"会计问题。我们需要特别关注所谓的生产性生物资产的状态。这涉及经济作物，如棕榈树和葡萄藤等，当这些作物达到生物成熟状态后，就可以在其使用寿命结束前不断生产制造出农产品。

对于像印度尼西亚这样一个农业在国民经济中占重要地位的国家而言，这个问题显得尤其重要。根据现有规定，棕榈树这类资产是按照公允价值进行计量的。而根据我们新的建议方案，这些资产应该和不动产、厂房及设备一样，按照成本进行计量。修订后，准则的实施成本将降低，并将消除对"净收益"的人为干扰。

结束语

女士们、先生们，非常感谢诸位能拨冗出席本次大会。希望你们在了解我们的工作举措后，能感受到我们为本地区和新兴经济体（如印度尼西亚）所作出的努力和承诺。虽然国际会计准则理事会总部离伦敦塔仅数步之遥，但我们并未将自己置身于象牙塔之中。我们的员工来自世界各地，他们充满了活力，干劲十足。我们开诚布公，广泛听取世界各地的声音和观点。我们需要你们的支持，正如你们需要我们的努力一样。在向全球统一的会计准则迈进的过程中，G20 建议我们特别关注新兴经济体的需求。因此，这是一个绝佳的机会，我们可以共同塑造全球财务报告的未来。

今天，我在这里伸出我的友谊之手，希望能与诸位共同努力实现国际财务报告准则的全面采用。我预祝本次大会圆满成功。

（张翔 翻译；乔元芳 审定）

国际财务报告准则趋同进展如何？
——跟踪通向全球会计准则的世界进展

2013年6月5日,"国际财务报告准则亚太政策论坛"在香港举办。汉斯·胡格沃斯特出席大会并发表题为《国际财务报告准则趋同进展如何？——跟踪通向全球会计准则的世界进展》的演讲。本文为演讲全文。

1983年,哈佛大学教授西奥多·莱维特将"全球化"这个术语引入商业领域。他说:"地球是圆的,但在绝大多数场合下,把它作为平的却符合直觉。"[1]如果退回到1983年,莱维特就想到经济世界是平的,那么在30年后的今天,经济世界也已经变成他所构想的图景了。

遗憾的是,支撑全球市场的监管体系未能同步前行。事实上,全球经济危机已经证明,国际监管中的套利交易十分盛行。自从危机爆发以来,各方均致力于创新全球监管基础,以使其适合21世纪的监管目标。

财务报告领域所取得的进步要早得多。亚洲金融动荡、安然和世通公司舞弊以及欧洲共同金融市场的创设,促成各方就全球会计准则达成共识,各相关国际组织已经明确表示支持国际会计准则理事会制定财务报告全球语言的工作。

G20领导人、国际货币基金组织、世界银行、金融稳定理事会、证券委员会国际组织以及巴塞尔银行监管委员会都公开表示支持这一重要工作。

那么,国际会计准则理事会是如何开展工作的？谁在使用国际财务报告准则？他们是如何采用国际财务报告准则的？迄今为止,我们基于所掌握的情况和大型会计师事务所的经验,对国际财务报告准则趋同情况作出了估计。但我们掌握的情况并不十分精确,结果导致人们经常怀疑趋同进展是否真的如我们设想的那么好。甚至有些人认为,很多国家所采用的是国际财务报告准则的本地修改版,因而实际上完全采用整套国际财务报告准则的国家(或地区)相对有限。

基于上述原因,我们感到有必要准确地掌握哪些司法管辖区已经采用和如何采用了国际财务报告准则。为此,2012年,受托人在战略审议中建议,对于国际财务报告准则通向全球会计准则的进展情况作出更为精确的评估。

在前国际会计准则理事会理事保尔·帕克特尔的领导下,工作人员连续工作9个月汇编相关信息。我们工作的第一步是面向全球会计准则制定者进行调查,然后再以其他来源的信息(包括证券监管者和大型会计师事务所)补充调查结果。

最后,我们要求每一个国家或司法管辖区的相关权威机构确认我们的结论。

今天,我们通过国际财务报告准则网站发布了首批66个司法管辖区采用国际财务报告准则的趋同概况。首批名单中包括G20的所有成员国和回应我们调查要求的其他46个司法管辖区。我们正在着手汇编其他50～60个司法管辖区的趋同概况,包括未回应我们首次调查的13个欧盟成员国。我们期待工作结束时,能够提供一幅国际财务报告准则趋同的世界图景。

本次发布的初步成果既引人关注,也令人倍受鼓舞。尽管这是一项定性评估,但我们仍然可以从中得到一些明确的结论。

首先,把国际财务报告准则作为唯一一套全球会计准则,几乎得到全球范围的支持。66个司法管辖区中的95%已经公开承诺,支持建立唯一一套高质量的全球会计准则。而且,除瑞士以外,所有管理区都表达了这样的理念,即国际财务报告准则应该成为唯一一套全球会计准则。那些尚未决定采用国际财务报告准则的管理区(如美国)也表达了上述看法。

其次,55个司法管辖区(占80%多)报告称,所有(其中的5个管辖区是"几乎所有")公众公司采用了国际财务报告准则。剩余的11个尚未采用国际财务报告准则的司法管辖区在通向采用国际财务报告准则方面,绝大部分已经取得重大进展。

考虑到这一变化是在十年多一点的时间内实现的,这的确是一个了不起的成就。

再次,已经采用国际财务报告准则的司法管辖区对国际财务报告准则作出的修改很少。对国际财务报告准则作出修改的绝大部分司法管辖区,修改也非常有限。例如,在欧盟的8 000家上市公司中,只有几十家公司使用从国际会计准则第39号中分拆形成的欧盟版本。

作出的修改要么是国家会计准则向国际财务报告准则过渡时的临时安排,要么对实务影响极小。对于国际财务报告准则被修改的所有情形,国际会计准则理事会日程表上都有正在进行的项目,包括农业、贷款损失准备、宏观套期会计、单独财务报表和收入确认。因此,最终的结果是,对国际财务报告准则的绝大多数修改将很有可能不复存在。

本次发布的汇编结果还显示对《中小主体国际财务报告准则》的大力支持。

66个司法管辖区中,有超过一半的司法管辖区已经采用或者计划近期采用《中小主体国际财务报告准则》。如果考虑到发布《中小主体国际财务报告准则》还不到四年的时间,这一结果更是成绩非凡。

在首批发布的趋同概略中,上述信息是唯一的一组明细信息,而且也没有理由相信随后发布的其他趋同概略会出现重大差别。我强烈推荐各位花一点时间,全面浏览一下我们网站目前所提供的国际财务报告准则应用情况信息。

相较其他全球标准(如巴塞尔委员会对银行的资本要求),使用本地改编版国际财务报告准则的情形非常有限。绝大多数国际财务报告准则采用者似乎有能力抵制修补国际财务报告准则的各种诱惑,这一事实真的不同寻常。为什么会出现这种情况呢?在演讲的下一部分,我将回答这个问题。

第一,我想绝大多数司法管辖区对国际会计准则理事会高度完善的应循程序感到满意。在我以前长期从事的公共政策制定职业生源中,从来没有像制定国际财务报告准则这样的透明环境,公众可以自由阅读理事会的所有文件,参加理事会的所有会议。

对于征求意见的期间和其他活动,国际会计准则理事会均有完整的要求,我们不太可能忽略全球提出的各种各样的问题。遵循充分详尽的应循程序所制定的会计准则,更有可能实现高质量,也更能经得起时间的检验。创立会计准则咨询论坛后,可以进一步确保准则制定的包容性。利用会计准则咨询论坛,我们期待准则制定获得及时和有洞见的信息和建议,这也将进一步缓释国际财务报告准则的非认可风险。

第二,国际财务报告准则基金会的治理结构已经实现了重大改善。监督委员会的建立,给予国际财务报告准则基金会一个更为坚实的公共监审平台。国际会计准则理事会亦对监督委员会负责，从而增加了额外的保证，即国际会计准则理事会不是一个随意漂浮的象牙塔，而且从来不是。同时，这样一个证券监管者形成的多边机构，可以抵制来自单一司法管辖区的不公正游说，增加了国际会计准则理事会的独立性。

第三，绝大多数司法管辖区对于自身存在且发挥作用的认可机制也感到满意。在几乎所有的司法管辖区，此类认可机制仅仅是通过简单的"是或否"决策来接受一项准则。几乎没有哪个司法管辖区存在一个为满足本地需求而对国际财务报告准则进行详细修改的复杂流程。

而且，这种认可机制在两个方面非常有效：一是认可机制将准则制定的最终主权赋予本地机构，因而创造了一个安全保护机制。二是由于存在认可不能通过的可能性，因而使得国际会计准则理事会不得不认真倾听各方意见。几乎没有司法管辖区不认可已经发布的国际财务报告准则，这一事实充分反映了国际会计准则理事会很好地听取了各方意见，接受了可能产生更好会计准则的意见与建议。

第四，我认为会计准则的技术性使得会计准则相对更容易接受。国际财务报告准则意在对经济事实作出中立的描述，而非构造经济事实，如巴塞尔委员会那样所描述的资本标准。

不错，会计准则离不开判断，少不了激烈的争议。有时会计准则甚至政治化了，特别是当会计准则曝光了隐匿的风险或者改变了传统做法，使得人们无法进行暗箱操作时，更是如此。绝大多数人接受这样的观点，即会计准则本质上是技术性的，而非政治性的。因此，绝大多数司法管辖区认为，只要保证应循程序和各方职责恰当，程序准确适当，会计准则的制定最好交由独立机构承担。

尽管存在这些安全保障机制，但依然有人认为不应存在一套单一的全球财务报告语言，他们希望我们转向巴塞尔式的全球原则，即修改并形成本地准则。我认为，这是一个灾难性的药方。事实上，这种方法在会计界曾经尝试过，但未获成功。

当时，国际会计准则委员会（国际会计准则理事会之前身）制定的会计准则意在作为国家会计规则的基础，结果却是各国接受了他们赞成的国际准则，改变了他们不赞成的国际准则。经过几十年的努力，国际会计准则委员会最终以国际社会承认失败而告终，并因此而创立国际会计准则理事会，赋予它制定单一套全球会计准则的新使命。

相关各方即使不赞成部分国际财务报告准则,他们也几乎总是抵制改变这些准则的企图。对于会计准则的本地调整,投资者总是持怀疑态度。因此,绝大多数司法管辖区就是简单地全盘照搬国际财务报告准则。同时,绝大多数人也接受这样的观点,即如果对国际财务报告准则的本地修改太多,就会损害全球准则所带来的益处。

金融危机已经证明,的确需要严格的经济准则以提供最大限度的透明度。本次发布的国家趋同概略表明,在向全球投资者提供透明度方面,国际财务报告准则已经取得很大进步。这既是值得我们庆祝已经取得成就的理由,也是我们未来工作的标杆。

那么,接下来还需要做哪些工作呢?首先,显而易见,部分大型和重要经济体尚未(全部)采纳国际财务报告准则。但即使在此类国家中,它们所取得的进步已经超出许多人的想象。

日本已经允许运用国际财务报告准则。目前,日本最大的17家跨国公司在国内报告中使用国际财务报告准则。日本商会和日本经济团体联合会估计,不久的将来,使用国际财务报告准则进行财务报告的日本公司将达到60家,约占日本证券交易所市值总额的20%。与多数人的想法不同,国际财务报告准则在日本活力十足。

在美国,2007年证券交易委员会允许在美上市的非美国公司使用国际财务报告准则的决定,具有里程碑意义。截至目前,有超过450家外国私营上市公司使用国际会计准则理事会制定的国际财务报告准则进行财务报告,涉及市值几万亿美元。因此,美国对国际财务报告准则的应用已经超越了起步阶段。

考虑到美国投资者对使用国际财务报告准则的世界其他地区的投资不断增加这样一个事实,就不难解释为什么美国证监会对国际会计准则理事会所取得的进展依然很感兴趣了。

中国的情况则有所不同,其选择了将所有上市公司与国际财务报告准则进行趋同的策略。中国取得极大的进步,已经与国际财务报告准则实现了实质性趋同。

中国还要继续努力,但我们也不得不承认,中国人已经迎头赶上。中国政府坚定地承诺,最终目标是实现与国际财务报告准则的全面趋同。

尽管国际财务报告准则的采用在世界范围内取得了巨大进步,但我们认为仅仅是"采用"还不够。显然,规范地"运用"同样重要。规范地运用国际财务报告准则的责任主要是编报者、审计师和监管者。在这方面,国际会计准则理事会的角色处于第二位,但在推动世界范围内规范运用国际财务报告准则方面,国际会计准则理事会的确起到了协助作用。

与此同时,显而易见,世界范围内非规范运用国际财务报告准则的风险,绝不是放弃全球会计准则的借口。即使全球准则的运用良莠不齐,比之运用得同样五花八门且数量众多的国家准则,它仍然能够提供更好的全球可比性。

事实上,只有存在共同语言,才有助于问题的显性化。

例如,伦敦城市大学卡斯商学院在 2013 年发布的国际财务报告准则下欧盟运用资产减值会计的情况分析[2],结论是欧盟对资产减值会计准则的运用总体良好,但仍有改进的空间。

但是,如果欧洲没有一套单一的会计语言,这样一份报告就无法完成。正是有了国际财务报告准则,该报告才能够清晰地识别特定司法管辖区在运用方面所存在的问题。

总体而言,G20 和国际组织承诺,最终目标是制定一套单一的高质量准则,即全球会计准则。今天发布的司法管辖区趋同概略,表明在实现最终目标的过程中已经取得了令人瞩目的进步,背离国际财务报告准则的情况极为少见。偏离国际财务报告准则的那些安排是过渡性的,而且国际会计准则理事会在新的工作日程中均考虑了这些问题。

同时,来之不易的成果必须加以保护。如果我们背叛了过去 12 年所取得的成就,历史都不会原谅我们。

为保护投资者利益,国际会计准则理事会需要完成它的使命,提供一套全球财务报告语言,G20 和国际社会必须继续坚定地支持国际会计准则理事会的工作。

谢谢诸位。

---

[1] 西奥多·莱维特.全球化市场.哈佛商业评论,1983(5).

[2] 卡斯商学院.资产减值会计:欧盟对国际财务报告准则运用情况的测试.www.cass.city.ac.uk.

(乔元芳 翻译并审校)

打破披露程式

2013年6月27日，国际财务报告准则基金会大会在荷兰首都阿姆斯特丹举行。汉斯·胡格沃斯特出席会议并发表《打破披露程式》的演讲。本文为演讲全文。

今天，我们要在相对较短的时间内，研究讨论诸多基础性问题。稍后，我的同事和高级职员会向各位提供全面的最新的国际会计准则理事会当前工作项目和未来工作计划。

今天上午，我的演讲集中在三个主题。首先，我谈一下G20设定的全球会计准则目标的进展情况。其次，我将简要地谈一下当前进行的三个重要项目，即贷款损失准备、保险合同和概念框架。最后是披露，这也是我今天演讲的主要议题，我将与各位分享使披露更为有效的十点计划。

一、全球会计准则

首先，我来谈一下全球会计准则。我们的目标是实现单一的全球会计准则，那取得了多少进展呢？

为了回答这个问题，我们进行了一项重要的研究。正如各位所知，本月初我们通过国际财务报告准则网站发布了首批成果。

对于国际财务报告准则的应用情况，本次调查深入透彻，结果特别令人鼓舞。首先，被调查的司法管辖区几乎一致地支持国际财务报告准则成为单一的全球会计准则。95%的司法管辖区已经作出公开承诺，支持单一的高质量全球会计准则。而且，几乎每一司法管辖区都确认（包括那些尚未决定采用国际财务报告准则的司法管辖区，如美国），这样一套单一的会计准则应该是国际财务报告准则。

其次，超过80％的司法管辖区的全部（其中5个为几乎全部）公众公司均采用国际财务报告准则。尚未采用国际财务报告准则的11个司法管辖区中，绝大部分也已取得重要进展。考虑到这一变化是在十年多一点的时间内实现的，这的确是一项了不起的成就。

再次，已经采用国际财务报告准则的司法管辖区对国际财务报告准则作出的修改很少。事实上，采用国际财务报告准则的司法管辖区中，超过40％为直接、自动地采用，无需认可。而且，作出修改的那些情况，可以视为有助于国家会计准则向国际财务报告准则过渡的临时安排。我们预期，绝大部分过渡性调整最终将消失。

当然，我们也清楚，个别大型且重要的经济体尚未（完全）采用国际财务报告准则。但是，即使在这些国家，它们所取得的进展也比许多人所想象的要大。

日本已经允许采用全套国际财务报告准则，而且最近已经扩大了可以采用国际财务报告准则的公司范围。

日本经济团体联合会预计，不久的将来，使用国际财务报告准则进行财务报告的日本公司将达到60家，约占东京证券交易所总市值的20％。另外，执政的自由民主党已经要求日本金融服务局制定一个路线图，以在2016年使300家左右的公司采用国际财务报告准则。

与多数人的想法相反，国际财务报告准则在日本活力十足。

在美国，2007年证券交易委员会允许在美上市的非美国公司使用国际财务报告准则的决定，具有里程碑意义。截至目前，有超过450家外国私营上市公司使用国际会计准则理事会制定的国际财务报告准则进行财务报告，涉及市值几万亿美元。因此，美国对国际财务报告准则的应用已经超越了起步阶段，这也是美国证券交易委员会对国际会计准则理事会所取得的进展依然很感兴趣的原因。

因此，归根结底，我们能够得出的结论是：尽管还有许多工作要做，但国际财务报告准则在世界范围内的采用已经取得奇迹般的进步。

二、当前工作

现在转向第二个主题，即国际会计准则理事会当前的工作情况。

首先是资产减值。众所周知，国际会计准则理事会和美国财务会计准则委员会均提出建议，用预期损失模型取代已发生损失模型。

经济危机期间已经清楚地表明，已发生损失模型存在一些严重缺陷，它为银行不确认损失轻而易举地留下了很大的空间,甚至在显而易见即将不可避免地发生损失时也是如此。尽管已发生损失模型的目标是压缩盈余管理空间,但有明显的迹象表明实务上存在巨大的差异。

今年早些时候,国际会计准则理事会公布了一个与美国财务会计准则委员会共同研究制定的预期损失模型简化版本,公开征求意见。我们认为,与现行的已发生损失模型相比较,该模型可更为及时地确认信用损失,忠实地反映基础交易的经济实质。而与此同时,美国财务会计准则委员会也制定了另一种不同的预计损失方法,它要求在初始确认相关资产时确认整个寿命周期内的预期损失。

尽管国际会计准则理事会和美国财务会计准则委员会的观点分歧令人不快,但各自的看法并非一无是处。两个委员会征求意见的时间存在交叉重叠,而且两个委员会都期望倾听对方的观点。

两个委员会都充分意识到,对于这样一个非常重要的领域,必须尽其所能实现趋同,至少是相当接近。我相信,今天晚些时候,欧洲央行理事会成员科拉斯·克诺特将会提醒诸位此项工作的重要性。

我要讨论的第二个领域是保险合同会计。保险行业非常重要而且业务十分复杂,集合投资总额往往以万亿美元计。保险行业的重要性确定无疑。

正因为如此,我们所不能接受的是,迄今尚没有一个恰当的会计准则核算保险合同。在世界范围内,保险公司在如何报告其财务数字方面,存在巨大差异而且格外复杂。无怪乎有投资者戏称,保险会计就是一个"黑箱"。

在计量负债时,许多保险公司依据过时的假设。事实上,部分公司清楚,当前的低利率环境导致行业生存艰难,因而仍使用多年以前的利率。

在日本,低利率已迫使部分保险公司破产,其他保险公司也不得不压低向客户承诺的回报。

许多保险公司还将负债的会计处理方法与所持有资产或欲持有资产的会计处理方法相挂钩。这就意味着,负债的计量受到资产的影响,即使事实上它们之间完全没有关系也是如此。这是保险行业缺乏可比性和透明度的另一个原因。

所幸,终结这一令人不太满意的局面,已经曙光初显。上周,国际会计准则理事会发布了新保险准则的第二次(也是最后一次)征求意见稿。根据征求意见稿的建议,保险公司要使用与负债相关的现行利率计量负债。这将使投资者更为可靠地分析观察保险公司的真实业绩,市场也将更为深入地洞悉保险公司如何有效地将其负债与资产相匹配。

建议的会计处理方法会导致更大的(收益)波动,而这恰恰可能是真实经济风险的反映。同时,我们还尽最大的努力,确保新准则尽可能减少非经济的、与会计相关的波动。为此,修改后的征求意见稿用了较大篇幅来阐述首次征求意见稿。当然,我们也承认,日益增加的复杂性也需要平衡。尽管我们认为已经很好地实现了方方面面的平衡,但在2014年该项目结束并发布准则之前,我们也诚恳期待听到各种观点。

我要讲的最后一个而且很重要的主题,就是进一步完善概念框架。最近,我们将发布一个讨论稿供各方评论。讨论稿明确了一些基础性会计主题的初步观点,如计量和其他综合收益的运用。尽管该项目已经耗费了十多年时间,形成了1 000多页的文档,我们也不能保证该讨论稿对所有会计问题都给出明确的答案。

我们明确了该项目的时间和范围。尽管目标宏大,但目前各项工作均按时间节点得以完成。虽然时间紧张,我认为我们还是能够发布一个可读性强、可以激发思想火花的讨论稿。相信这个讨论稿将是深入地进行公开讨论的坚实基础。

我们期望多年来困扰准则制定者的一部分最为复杂的问题能得到更多的关注,期待与相关各方共同努力,也有信心取得进步。

三、打破程式,改革财务披露行为

第三个也是我要讨论的最后一个主题是必须改进财务报告的披露。很多公司的年度报告不断膨胀,有用信息量与一些不必要的披露都在同步扩张。年度报告仅仅成为一份合规性文档,而不再是沟通传递信息的工具了。

今年1月份,也是在这个房间,我们组织监管机构、财务报告编报者、审计师、财务报告使用者和会计准则制定者进行讨论,直到所有各方均认识和理解了问题之所在。一个共同的结论是,财务报告披露所存在问题的许多方面,与行为因素有关。

例如,财务报告的许多编报者过度谨慎,无论什么东西都放到披露中,因为他们实在不想承担被监管机构要求重述财务状况的风险。毕竟,一个首席财务官不会因为披露信息量过大而遭解雇,但报表重述则可能是职业自杀。而且,通过过度披露来掩盖对公司不利却非常相关的那些信息也简便易行。某些时候,比之费时费力地使信息更有助益和更可理解,简单地照章行事则更为轻松。

总之,财务报告编报者、审计师和监管机构众所周知的风险厌恶,导致了目前这种在选项框中画勾的心理,结果是损害了财务报表传达信息的价值。那么,要改变这种文化,我们能做什么呢?打破藩篱,我们又能做什么呢?

首先,国际会计准则理事会将率先垂范,决定把《2012年国际财务报告准则基金会年度报告》及相关披露在2011年基础上压缩25%,同时还要增加有用信息的数量并使之更易于阅读。

对此,国际会计准则理事会内部进行了深入的讨论,与审计师进行了全面沟通。我深信,上述目标一定能够实现。

更为重要的是,国际会计准则理事会最近发布了一份《反馈公告》,汇总描述了前已述及的披露事项中我们获得的方方面面的关键信息。基于上述文件,今天我很高兴提出十点计划,以使财务报告的披露取得实实在在的改进。

其中,八项举措将在短期内取得看得见的效果。这些措施没有一项是革命性的重大改革,大部分措施甚至十分简单。但是,根据我在政府部门工作的经验,解决看起来复杂艰巨的问题,最简单的办法往往最管用。

1. 将在国际会计准则第1号中明确:重要性原则并不仅仅是指财务报告应当包括重要的项目,而且还意味着最好排除那些不重要的披露。披露的明细信息太多,反而使重要的信息更难理解。公司应主动积极地减少那些杂乱无章的信息。换言之,少即是多,宁缺勿滥。

2. 将进一步明确,重要性评估适用于包括附注在内的财务报表整体。许多人认为,一个项目如果未成为主要财务报表表内的行项目,就应该在附注中披露,以便确定其存在。我们不得不澄清的是,情况并非如此。如果一个项目不重要,在财务报表的任何地方都不需要披露。

3. 将进一步明确,即使一项准则与主体的财务报表相关,也并不意味着该准则中的每一披露要求均能提供重要的信息。事实上,披露是否具有重要性,应独立地逐项判断。

4. 删除国际会计准则第1号中那些被理解为规定财务报表附注顺序的表述,方便主体以更为逻辑、更为一体化的风格传递它们的信息。

5. 国际会计准则第1号要确保公司在财务报表的哪个地方披露会计政策的灵活性。在财务报表中,重要的会计政策应更为凸显,不太重要的会计政策则应转移到财务报表后面。

6. 根据全球很多财务报表使用者的要求,将增加净负债调节表。采取该项措施后,不仅可以向财务报告使用者清晰地展示被公司称作"净负债"的那些负债,而且还可以归并和关联那些散布在财务报表披露中的负债。

7. 编制有关重要性的一般应用指引或培训材料，就什么是重要信息，向审计师、财务报告编报者和监管机构提供更为清晰、更为统一的观点。关于此项重要的工作，国际会计准则理事会将与国际审计与鉴证准则委员会和证券委员会国际组织共同开展工作。

8. 在制定新准则时，尽量少用硬性披露措辞，重点关注披露目标和满足披露目标的披露案例。最近发布的会计准则已经开始这样做了，为判断重要性提供了更为明确的空间。

最后，我们将着手开展两项工作，以实现中期改进。

9. 2013 年下半年，国际会计准则理事会将启动一个研究项目，以全面复核国际会计准则第 1 号、国际会计准则第 7 号和国际会计准则第 8 号。该项目将重新审视财务报表列报项目已经做的部分工作，目标是取代上述准则，并创立实质性新型披露框架。

10. 最后，上述准则的复核工作结束后，我们将对现行准则的披露要求进行全面的复核。

我深信，上述举措还有极大潜力，仅仅是前已述及的 8 项措施就会产生很大效果。上述举措综合发挥作用后，应能消除提供程式披露的大部分借口，肯定有助于激发财务报表编报者、审计师和监管机构作出迫切需要的思维变革。国际会计准则理事会将继续与相关各方（其中，财务报表使用者尤为重要）共同努力，减少不加选择的随意披露，使披露提供更多有意义的信息。

四、结论

女士们，先生们，十分感谢各位的关注。在开幕致词中，我已经涉猎了大量基础性议题。我也谈及，国际财务报告准则的调查资料，为国际财务报告准则所取得的成功提供强有力的证据。我还说明了国际会计准则理事会当前所做的主要项目，并提出了改进财务披露的十点计划。

我们为本次会议安排了精彩的议程，我期待今天将是而且无疑是激发思维活力的一天。

谢谢。

（乔元芳 翻译并审校）

欧洲与通向全球会计准则之路

2013年9月9日,2013年安永国际财务报告准则大会在德国首都柏林举行。汉斯·胡格沃斯特出席并发表题为《欧洲与通向全球会计准则之路》的演讲。本文为演讲全文。

尊敬的女士们、先生们:

虽然我不是柏林人,但我仍想在我演讲的开头用德语说两句。来到柏林总是令人心情愉悦,对安永会计师事务所的邀请,我表示衷心感谢。

作为欧洲最重要的经济体,德国是国际会计准则理事会的重要合作伙伴。在接下来的演讲中,我将会提及,未来一段时间,国际会计准则理事会的工作既重要又繁忙。在此期间,德国的远见卓识会起到重要的作用。今天我出席会议,不只是宣传国际会计准则理事会及其取得的成就,也想倾听大家的心声与诉求。诸位的任何意见和建议,都会使我振奋不已。

柏林是欧洲的正中心,我想利用这个机会,从所观察到的欧盟与国际会计准则理事会以及与国际财务报告准则的关系入手,开始我的演讲。

众所周知,欧盟委员会委员米歇尔·巴尼尔已要求欧洲投资银行前主席菲利普·马斯塔德研究制定一份提案,强化欧盟对国际财务报告准则的贡献。感谢马斯塔德先生利用这个机会贡献他的研究成果,我们期待今年晚些时候发布的最终报告。

欧盟的组织管理与运作,是欧盟自身的事,我不想以任何方式来揣测马斯塔德先生将会提出什么样的最终建议。我把演讲限制在仅仅指出支配着欧洲与国际会计准则理事会关系的部分重要事实。

首先,可以毫不夸张地说,国际财务报告准则的成功历程,同样也是欧盟的成功故事。2005年,欧盟决定采用国际财务报告准则,给予国际财务报告准则成为全球单一会计准则所必需的可信度和关键数量。欧盟采用国际财务报告准则,成为许多司法管辖区采用国际财务报告准则或启动趋同进程的决定性因素。目前,世界上有100多个司法管辖区要求或允许使用国际财务报告准则。如果没有欧盟的引领示范,能否出现今天的局面,真的值得怀疑。

同样毫无疑问的是,用国际财务报告准则取代欧洲复杂多样的会计语言,让欧洲资本市场受益颇丰。重要的是不要忘记,欧洲采用国际财务报告准则的行动,部分地克服了20多年来为实现高质量的欧洲会计准则所经历的重重困难。

国际财务报告准则的引入,不仅为解决欧洲范围内会计准则的多样性提供了现成方案,而且极大地增强了透明度,有效降低了上市公司的资本成本,欧洲资本市场的执行力得到极大改善,欧洲证券与市场管理局识别、确认欧洲范围内会计准则执行过程中各种问题的能力得到极大提高。

除国际会计准则第39号外,欧盟执行了其他全部国际财务报告准则。欧盟对国际会计准则第39号设定了豁免条款,但在欧盟9 000多家公司中,仅有20家左右使用这一条款。

既然欧盟采用国际财务报告准则的进程已接近完成,这是否意味着欧盟将会计领域的主权让位给了国际会计准则理事会呢?如果诸位拜访过位于伦敦堪农街30号的国际会计准则理事会总部,就知道事实并非如此。

任何一项国际财务报告准则是否在欧盟采用,欧盟都有权决定,并为此采取认真、严谨的认可程序。事实上,在所有已经采用国际财务报告准则的司法管辖区中,欧盟采用的认可程序最为严格。多个欧盟组织参与了国际财务报告准则的认可程序,其中包括欧洲财务报告咨询小组、国家会计准则制定机构、欧盟会计监管委员会、欧盟、欧盟成员国和欧洲议会。

大部分司法管辖区采用的认可程序比较简单。各位知道,国际会计准则理事会最近发布了国际财务报告准则采用情况的首批国别分析报告,详细描述了各司法管辖区采用国际财务报告准则的方式和路径。该项研究表明,在超过40%的司法管辖区,国际会计准则理事会发布的会计准则自动生效,无须认可。剩余60%中的绝大部分司法管辖区,仅由专业会计机构、证券监管机构共同或者单独进行认可,程序相对简化。除欧盟外,只有新西兰和澳大利亚的议会参与国际财务报告准则的认可。

还有一个重要的方面需要指出,在采用国际财务报告准则时,未作重大修改的并非只有欧盟,绝大多数司法管辖区也是这么做的,对此各位不必感到惊讶。毕竟,G20反复强调,建立一套唯一的全球会计准则是终极目标。如果所有司法管辖区都对国际财务报告准则进行修改以适应当地需要,上述目标就永远不可能实现。

当然,某些大型经济体尚未全面采用国际财务报告准则也是事实。但是,这些经济体中的大部分,在采用国际财务报告准则进程中取得了重大进展,而且这些进展还在持续不断地推进,通常这些进展并不为公众所熟知。以日本为例,在不久的将来,占东京证券交易所市值总额20%的一大批公司,将有望使用国际财务报告准则。尽管美国证券交易委员会尚未下定决心要求美国国内公司使用国际财务报告准则,但是,市值总计达数万亿美元的450家外国上市公司,已在美国市场中使用国际财务报告准则,从而使美国成为国际财务报告准则的重要利益相关方。

最后,在国际会计准则理事会制定会计准则的过程中,欧盟积极主动、地位凸显。事实上,欧洲财务报告咨询小组和国家会计准则制定机构(如德国会计准则委员会)积极参与国际财务报告准则制定的宣传推介、实地测试和咨询反馈,在这方面,欧盟比世界上任何其他司法管辖区投入的资源都要多。

欧盟的这些努力并没有付之东流。在国际会计准则理事会的准则制定过程中,单单是欧洲财务报告咨询小组就明确指出了可以有所作为、能够发挥积极作用的诸多领域。最近,国际会计准则理事会成立了会计准则咨询论坛,借助该论坛,欧洲的声音将更为强劲,欧盟可以扮演更为重要的角色。

我可以明确地告诉各位,世界其他国家和地区一直认为欧盟在国际财务报告准则制定过程中发挥着重大作用。事实上,欧盟之外的许多利益相关方也都在担心,欧盟这个巨无霸在国际财务报告准则制定中的影响力太过强大。

我认为,欧盟与国际会计准则理事会、与国际财务报告准则之间的关系,总体上运行良好、协调平衡,发挥着建设性作用。

为实现全球会计准则的这一共同目标,进一步深化欧盟与国际会计准则理事会的合作,我们欢迎任何意见与建议。

那么,国际财务报告准则的情况如何?现行工作项目的进展如何?今天下午,国际会计准则理事会德方委员马丁·埃德尔曼将对金融工具会计准则进行详细解读,今天上午我仅对国际会计准则理事会的一些重要项目作一总体介绍。

趋同

在过去的几个月里，为完成留存的几个趋同项目，我们采取了几项重大措施。

首先，今年秋季我们有望发布一项新的会计准则——收入确认。在起草征求意见稿的过程中，我们仍然需要处理一些棘手问题，但我们有信心不久将完成全部的工作。由于收入是损益表的首行项目，收入确认影响到所有公司，因而该准则十分重要，为此我们花费了大量时间。新发布的收入确认准则，指南较少，它将取代有上千页应用指南的美国准则和相应的国际财务报告准则。我把与美国财务会计准则委员会的趋同项目，称为"皇冠上的明珠"，原因就在于此。

租赁会计

第二个项目是租赁会计，这是另外一个困难重重但也非常重要的领域。目前，尽管绝大部分租赁合同通常都包含重大融资成分，但都没有确认进入资产负债表。对于诸如航空公司和铁路公司之类的大部分公司而言，表外融资额巨大。据估计，由于租赁隐藏了杠杆比率，导致长期债务低估了20%。那些小公司的情况就更加糟糕了。

而且，提供融资租赁服务的公司，多半是银行或者银行的子公司。如果一个公司先贷款，然后再用贷款来购买资产，这种融资形式就必须确认记录。但是，当把它称为"租赁"时，它就轻而易举地从账簿中消失了。

依我之见，外形似鸭，游泳时像鸭，而且还如鸭一般嘎嘎叫，那最大的可能，它就是一只鸭子。债务也是这样，不管以租赁还是以其他什么形式出现，它都是债务。

目前，对于公司隐藏杠杆的程度，绝大多数分析师都颇有经验地进行估计与猜测。当然，对于租赁业务内含的真实杠杆，有些人低估了，而有些人却高估了。

正是因为如此，财务报告使用者向国际会计准则理事会一再强调，他们需要的是严格规范、信息可比的租赁会计准则。

我们认识到，要实现租赁会计的变革，财务报告编制者就必须付出一定的代价。当然，为确保成本的最小化，国际会计准则理事会已经作出了一些务实的决定，例如将短期租赁和可变租赁付款额排除在外。另外，对于绝大部分要求披露的信息，现行国际会计准则第17号已经要求在附注中披露。实际上，能够全面控制其租赁承诺的公司，对于会计准则要求披露的绝大部分信息，都可以信手拈来。

我还要强调的是，将租赁业务在资产负债表中进行记录，财务报告编制者本身亦将受益。

如果说许多首席执行官仅仅模糊地、粗略地意识到租赁合同所隐藏的全部债务，我一点也不奇怪。通过使隐藏的债务清晰化和显性化，公司对资本分配就能作出更加理性的决策。租赁业务当然不会消失，但公司却可以就购买资产和租赁资产作出更为合理的决策。

资产减值

关于资产减值，国际会计准则理事会与美国财务会计准则委员会的分歧颇大，难以趋同。事实上，两个委员会都对资产减值项目作出了艰苦的努力。在过去的三年中，两个委员会制定了至少6个不同的资产减值模型，而且到目前还没有结束。

我们双方一致认为，现行的已发生损失模型，为银行长时间推迟确认不可避免发生的贷款损失，留下了太大的操纵空间。已发生损失模型确认的贷款损失金额较少、时间较晚，是问题的症结所在。为此，两个委员会都同意，应该用更具前瞻性的预期损失模型来取代已发生损失模型。

然而，关于预期损失模型的具体构建方法，双方难以达成一致意见。美国财务会计准则委员会希望银行在贷款的首日就确认可能发生的全部损失；而国际会计准则理事会认为，只有信用风险已经发生而且出现重大上升时，才能识别和确认贷款损失。

我们发现，双方之所以无法达成一致意见，其中一个原因是预期损失模型需要处理未来不确定的结果，而如何确定与处理未来不确定的事项并没有明确、统一的答案，因而预期损失模型本身就具有高度的主观性。

国际会计准则理事会提出的最新模型最终得到了各界的广泛支持，该项目即将圆满结束，这是一个令人欣慰的好消息。与此同时，我们仍然希望国际会计准则理事会与美国财务会计准则委员会各自的模型能够缩小差距，更加协调。今年9月份，我们双方将在伦敦再一次召开联合会议，分析研究我们取得的进展。

保险合同

我要讨论的第四个领域就是保险合同会计。保险行业是业务异常复杂且十分重要的一个行业,集合投资超万亿美元,系统重要性毫无疑问。

正是因为如此,至今尚无良好的、适用的保险合同会计准则,令人无法接受。由于保险业缺少恰当的会计准则,导致世界范围内保险公司的财务报告复杂多变、无法统一。投资者私下抱怨,保险会计就是一个"黑箱"。

许多保险公司在计量负债时使用过时的假设,部分保险公司甚至使用多年以前的(高)利率。我们都清楚,当前的低利率环境,使得保险行业经营艰难。

作为欧洲保险行业的监管机构,欧洲保险和职业养老金管理局对于因长期持续低利率对保险业所造成的影响敲响了警钟。欧洲保险和职业养老金管理局担心,部分保险公司将不能满足其资本要求。欧洲保险和职业养老金管理局以日本为例进行了分析,认为日本的部分保险公司就曾因为持续低利率而破产,其他保险商不得不下调对客户承诺的投资回报率。[1]

如果说保险业是金融危机的受害者,那么,它绝对是一名沉默的受害者。保险业未能成为新闻头条的部分原因,是因为缺少恰当的会计准则,从而使存在的问题无法全部暴露出来。

所幸的是,终结这种不能接受的局面,已经曙光初现。最近,国际会计准则理事会第二次、也是最后一次发布新保险合同会计准则的征求意见稿,建议用现行市场利率计量保险公司的负债,使投资者更好地了解保险行业的真实业绩。市场也将获得更多关于保险公司负债与资产有效匹配方面的信息。如果我们建议的新方法导致保险公司收益出现更大的波动,那这种波动可能正好反映了真实的经济风险。

与此同时,我们还在积极努力,确保使新准则最大限度地减少非经济因素的收益波动以及与会计相关的收益波动。第二次征求意见稿提出的方法,有助于消除人们在这方面对第一次征求意见稿的担心与顾虑。但是,我们也的确承认,对于由此而增加的操作复杂性,我们也要进行权衡和取舍,但在2014年新准则发布之前,我们还是想诚恳地听取各种观点与建议。

未来工作日程

今年7月份,国际会计准则理事会发布了《概念框架》讨论稿,公开征求意见。尽管该项目内容广泛、目标宏大，但为了按时完成，我们还是决定充分考虑时间限制和内容范围，集中精力开展工作。尽管时间紧张，我仍然认为此次出台的讨论稿既具有可读性，也能够启迪思维、激发灵感。我深信，该讨论稿将为开展影响深远的公众讨论，奠定坚实的基础。

该讨论稿提出了国际会计准则理事会对会计计量、其他综合收益使用等部分基础性会计问题的初步观点。

该讨论稿明确：国际会计准则理事会继续将损益作为企业财务业绩的关键指标，并不仅仅关注资产负债表。就其他综合收益的重要性以及如何规范其使用，讨论稿也给出了初步答案。尽管前后历经十年，产生了上千页文档，但我们仍不能夸大其词，因为讨论稿并不可能对所有会计问题都给出确定无疑的答案。

在我们的工作任务中，与概念框架相关的一个主题是改进财务报告的披露。许多公司的年度报告内容庞杂、篇幅膨胀，而披露所内含的有用信息量却没有同比例增长。

许多人都同意这样的看法，即披露存在的问题，主要是行为问题。例如，许多财务报表编制者为避免监管机构查出问题，就一股脑地把无论什么内容都塞进财务报告，作为披露的内容。毕竟，没有哪个首席财务官会因为披露信息量过大而遭解雇，但报表重述无异于职业自杀。

另外，过度披露甚至还是隐匿不利却非常相关的信息的简便办法。

而且，要使提供的信息有益且可理解，需要费时费力，而按会计准则规定的披露清单照单披露，则省时省力，容易得多。

总之，由于财务报告编制者、审计师和证券监管机构都存在风险厌恶，因而导致披露信息时的"机械勾选、依规填充"心态，结果使财务报表应有的传递有用信息的价值大打折扣。如何才能打破这种机械的披露模板呢？

首先，国际会计准则理事会决定率先垂范，作出表率。我们力争使国际会计准则理事会 2012 年年度报告的篇幅比上一年度压缩 25%。同时，增加有用信息量和可读性。国际会计准则理事会内部进行了深入的讨论，与审计师进行了沟通，我们将确保实现上述目标。

最近，我提出了使财务报告披露得到实实在在明显改进的十点计划，其中的大部分要求都很简单。例如，明确规定，如果一项信息不重要，最好不要提供，连附注中也不要披露。

我们也希望给予主体更多的自由度，方便主体把重要的披露或会计政策置于更为突出、显要的位置。

通过实施这些简单的措施,我们希望能够消除那些发布僵化的模板式披露的种种借口,也希望能够有助于公司更有效地传递公司战略方面的信息。当然,这些措施也有助于唤起财务报告编制者、审计师和证券监管机构亟需的思维倾向的重大变革。国际会计准则理事会将继续与各利益相关方(特别重要的是投资者)协同工作,为减少披露的随意性、增加信息的有用性而共同努力。

女士们,先生们,我的演讲即将结束。

刚刚过去的全球金融危机警示我们,资本市场应该独立运作,不受其他因素影响,而且全球需要统一的财务报告语言,这也恰恰是国际会计准则理事会应予认真对待、不可推卸的责任。对国际会计准则理事会的工作,欧洲各界持续给予支持,对此我们深表感激,同时你们对国际会计准则理事会的承诺和支持,也会得到应有的回报。

祝大会取得圆满成功,谢谢各位。

---

[1] EIOPA.长期低利率环境下的监管响应,2013-02-28.

(乔元芳 翻译并审校)
(原文德文部分翻译 朱丹)

强化会计准则制定机构
之间的协调配合

2013年9月23日,国际财务报告准则基金会"会计准则制定机构全球大会"在英国首都伦敦举行。汉斯·胡格沃斯特出席会议并发表题为《强化会计准则制定机构之间的协调配合》的演讲。本文为演讲全文。

引 语

女士们,先生们,来自各国会计准则制定机构的同行们,欢迎各位参加本次"会计准则制定机构全球大会"。

1991年,也就是国际会计准则理事会创设之前的第十个年头,全球会计准则制定机构召开了首次会议。回望彼时,国际会计准则制定机构抱负有限、目标较低,仅仅是希望减少各国会计准则之间的差异。

今天,国际会计准则理事会的使命已经提升为"建立一套单一的高质量全球会计准则"。国际会计准则理事会的这一使命,得到G20的支持,我们承诺要全面实现这一目标。

但是,建立"一套单一的会计准则"并不意味着只能存在唯一一个会计准则制定机构。长期以来,国际财务报告准则制定工作得到了全球会计准则制定机构的支持,因为国际会计准则理事会只有大约60名技术人员、16名理事,而利益相关者涉及全球100多个国家和地区,工作无法全面深入。如果没有在座各机构的大力协助与支持,国际会计准则理事会将疲于应付公司和投资者应用新会计准则时面临的诸多实务问题和疑难敏感问题。

我们的合作关系,在国际会计准则理事会新的工作计划中得到清晰反映和印证。例如,如果没有亚洲—大西洋会计准则制定机构组(AOSSG)成员国(特别是马来西亚)的前期工作,那么,修改《国际会计准则第41号——农业》准则中有关生产性生物资产的相关条款就不能实现。上周,我们开始讨论同一控制下的企业合并,而这项工作的起点则是意大利会计准则制定机构、欧盟财务报告咨询小组和新兴经济体小组成员国的会计准则制定机构的前期工作。类似的事例还有很多,不胜枚举。

要建立唯一的全球会计准则,保证准则的高质量,那就只能有唯一的准则仲裁者。因此,国际会计准则理事会必须与在座诸位紧密合作,共同努力。

要一致地应用和执行国际财务报告准则,国际会计准则理事会也遇到与制定会计准则时同样的挑战与难题,因为我们没有强制要求实施或者豁免执行国际财务报告准则的资源和权力。

在过去的十多年中,国际会计准则理事会与全世界合作伙伴合作完成的大部分工作均以非正式的方式进行。然而,自上一次会计准则制定机构全球大会以来的12个月中,在加强国际会计准则理事会与全球会计准则制定机构之间的紧密关系方面,我们迈出了重要的步伐。下面,我将与诸位分享部分重要进展。

各司法管辖区趋同情况汇编

首先,我最常被问及的一个问题是:哪些国家或地区真正使用国际财务报告准则?以前,充其量我们只能进行非正式的估计与推测。但是,国际会计准则理事会居然不能精确描述推动实现全球会计准则的进展情况,人们对此总是多多少少感到不太满意。

为了获得世界范围内使用国际财务报告准则的总体情况,在去年的大会上,我们展示了最初的工作情况和初步成果。自那以后,在各位的帮助下,由保尔·帕克特尔带领的工作团队取得重大进展,完成了81个司法管辖区的趋同情况汇编,不久还会披露更多司法管辖区的趋同情况。

本次调研的结果,使我们倍受鼓舞,信心大增。例如,已经完成趋同汇编的81个司法管辖区中,78个已经公开承诺执行单一的全球会计准则,85%已经在其资本市场中采用国际财务报告准则,已经采用国际财务报告准则的司法管辖区几乎未对国际财务报告准则作出修改,对国际财务报告准则作出的极少修改绝大部分是全面采用国际财务报告准则计划的暂时性措施。

稍后，保尔·帕克特尔会就该项工作的简要情况，向各位进行更为全面的阐述。当然，取得这样的工作成果，开局重要，结果良好。如果没有各位的支持，就不可能实现。顺便要提及的是，对于尚未提供趋同情况的司法管辖区，保尔将与你们联络并开展相关工作。我要提醒各位，如果保尔没有得到他所需要的全部信息，他是不会善罢甘休的。

证券委员会国际组织

国际会计准则理事会与证券监管机构全球组织——证券委员会国际组织（IOSCO）签订了合作协议，是我们取得的第二个重要进展。协议规定了要采取的一系列措施，意在使两个组织更加紧密合作，协同开展工作，把国际财务报告准则在全球范围内的一致应用，提升到一个更高的层次。

一致地应用会计准则，与会计准则本身同样重要。我们双方的协议是机构之间必要的协同安排，目的是促进会计准则的一致应用。证券监管机构是会计准则制定机构为数不多的朋友，我们应充分利用这种友谊和关系，强化合作。

会计准则咨询论坛

第三项重要的进展是成立了"会计准则咨询论坛"（ASAF），为加强国际会计准则理事会与全球制定会计准则的团体之间的合作提供一个重要机制。会计准则咨询论坛的第一次会议由各机构派员出席，第二次会议是视频会议，第三次会议将于本周晚些时候在伦敦召开。

我认为，会计准则咨询论坛是一个积极的进展，而且通过论坛参与者最近的发言，我也注意到他们也持有同样的看法。正是因为有了会计准则咨询论坛，对国际会计准则理事会各种建议与改革措施的反馈和回应才成为多边的共同努力，而不再仅仅是双边行为。论坛成员并不仅仅与国际会计准则理事会进行讨论，他们相互之间也进行交流与讨论；他们的观点不仅需要得到国际会计准则理事会的信任，论坛成员之间也要就各自观点的是非曲直展开讨论。最终的结果是，不仅参与者对各种不同的竞争性观点有了更好的理解，国际会计准则理事会也能够更好地将各种反馈和意见融入自身的考虑和思考。

重要的是，会计准则咨询论坛不仅反映成员组织的观点，还反映全部会计准则制定团体的观点。格外重要的是，亚洲—大西洋会计准则制定机构组、欧盟财务报告咨询小组、拉丁美洲准则制定小组、泛非会计师联合会等地区性准则制定机构代表的是整个地区，从而确保了会计准则咨询论坛不被外界视为一个排他性的俱乐部。

之所以仍然需要"会计准则咨询论坛"这样一个世界性准则制定机构的存在，包容性也是一大原因，因为这个机构是全部准则制定机构相聚与交流的唯一平台。我也知道，"会计准则制定机构国际论坛"(IFASS)的部分成员出现了会议疲劳症，特别是那些同时也是"会计准则咨询论坛"成员的人士。为了减少交叉重复和频繁出行，我们很乐意与"会计准则制定机构国际论坛"进行讨论沟通。但是，我认为，把"会计准则咨询论坛"这样一个世界性准则制定机构作为至关重要的平台，是我们双方的共同责任，因为它是迄今为止代表性最广、包容性最强的平台。

会计准则制定者的角色和定位

最后一个讨论的主题，我称之为"准则制定悖论"。纵观会计准则发展史，最需要改进的是透明度，但它又是争议最大、最难突破的领域。例如，把股票期权费用化，显然是正确的选择。但是，既得利益集团十分强大，到处游说，声称没有任何成本的股票期权，可以使经济增长的神话保持相当长时间。如果大家对"会计的角色是使资本主义保持诚实可信"的观念深信不疑，那就值得进行这种针锋相对的论争，这也是大幅改进透明度、保护投资者的方式和方法。

当然，并非所有的论争都是既得利益集团游说的结果。毕竟绝大多数论争都是因为准则制定者在提出改革建议时措施和方法尚不成熟，或者是改革的结果违背了初衷。国际会计准则理事会的应循程序提供了一个会计准则质量控制机制，对此我们应予珍视，充分发挥其作用。对国际财务报告准则技术和实务上的正当、合理的考虑和诉求，都应该得到充分表达，这也是我们的职责所在。

然而，要区分哪些是游说行为，哪些是合理诉求，甚为困难。因为既得利益集团的游说与那些意在提高会计准则质量而代表公众利益的反馈意见，并不总是泾渭分明，而且既得利益集团的游说在经过包装后，表面上看来都是为公众利益而建言献策。有的时候，信息使用者也想维持现状，不愿变革；分析师也特别钟爱自己建立的分析模型，不想通过会计准则把复杂的问题显性化。

强化会计准则制定机构之间的协调配合

包括国家会计准则制定者在内的所有准则制定者都面临着一个中心任务，就是要把合理诉求与维持现状的保守主义区别开来。国际会计准则理事会既需要在座各位识别并指出我们的各种建议与改革措施在技术和实务上的不足与疏漏，也需要大家协助国际会计准则理事会阻断既得利益集团的游说。这项工作有不少困难、不受欢迎，有时还要冒犯既得利益集团，但这项工作异常重要，单靠国际会计准则理事会无法完成。只有争取所有可能争取的支持与帮助，国际财务报告准则才能达到必要的严格规整、规范条理。

在接下来的几年中，我们要争取完成保险合同、金融工具、租赁和收入确认四个重要项目，以上所言就尤其重要。在进行上述所有项目的过程中，我们将尽一切可能，尽量不出现非预期的结果。高质量的反馈和实地测试，对于完成我们的工作具有不可估量的价值。当然，我们还必须时刻警惕，防止非常规的游说活动。准则制定工作就是一项管理变革的实践活动。但是，即使是追求更好状态的变革，也是不受欢迎的。国际会计准则理事会需要诸位的大力协助，实现变革的目标。

女士们，先生们，预祝本次大会取得圆满成功。我期待在接下来的两天时间里，与各位深入讨论我们所面临的挑战。

（乔元芳 翻译并审校）

期待美国尽快作出采用
国际财务报告准则的承诺

2012年12月4日,美国注册会计师协会召开大会,会议主题是"美国证券交易委员会与美国公众公司会计监督委员会进展现状"。汉斯·胡格沃斯特出席会议并发表演讲。本文为演讲全文,标题为译者所加。

去年的这个时间,我向各位介绍了将国际财务报告准则建设成为全球财务报告语言的进展情况。今天,我很高兴地向大家汇报这项工作在全球取得的持续进展。目前,100多个国家和地区使用国际财务报告准则,这其中包括了3/4的G20成员国。包括俄罗斯、土耳其等非欧盟国家在内,几乎全欧洲都使用了国际财务报告准则。在非洲,承诺使用国际财务报告准则的国家和地区不断增加,亚洲和中东的大部分地区也是如此。在美洲,几乎所有国家都在使用国际财务报告准则,包括巴西、阿根廷、墨西哥和加拿大。当然,位于墨西哥和加拿大之间的美国,尚未承诺使用国际财务报告准则,下面再作详细讨论。

在2002年国际会计准则理事会与美国财务会计准则委员会签订诺沃克协议时,很多人认为国际财务报告准则是欧洲与美国之间的一个双边项目与安排。当前,会计准则制定的环境已经大为不同。驱动全球经济增长的大部分新兴经济体支持和赞同国际财务报告准则,它们希望在制定会计准则的领域中占有一席之地,能够发出自己的声音,对此我们表示理解。国际会计准则理事会正在亚洲和拉丁美洲尝试建立地区性会计准则论坛,作为对欧洲此类机构的一个补充。

由于国际会计准则理事会与美国财务会计准则委员会的趋同项目即将完成,国际会计准则理事会正在探索新的多边机制与方法,与多个准则制定机构一道制定国际财务报告准则。我们建议,新机制要允许全球会计准则制定机构在制定会计准则过程中更加深度地合作,对此上个月我们已经发布征求意见稿,广泛征求各方意见。我们希望并期待美国财务会计准则委员会全程参与并成为这一新的全球论坛的签约伙伴,我们也仍然需要美国同行认可的优秀专家。

鉴于全球化势不可挡,G20反复呼吁建立全球会计准则。在推动单一全球会计准则的进程中,美国扮演了重要角色,应该为此而感到自豪:1973年,创建国际会计准则委员会(国际会计准则理事会的前身)之际,美国发挥了关键作用;重组国际会计准则委员会、建立国际会计准则理事会之际,美国证券交易委员会确定无疑地表示,国际会计准则理事会与美国财务会计准则委员会极为相像;国际财务报告准则基金会受托人首任主席是保尔·沃尔克;1/4的国际会计准则理事会委员和3/4的受托人来自北美。

最近,我们任命了一些优秀的美国人进入国际会计准则理事会:来自毕马威会计师事务所的玛丽·托卡,以前曾在美国证券交易委员会工作,将于明年1月份加入国际会计准则理事会;来自摩根大通、令人十分尊敬的首席执行官海蒂·米勒将出任受托人。除了直接参与之外,美国财务会计准则委员会与国际会计准则理事会之间历经十多年的趋同进程,也对国际财务报告准则的制定发挥着巨大的影响。基于上述分析,我们认为,美国已经为成功采用国际财务报告准则做好了充分准备。[1]

上述一切工作,目的都是期待美国成为制定、使用和监管单一全球会计准则的坚定参与者。2007年,美国财务会计基金会和财务会计准则委员会向美国证券交易委员会提交的评论信对此阐述得明白无误:"如果所有美国公众公司均使用由单一全球准则制定机构发布的会计准则来编制财务报告,投资者利益将得到更好的保护。而要求美国公众公司实行改进后的国际财务报告准则,则能较好地实现上述目标。"

在去年的演讲中我也谈到,要求美国证券交易委员会下定决心采用国际财务报告准则,绝非易事。我当然不会天真地希望美国所有公司从某一天统一采用国际财务报告准则。但是,规划出实行国际财务报告准则的路线图,却是全世界对美国证券交易委员会的合理预期。

然而,众所周知,美国证券交易委员会最初计划于2011年作出是否采用国际财务报告准则的决定,现在又再次推迟到2012年。自我设定的时间节点通常都没有约束力,我们作为会计准则制定机构对此一清二楚。我也意识到多德·弗兰克面临着巨大的压力,而且时值总统选举,这也不是证券交易委员会作出决定的最佳时机。

美国在采用国际财务报告准则问题上的停滞不前,如果是在五年前,则对国际会计准则理事会确实后果严重。因为如果美国不采用国际财务报告准则,欧洲就会自行其道,亚洲就会制定自己的地区性会计准则。但时至今日,上述情况已经一去不复返。我所接触的许多国家由于已经发生向国际财务报告准则过渡的转换成本,因而没有哪个国家愿意停止采用国际财务报告准则,再倒回来执行国家或地区准则。国际财务报告准则已经赢得全球影响,这个趋势不会发生逆转。因此,即使美国不采用国际财务报告准则,国际财务报告准则也没有分崩离析的危险。

但是,如果美国不以某种姿态和形式融入国际财务报告准则大家庭,则美国在国际财务报告准则制定和实施过程中是否还具有强大、持续的影响力,各方面都表示出极大的担忧。

我相信,美国仍将是国际会计准则理事会及其活动的重要参与者。但显而易见的是,美国的影响大小,与其向国际财务报告准则的承诺是成比例的。这里只举一个例子:把美国财务会计准则委员会的职责定位于认可国际财务报告准则,还是一个不负责推动国际财务报告准则的国家会计准则制定者,在这两种不同的情况下,美国的影响力则有天壤之别。

的确,目前的现状暗含退到从前、重走老路的巨大风险。美国证券交易委员会如何作出决定存在着不确定性,不利于我们完成剩余的趋同项目。在某些问题上,双方要达成共识、形成共同方案,变得越来越困难。如果我们对趋同协议中的项目都无法实现趋同,那趋同协议结束后,还怎么能保持趋同呢?如果两套准则差距加大、分歧增加,则风险巨大,这将是多么大的资源浪费啊。

国际财务报告准则与美国公认会计原则的趋同进程已历经十载,双方孜孜以求、不厌其烦甚至痛苦前行,单是分析和报告写作就花了两年时间。因此,全世界许多人都期待美国就采用国际财务报告准则问题作出清晰规划,给出明确愿景。

这就是我们需要美国就继续承诺单一全球准则给出确切信号的原因。仅仅追求准则之间的可比性是行不通的,不可能实现单一准则的目标。实践证明，我们在20世纪90年代的努力已经失败[①]。如果美国不发出可靠、确切的信号，"国际关切"就会变成"国际怀疑"，G20关于全球会计准则的呼声就会显得空洞乏力、虚无缥缈。国际会计准则理事会绝不能容忍这种情况的出现。

女士们，先生们，在过去的十年间，在全球绝大部分地方，国际财务报告准则已经成为事实上的全球会计语言。遍布全球的投资者依靠国际财务报告准则作出投资决策，使世界保持安全稳定。我真的不知道，哪项全球经济准则或组织能够缺少美国的主导。正是因为如此，缺少美国和美国证券交易委员会主导的国际财务报告准则不可想象。但是，美国要取得主导地位，就需要远见卓识、勇往直前和毅然决然的决策，而美国恰恰不缺乏这些品质。

请诸位原谅我开幕致辞的率真直白。荷兰人因直言不讳而名声不佳，而我恰恰就是一个荷兰人。但是，作为生活和工作在美国的一个荷兰人，我清楚美国人谈话也喜欢直来直去。诚挚感谢诸位认真倾听我的演讲。

---

[1] 国际财务报告准则基金会工作人员对美国证券交易委员会关于采用国际财务报告准则的最终报告的分析。www.ifrs.org.

（乔元芳 翻译并审校）

---

① 国际会计准则委员会(IASC)由9个"发起成员"创立。美国注册会计师协会是其中之一，代表美国。当时的设想是，由于国家会计准则制定者基于国际会计准则委员会的准则来制定本国准则，因而应实现最大的可比性。但是，经过25年的努力，最初的9个发起成员所使用的准则没有一个与国际准则接近。各国各取所好，它们仅留下国际准则中所同意和喜欢的部分和内容，修改它们不需要和不喜欢的部分和内容。为此，国际社会再次凝聚在一起，探求应该采取何种行动，并于1997年发布了一份战略报告，建议重组国际会计准则委员会，将制定和实施单一全球准则作为其职责和使命。

为什么金融业与众不同：
金融业按现值计量的相关性

2013年12月3日，英格兰及威尔士特许会计师协会与国际财务报告准则基金会联合举行"金融机构国际财务报告准则大会"。汉斯·胡格沃斯特出席会议并发表演讲。本文为演讲全文。

尽管国际会计准则理事会如此重视金融工具会计准则，却没有为金融工具制定充分适用的会计准则，而且制定的会计准则也不令人满意。自2008年开始，我们就致力于研究制定国际财务报告准则第9号，目前仍在一丝不苟地全力推进。

认真地说，目前看来，所幸征途已现曙光。国际财务报告准则第9号即告完成，而且是不久便将大功告成。但不可否认的是，我们仍偶有纠结、游移不定。当然，对金融工具会计处理游移不定的不仅只有国际会计准则理事会，我们的同行——美国财务会计准则委员会也同样如此。

会计准则制定者之所以殚精竭虑全力解决金融工具会计问题，原因有两个。首先，金融工具自身极为复杂，而且更为重要的是，金融业对会计规则又极为敏感。即使会计规则发生相对微小的变动，也会导致银行（会计报表）呈现出天壤之别。由于会计透明可能导致对银行业采取进一步紧急救助行动，对最大化会计透明度的追求热情也会因此降温。因此，国际会计准则理事会所提议的每一项变革，都务求深思熟虑。

为什么会出现这种情况呢？金融业会计与其他行业会计的区别究竟是什么呢？为了回答这些问题，我首先就非金融主体会计作一描述。

人们经常批评国际会计准则理事会过度关注资产负债表和公允价值计量，从而导致审慎性缺失，会计数字极度波动。

我一直认为,从总体上讲,这些批评有失公正。国际会计准则理事会发布的概念框架讨论稿已经非常明确地阐明了下述观点:损益是衡量业绩的关键指标;资产负债表没有优先地位;国际会计准则理事会既没有赋予公允价值会计优先地位,当然也未把公允价值会计妖魔化。

国际会计准则理事会所选择的路径和方法,与资产负债表法和收益表法都有细微的差别,个中原因并不难理解。事实上,对不同的行业,资产负债表的重要性差别极大。对于绝大多数制造业企业和服务业企业而言,资产负债表仅能部分地反映主体的财务状况。

在制造业企业和服务业企业,为了生产产品或提供服务,大部分资产均与其他资产一并联合运用。因此,大部分资产的现值并不具有特别的重要性。

在持续经营的绝大多数情况下,不动产、厂场和设备的公允价值对决策的相关性极为有限。例如,对于汽车制造商(或其投资者)而言,如果他们意在利用机器人生产汽车,那么知悉机器人的现行市场价值并不具有特别的相关性。而且在许多情况下,按公允价值来估价不动产、厂场和设备,不仅代价高昂,同时还为盈余管理留下空间。如果损益中包括对不动产、厂场和设备公允价值的经常性调整,那么主体的盈余就会变得格外混乱不堪、无法理解。

但这并不是说,以成本为基础进行会计处理就没有什么严重缺陷。特别是在通胀环境下,历史成本很快就会丧失相关性。此外,按成本编制的资产负债表有碍投资者识别隐藏的潜在价值(例如,破旧办公楼所占用土地的价值)。但总体而言,考虑折旧以后的历史成本通常被认为是计量非金融业大部分资产、符合成本—效益原则的方法。

之所以说资产负债表仅仅能部分地反映许多公司的真实经济状况,无形资产的会计处理是另外一个原因。像苹果和谷歌这样的高技术企业,技术、设计或者市场控制力对未来盈利能力的重要性,要远远大于不动产、厂场和设备的价值。但是,即使无形资产显而易见地存在,却由于绝大部分无形资产无法可靠计量,也没有纳入资产负债表。

所有这一切,并不意味着非金融业资产负债表无关紧要,因为资产负债表包含一个主体重要的杠杆信息,这也正是我们对即将出台的租赁准则投入如此多精力的原因。资产负债表还为投资者提供了存货以及不动产、厂场和设备状况方面的信息,但要预测未来现金流量,在许多情况下,投资者还需要对盈余和无形资产进行更为深入的分析。

国际会计准则理事会充分意识到，过度关注资产负债表，并不能向投资者提供有用的信息。

金融业却与众不同。银行和保险公司的资产负债表金额庞大、影响巨大，资产负债表的相对较小变化，都会对盈余产生巨大的影响。银行和保险公司的未来现金流量高度依赖于资产负债表上的金融工具。

对于大多数金融工具，其现值才至为重要。部分金融工具在金融市场上交易活跃，理所当然地受到市场波动的影响。因此，相对于非金融业，金融业的资产负债表和现值计量技术（包括但不限于公允价值会计）更为重要。

尽管现值计量技术的重要性无可质疑，但金融会计也因此而卷入争议的漩涡，也是不争的事实。现值计量能够更好地发现资产与负债的错配，对市场波动也更为敏感。

因此，现值计量可能导致更大的波动。从这个角度考量，银行与保险公司与其他财务报告编制者并不二致：它们都厌恶波动。

而且，如果他们意识到波动是由会计导致的，那就更加厌恶这种波动。

在金融危机最严重的时候，银行业人士都认为，他们是公允价值会计导致的人为波动的牺牲品。他们认为，无论经济是上行还是下行，依赖市场价格都会使经济循环不断恶化。这些批评者深信，公允价值会计助长了顺周期效应，从而人为地制造了波动。

事实是，绝大多数银行对公允价值会计的运用极为有限，主要是交易账户和衍生工具运用公允价值会计。绝大多数人都认为，对于此类金融工具，除公允价值会计外别无选择。而且，绝大多数银行的账簿由贷款等传统资产构成，而它们却继续以摊余成本计量。

因此，对于绝大多数学术研究得出的公允价值会计对金融危机并无重要影响的结论，就不足为奇了。

在公允价值确实发挥作用的领域，公允价值计量通常有益无害。持有有毒担保债务凭证（CDOs）的银行使用公允价值计量，通常能够更快地认识到所面对的危险。尽管使用公允价值可能被视为不够谨慎，但如果把公允价值作为减值的迹象，则是能够做到的最为审慎的事情。

事实上，会计所做的事情，只不过是反映真实的经济波动，而这种波动正是银行业商业模式的核心所在。现实情况是，很难想象有一个行业像金融业那样对现实经济波动如此敏感。

银行资产负债表的左右两边都很脆弱。银行的资产中,不管是衍生工具还是提供了房产抵押的贷款,对经济周期都十分敏感。诸如抵押贷款这样的传统银行贷款,长期以来都被视作收益稳定、老套常规的业务。然而自2007年以来,我们都明白了,房价的长期趋势以及监管的失误,很可能导致重大误导。正如我们看到的爱尔兰和西班牙的情况,即使3A级金边政府债券也会快速恶化,变得一文不值。

银行业资产负债表的负债一方,脆弱得同样声名狼藉。不管是大规模获得的融资,还是零星获得的融资,都可能在鼠标轻点之间而瞬间蒸发。

这似乎还不是全部的风险,银行业的经营基于微薄的资本才是问题的关键。就在金融危机发生之前,许多银行的有形普通股权益资本已经成为负数。有形普通股权益资本通常只占资产负债表风险加权资产的1‰~3‰,有些银行的净有形权益甚至都是负数。

所幸国际会计准则理事会对合并财务报表要求严格,银行的超常规杠杆水平才得以暴露在公众面前。但市场参与者却无视这些信息,从而成为经济史上最令人震惊的集体认知失调案例。

尽管会计在经济危机中至多只扮演了次要的角色,各方却施压要求降低公允价值会计的影响,为此美国财务会计准则委员会和国际会计准则理事会承受了巨大压力。尽管会计准则作出的变化并不太大,但由于银行业的状况如此糟糕,因而会计准则的改进无论多么微小,甚至只具有装点门面的作用,都被认为对银行业大有裨益。由于银行的状况过于难看而无颜面对公众,为了使其看上去漂亮些,会计规则被迫屈服,这实在是一个经典案例。如果银行资本充足,会计准则发展史上如此丑陋不堪的一幕就不该发生。

我们承认,国际财务报告准则有一项规定,即所谓"自身信用"的会计处理,的确可能导致有违直觉的结果。在金融危机最严重之际,处于重压之下的银行自身债务公允价值下降,导致对自身信用进行公允估价反而会报告利润,结果荒诞。

国际财务报告准则第9号已经解决了这个问题,而且最近还决定,将上述方法作为一般套期会计变革的一部分,允许单独运用。

金融危机也同样清楚地表明,现行的减值模型运作效果不佳。目前使用的已发生损失模型,意在防止通过提取"洗大澡"准备金而进行盈余管理。

而金融危机已经证明,该模型对不同的盈余管理手法都束手无策。例如,过分地推迟确认损失,甚至在充分证明损失已不可避免的情况下仍不确认损失。这就是为什么要用预期损失模型取代已发生损失模型的原因所在。

目前,我们已经研究制定了一个具有操作性而且比已发生损失模型更具有未来取向的减值模型。

一旦金融资产的信用风险出现重大上升,就必须确认寿命期间内的全部预期损失。新减值模型还将阐述摊余成本会计的一个主要缺陷,即它很容易掩盖不可避免的未来现金流量短缺。我们进行的实地测试显示,此举将导致准备金水平出现重大上升。

金融危机还促使国际会计准则理事会加快了以国际财务报告准则第9号取代国际会计准则第39号的步伐。国际财务报告准则第9号将继续采用混合计量方法,但我们已经努力把分类和计量建立在目标的基础之上。

金融工具的分类既取决于现金流量的性质,也取决于商业模式。概而言之,如果一项金融工具具有基本贷款特征,而且是以持有并收回为商业模式,该金融工具就应以摊余成本计量;如果一项金融工具不具有基本贷款特征且商业模式是为了进行资产的交易,该金融工具就应以公允价值计量且公允价值变动计入损益;如果持有一项资产,既有出售的目的,也有收取合同现金流量的目的,该金融工具就应以公允价值计量,但公允价值变动计入其他综合收益。

国际财务报告准则第9号并不会彻底改变现状,银行的绝大多数资产仍以成本计量并报告。那么,这是否意味着银行业将在摊余成本提供的无忧无虑的稳定状态中持续生存?显然,这个问题太过夸大其词,因为众所周知,现实情况远比这复杂。

20世纪80年代发生在美国的存贷款危机,是摊余成本会计存在局限性的典型案例。在20世纪80年代早期,由于银行的存款利率与对外贷款组合利率严重错配,存贷款行业事实上已经破产。当时的美联储主席保罗·沃尔克大幅度提高利率,存贷款业被迫支付更多的存款利息,而长期抵押贷款的利息收益却大多相对固定。显然,摊余成本会计并没有揭示不可避免的全部损失,它所描述的"稳定"是一种假象,而所有人都知道它的描述并不正确。

30多年后的今天,确保利差幅度已经成为银行高管们的中心任务,而且比以前任何时候都更为重要。

现实情况是,银行业错综复杂,远不是一手取得存款,另一手收取合同现金流量那么简单。银行业务的本质是赚取稳定的净利息差,这需要进行非常复杂和动态的资产负债管理。

当银行负责贷款的人员悠闲地收取贷款的合同现金流量时,资金部的同事们却在紧盯利率市场,每天都在管控利率风险。此类管控活动基于利率风险的现值计量,要求大量使用以公允价值计量的衍生工具等金融工具。

因此,如果收取合同现金流量仅仅是银行业务模式的一部分,那也显而易见,仅仅使用摊余成本计量也不能忠实地陈报银行的财务状况。事实上,用来管理利率风险的金融工具,通常以公允价值计量。因此,这种混合计量方法造成的不可避免的结果就是,银行财务报表中充斥着摊余成本与公允价值的会计不匹配。

由于存在会计不匹配,银行很难向投资者解释说明其财务业绩。因此,绝大多数银行积极采用一般套期会计准则解决这个问题,成功地规避了部分会计波动。但众所周知的是,现行套期会计规则使用随心所欲的标准,也只处理了部分套期关系。更为要命的是,现行套期会计并不能恰当地反映对开放式组合净头寸的管理情况。

正因如此,国际会计准则理事会目前正在制定一个讨论稿,开发一个新的宏观套期模型。该模型将使会计能够更好地反映与开放式组合有关的风险管理活动,而不再将套期会计仅仅局限于特定的金融工具。总的来说,宏观套期会计使得开放式组合中所嵌入的利率风险现值与对冲该风险的衍生工具公允价值的匹配成为可能。

最近在阅读美国财务会计准则委员会前主席鲍勃·赫兹回忆录时,我发现国际会计准则理事会拟议的宏观套期会计方法与赫兹关于金融工具会计处理的设想非常接近。在这本可读性很强的著作[1]中,赫兹说他努力说服同事们,希望采用的金融工具计量模型应基于按现行市场利率折现的现金流量现值。

他的建议实质上是会计的"第三路径",试图避免摊余成本会计和公允价值会计这两种方法的缺陷。与摊余成本会计相比,折现现金流量模型既能更好地洞察利率和期限错配问题,又能避免公允价值会计的某些"噪音"(这些噪音是由一般市场和流动性因素导致的)。彼时,他并没有成功说服美国财务会计准则委员会中他的同事们。但是我认为,国际会计准则理事会即将发布的宏观套期讨论稿,肯定认可赫兹的某些设想。现金流量现值对于银行的风险管理以及国际会计准则理事会建议的会计处理方法,都很重要。

如果对这一新方法能进行良好的设计和恰当的运用,它就能更好地反映银行的实际商业模式,实质性地减少会计不匹配情况的发生。我要强调的是,"良好的设计和恰当的运用"是一个前提,因为如果没有充分的约束和严格的规范,宏观套期也会堕落成为缺乏严谨或者缺乏可比性的、由用户根据需要自行定制的会计。

我们的目标是改善透明度,而不是掩饰经济波动。正因如此,在提出建议方案时,我们总是小心翼翼、谨慎前行。

要完成我们提议的宏观套期会计,显然还需要相当长的时间。因此,我们把宏观套期会计从国际财务报告准则第9号中独立出来。国际财务报告准则第9号事实上已经完成,不久即将接受认可。鉴于国际财务报告准则第9号在金融工具分类和计量、一般套期和减值方面进行了重大改进,无疑将得到全球的认可。

由于时间的限制,刚才我较少谈及保险合同会计。那些密切关注新保险合同会计准则研究制定进程的人士都知道,国际会计准则理事会建议的模块化保险合同会计模型同样具有我刚才谈及的"第三路径"会计特征,它既不基于成本,也不基于公允价值,而是一个使用现行利率的折现现金流量模型。

尽管对上述建议模型还有很多公开争论和不同意见,但绝大多数市场参与者认为,要使保险负债的列报为投资者提供具有决策意义的信息,唯一的方式就是使用现值。特别是在利率被长期打压的当前宏观经济环境下,使用历史利率显然将生成误导的信息。因此,现值计量技术对保险业同样至为重要。

女士们、先生们,现在我作一个简要的小结。我希望我已经清楚地阐明,总体而言,国际会计准则理事会并没有给予资产负债表优于损益表的地位。当我为金融业激辩,认为资产负债表的确事关重大时,我认为这种阐述是多此一举。

我希望在座的大多数人士同意这样的观点,即许多金融工具的现值计量,对金融业的风险管理绝对至关重要。实际上,银行经理如果未按现值进行日常风险管理,就必定会受到监管者的严密审核和监管。

国际会计准则理事会全力以赴工作,目的就是使银行业的会计报表更好地反映风险管理活动。我们需要诸位的真知灼见和大力支持,以便使国际会计准则理事会建议的方案与设想能够付诸实施。因此,在国际会计准则理事会达成金融工具和保险合同相关建议方案过程中,建议各位全面积极地参与。谢谢大家。

---

[1] Bob Herz. Accounting Changes,Chronicles of convergence,crisis and complexity in financial reporting.2013.

(乔元芳 翻译并审校)

A Time for Change? The Objectives of Financial Reporting

Speech by Hans Hoogervorst at conference organised by the European Commission Financial Reporting and Auditing in Brussels, Belgium
09 February 2011

In the past three years, I have participated in many intense debates on accounting questions. Two questions have dominated these debates. The first question that always pops up, is to which audience financial reporting should primarily be directed: should they primarily be targeted towards investors, or should they address a more general public, including for example prudential regulators? A second, related question is whether accounting standards only serve the goal of transparency, or if they should also have a financial stability objective.

I was often puzzled by the intensity of these debates, given the fact that I think these questions can be answered in a fairly straightforward way.

Let us first try to answer the question to which audience financial reporting should primarily be directed.

Nobody will disagree that the purpose of financial reporting is to provide as faithful a picture as possible of the financial position of a company or organisation. Financial statements should contain information that is as unbiased and reliable as possible.

It goes without saying that financial statements are most relevant to the investor. After all, financial reporting was born out of the necessity to give investors adequate information on company they are providing capital for. The interest of the investor will always remain the main focus of accounting standard setting.

At the same time, it is important to realize that if the purpose of financial reporting is to be as faithful as possible, it is less relevant who the user of the financial statement is. If a financial statement of a company is as accurate as possible it cannot be accurate in 10 different ways. It could not possibly become more or less faithful depending on the question whether an investor, a depositor or a regulator is using it.

Moreover, while it remains undeniable that financial statements are of primary importance to investors, in our modern economy so many entities are working with "other people's money" that financial reporting is of importance to much wider interests. High quality financial reporting is of essential importance to depositors and their protectors, the prudential regulators, to suppliers, to creditors in general.

Indeed, reliable financial reporting is such an important ingredient for building trust in our global market economy, that it can be said to be of public interest. That is why the IFRS Foundation mentions in the first paragraph of its constitution that it works "in the public interest".

It is hard to underestimate the public interest of IFRS. IFRS is already the common business language of well over 100 nations. It is indeed the only set of standards that has the potential to be used all over the world. IFRS is an engine for economic modernisation, linking industrialized nations with growth markets around the world. Only IFRS can unleash the full potential of a truly global capital market. It can make an enormous contribution to economic growth by enhancing transparency and liquidity around the world. This is a global public interest which I will be proud to serve.

The second hotly debated question is the question whether the purpose of financial reporting should primarily be to provide transparency, or that it should also serve the goal of stability.

In this debate, transparency and stability are often juxtaposed as if they were conflicting goals. I think this is essentially a false contradiction. In my view, it is clear that transparency is a necessary precondition of stability. The current credit crisis has to a large extent been caused by a lack of transparency in the financial markets. Huge risks were allowed to build up on and off balance sheet without being noticed. Without proper transparency about risks, stability is bound to collapse in the end. Stability is not the same as transparency, but there can be no durable stability without transparency.

So accounting standards can contribute to stability by enhancing transparency. There are plenty of recent examples of how accounting standard setters are doing just that, often in close consultation with the prudential community. I am referring to the tightening up of conditions for off-balance sheet financing; the proposed convergence to eliminate differences between US GAAP and IFRS in the netting of financial assets and liabilities; the proposed introduction of the expected loss model to enhance loss recognition in the loan portfolio in a timely stage.

Accounting standards can also be useful for stability purposes by avoiding artificial noise in the balance sheet and the income statement. This was an important reason for the IASB to continue with a mixed attribute system with regards to financial instruments. Financial instruments that have basic loan features and which are managed on a contractual yield basis are valued at amortized cost. For such instruments, cost is deemed to provide more relevant information than short term market fluctuations. This method can indeed prevent unhelpful noise, yet it should not imply that market expectations are irrelevant, as I will explain later.

The distinction between the P&L and Other Comprehensive Income is another example of accounting standards being sensitive to preventing noise in the income statement. While the definition of OCI is in need of a firmer theoretical underpinning, it is a pragmatic way of shielding the P&L from volatility in the balance sheet that does not truly reflect the financial performance of the entity.

So accounting standards can make a very important contribution to stability by providing maximum transparency, and by avoiding artificial noise.

However it is important to keep this in perspective. Stability should be a consequence of greater transparency, rather than a primary goal of accounting standard-setters. For this, accounting standard setters simply lack the tools. For example, they cannot set capital requirements for the banking industry. This instrument belongs to the prudential regulators who do have stability as their main mission.

What accounting standard setters can also not do is to pretend that things are stable which are not. And, quite frankly, this is where their relationship with prudential regulators sometimes becomes testy. Accounting standard setters are sometimes suspicious that they are being asked to put a veneer of stability on instruments which are inherently volatile in value.

Whereas the search for transparency is the natural focus of accounting standard setters, this is not necessarily the case for prudential regulators. They are bound to strict confidentiality rules and often feel an understandable need to work out problems behind closed doors. After all, maximum transparency may not always be the best way to prevent a bank run.

More generally, transparency does not always come spontaneously to an industry that is as vulnerable as the financial sector. It is indeed hard to imagine a riskier business model than the current banking industry. Both sides of a bank's balance sheet are prone to volatility. Its assets can be very sensitive to the economic cycle, whether they are based on derivatives, bricks and mortar or sovereign risk. Gold-plated triple A can turn sour very quickly, as we have seen in the case of Ireland. The banking industry's liability side is also notoriously vulnerable. Funding can evaporate with the speed of a mouse-click.

As if this is not risky enough, the banking industry has been allowed to run on the flimsiest of capital margins. The capital cushion of the banking industry has been allowed to shrink dramatically in the last century. Just before the crisis, tangible common equity of most banks was lower than 2% and in many cases close to zero!

It is no surprise that this business model experiences recurrent crises all around the world. More than occasionally, banks need to be rescued by government intervention or massive budgetary stimulus. Even more frequently, the financial industry needs to be propped up by free supply of raw material by central banks in the form of artificially low interest rates. The implicit or explicit government guarantees that many banks enjoy, allow them to borrow at rates that are in effect subsidized. In effect, the financial industry is among the most heavily state-supported sectors of the world economy.

Many weaknesses of the current system are being addressed. Capital requirements are being increased; underwriting standards are being improved; the infrastructure of the derivatives markets will be strengthened. But many vulnerabilities will remain. Even under Basel 3, triple-A sovereign risk carries zero risk weights, while we should know by now that zero risk does not exist. The new leverage ratio-while a great improvement in itself-will (at 3%) still be low in the light of the massive losses that were experienced during the current crisis.

One cannot envy the prudential authorities for being responsible for such an inherently unstable system. In these circumstances, it is also understandable that they can be uncomfortable with accounting rules that force problems into the open. It is only natural that banking supervisors try to buy time for the banking system to get back on its feet. It must also be admitted that in the past this approach has occasionally been effective. Paul Volcker-the greatest central banker of all time-still remembers with pride how by hiding the fact that the American banking sector was basically broken during the Latin American debt crisis, he created time for the banks to repair their balance sheets.

However, I sincerely doubt if this method still works in the 21st century. In these days of the information revolution on the internet, of intensely prying media, institutional investors and activist shareholders, it is an illusion that you can keep real problems hidden for very long. Indeed, a perception that regulators may not be transparent about the true nature of the problems may serve to fuel undue unrest in the market.

The July 2010 stress test of the European banking sector is a case in point. The markets immediately perceived this stress test as a lacking in rigor. One reason for scepticism was that sovereign bonds on the banking book were deemed to retain their full value, despite the fact that many were trading at steep discounts in the market. The fact that some Irish banks that had passed the test later turned out to be insolvent only served to reinforce the doubts in the market.

I also wonder what kind of message this stress test gave to auditors. The European Commission is asking questions about the fact that auditors gave clean bills of health to almost all the banks that failed during the credit crisis. But how critical will auditors be when they see that regulators consider that severely discounted securities carry no risk?

By the way, the introduction of an expected loss model is very high on the wish list of prudential regulators, to promote more timely recognition of losses. How credible can that be if currently obvious signals pointing at impairment are ignored?

The amortized cost model for banking book securities can only be credible when impairments are booked in a timely fashion. If too wide a divergence between market valuations and the book value of such securities is maintained, ultimately investors will start clamouring for extension of fair value accounting.

The truth is that investors around the world have had little faith that the financial industry has been facing up to its problems in the past years. In such circumstances, markets often become suspicious and they tend to overreact. Thus, lack of transparency directly feeds into lack of stability.

There is one final reason why I think that both the accounting and prudential community should be fully committed to transparency. That reason is that preventing a crisis through full risk transparency is much less costly than letting things go and cleaning up afterwards. Should a clean-up be inevitable, time should not be bought by trying to hide problems, but by making them manageable through better support and resolution mechanisms such as are currently being designed.

My career has been fully devoted to the public interest and I am strongly motivated to work closely with all stakeholders, including the prudential community for the common good. But while we cooperate, we should respect each other's mission and responsibilities.

Accounting standard setters should remain committed to their main goal of providing transparency. By providing transparency, they give a great contribution to stability. The difficult task of making the financial industry safer is the responsibility of the banking supervisors. I am convinced that they can strengthen their mandate of guarding stability by using more effectively transparency as a preventive instrument. The regular publication of rigorous stress test, such as mandated by the Dodd-Frank Act, can do a lot to help them in their difficult task of imposing adequate capital levels on the financial industry.

In the final part of my speech, I would like to make some observations about another sensitive issue, namely the relationship between independence and accountability in accounting standard setting.

When you look at the fundamentals of IFRS, it is striking that most of them are based on plain, economic sense. Despite its complexity, IFRS is actually a quite elegant system of economic reasoning, firmly rooted in common sense.

At the same time, we have to recognize that financial reporting is not an exact science. Asset valuation is in many respects more of an art than a science. Many assets are not homogenous and they often have no active of liquid markets that give reliable price signals. In many cases, asset valuation requires a lot of judgement and/or common sense. Often there is room for legitimate differences in opinion.

But often, accounting disputes are not fed by genuine intellectual debates, but by naked financial interests. It was not in the interest of CEO's to run share based payments through the P&L. That is why they fought it tooth and nail when accounting standards were forcing them to do so.

It was also not in pleasant for companies to have their pension liabilities fully visible on their balance sheet and therefore IAS19 on employee benefits met fierce resistance. Though these changes forced changes in some business practices, it is clear that they were for the good, bringing hidden costs or liabilities out into the open.

Accounting standard setting should therefore be sensitive to legitimate business concerns but be firm and independent in the face of special interests. Independence is an essential precondition for durable public trust in accounting standard setting.

At the same time, I fully realize that independence does not come automatically. The IASB should never be perceived as an Ivory Tower. Independence will only be respected if there is a strong sense of ownership among the user community and among the public authorities that endorse the standards. This is a huge challenge, especially for a young organisation that has conquered so much territory in a very short time.

I see four ways to strengthen the worldwide sense of ownership of IFRS. First of all, the quality of the IASB's standards should always be first-rate. We may have differences of opinion about content; the quality of the IASB's work should always be beyond doubt.

Secondly, we need a first-rate system of due process. The IASB already follows very strict rules for due process in which exhaustive consultation takes place around the world. The IASB's deliberations and voting procedures are broadcast live on the internet, making it one of the most transparent standard setters in the world. Still, we need to build on existing outreach efforts to ensure that participants around the world are heard and their views given due consideration by the Board. The opening of a regional office in Japan is an important step in that direction.

Thirdly, the IFRS-foundation needs to be fully aware of the challenges that can be involved in the implementation of the standards. While standards need to adapt to rapid economic developments, in the timing of changes we need to take into account the user's capacity to digest them.

Finally, independence needs to be accompanied by a strong system of accountability. The governance of the IFRS Foundation is now being reviewed by the Foundation itself and by the Monitoring Board. I believe the governance of their relationship can be strengthened and I look forward to proposals to that effect. It is very important that we develop a governance structure that is more inclusive and in which all jurisdictions using IFRS feel adequately represented.

At all costs we should avoid the impression that the IFRS Foundation is dominated by a small group of countries. As a global organization, I feel it is very important that all participants have a sense of ownership. Obviously it is a huge challenge to make a homogenous body of a young, international organisation. Throughout my career in public services I have met many challenges. I even enjoy them. So I am very much looking forward to chairing the IASB in the coming years.

China and IFRS—An Opportunity for Leadership in Global Financial Reporting

Speech by Hans Hoogervorst in Beijing, China

26 July 2011

Introduction

I am greatly honoured to address such a prestigious gathering on my first visit to China as the new Chairman of the IASB.

I would like to thank Director General Yang Ming of the Ministry of Finance and her staff at the Accounting Regulatory Department for convening this event. I would also like to thank President Liu, Trustee of the IFRS Foundation as well as my friend and fellow Board member Dr Zhang Wei-Guo for their work supporting of the goals and ambitions of the IFRS Foundation.

The topic of my speech has been chosen deliberately. China has become or is becoming a world leader in so many areas—from manufacturing to academic research. China is rapidly regaining its historic position as one of the largest economies in the world. Because of this when China speaks, the world listens. In accounting, China has made tremendous progress by building an accounting profession and setting in place a process of continuous convergence with IFRS. This is an achievement of which China should be justifiably proud. This development is also welcomed by important international bodies like ESMA, the European securities regulator and the World Bank.

Still, I believe that China's path to becoming a global leader in financial reporting is not fully fulfilled. If China does want to become a global leader in financial reporting, then the IASB stands ready to support this ambition.

The next 12—18 months will be very important for the future direction of international financial reporting. The people in this room have a significant stake in the outcome. Now is the time to speak up, to ensure China's voice is heard and acted upon.

Before I come on to this, as a newcomer to the financial reporting community I feel I should provide some perspectives on why the IFRS Foundation Trustees chose me as a successor to Sir David Tweedie, who achieved so much in his ten years as Chairman of the IASB, and why I am genuinely excited to lead the IASB to a second decade of success. I would also like to share with you my analysis of the priorities for the IASB in the coming years.

My background and interest in financial reporting

Let me begin by sharing with you a series of experiences that triggered my interest in financial reporting and ultimately led to my appointment as Chairman of the IASB.

I've actually been involved in financial reporting matters for some time. I previously served as a Dutch Minister of Finance and more recently as Chairman of the Authority for the Financial Markets, the Dutch securities and markets regulator which is comparable to the China Securities Regulatory Commission here in China.

It was during the darkest days of the financial crisis that I gave my first public speech on accounting, stressing the importance of maintaining the highest levels of transparency in financial reporting. While the accounting was not perfect, I felt strongly that some were seeking to use the accounting standards as scapegoats for failures elsewhere in the system. This was much to the annoyance of those, and there were many, who believed the accounting should be neutered in order to protect investors from themselves and to avoid the markets from being spooked.

Perhaps that is why in 2008 the IASB and the FASB invited me to co-Chair the Financial Crisis Advisory Group, a group of international leaders with broad experience of financial markets. It was a great experience. The FCAG was a very diverse group, consisting of both proponents and adversaries of fair value accounting.

We had fierce discussions, but gradually developed a clear consensus and produced a report that was widely appreciated.

That is when my interest in accounting was truly ignited. I discovered that accounting is not boring at all but intellectually challenging. I discovered that in accounting, the power of the argument can bring people together. People can actually convince each other of their opinion (unlike often in politics).

These experiences triggered a personal interest in accounting, but two factors convinced me of the importance of this work to the broader global economy and my desire to lead the IASB as it adapts to become the global accounting standard-setter.

First, that it is hard to overestimate the importance of maintaining public trust in high quality financial reporting. As both a policy maker and a regulator, I have devoted most of my career to the pursuit of the public interest. The primary public interest that we serve is to provide investors and other market participants with financial information to make investment decisions. But the public interest role of accounting standards is deeper than this definition might imply. Sound economies rely on the provision of faithful, reliable financial information to maintain public trust and ensure the flow of capital to fuel growth.

The recent financial crisis provided a real-world example of what can happen when confidence is lost in published financial information.

The crisis was to great extent caused by fatal flaws in economic assumptions, such as credit underwriting standards, the standards of credit rating agencies and widespread gaming of the Basel capital ratios for banks. To a lesser degree, even accounting standards played a part by providing too much room for off-balance sheet financing and avoidance of impairments of shaky assets.

Many of these issues had been building for years, but it was when investors felt they could no longer reply on published financial information that panic ensued and the markets went into free-fall. It showed why high quality accounting standards are a prerequisite to maintaining public trust, without which no economy can properly function. IFRSs provide that trust.

Second, in addition to their public interest role, high quality, international financial reporting standards are a force for economic progress. When a country adopts IFRSs, it is making a public commitment to maintain the highest standards for financial reporting. As a result, for most countries, inward investment flows, the cost of capital is reduced, and the overall prosperity of a country is likely to increase—raising living standards for all. Investors similarly will be more able to diversify their portfolio and benefit from increased comparability. IFRSs support economic growth and establish a high-quality level playing field for globalised markets. Like no other standard, IFRSs link the new growth economies in the East with the more established economies in the West.

For these reasons it is very exciting to be part of this adventure.

While I am not a technical accountant by training, I hope that my experience and contacts outside of the pure financial reporting world can assist the IASB as it takes its rightful place as an important cog in the global financial system. I am fortunate to have a strong Vice-Chairman in Ian Mackintosh, former Chairman of the UK ASB, and together with my fellow IASB members we will share much of the international outreach and technical work.

My priorities

I would now like to turn to what I see as the IASB's priorities for the near future. These priorities are largely determined by the two factors I have already discussed. As an organisation that serves the public interest and promotes economic progress, our main output, financial reporting standards, must be of the highest quality. They must be developed following a robust process that takes into consideration the requirements of those who use them, and must be recognised, understood and accepted internationally.

To me, this translates into four specific priorities.

1. Completing our convergence programme

First, we must complete the remaining convergence projects with the US standard-setter to the highest possible standard, and to do so in a way that benefits from the input that we receive from the entire global financial reporting community. These remaining convergence projects address some of the most difficult and important areas of financial reporting.

Our work to improve international and US revenue recognition requirements is at an advanced stage. After a final re-exposure, the new joint standard will replace US requirements that are generally considered to be too detailed and international requirements that are not detailed enough.

Our project to improve lease accounting requirements-which is also well advanced-will provide investors with better information on the rights and obligations companies have through their lease commitments. This project represents an important step in our work to push back off-balance sheet financing.

Our work to improve and align our respective financial instruments accounting standards is also much needed. This is perhaps the most pressing item on our plate right now. The two boards have already proposed moving to an expected loss impairment model. Last week the boards took important steps to come to a common solution.

The IASB is re-deliberating our proposal on hedge accounting based on public comments we received, and we are midway through developing proposals that address the challenging topic of portfolio hedging.

Although it is not part of the Memorandum of Understanding between the IASB and FASB, completion of the Insurance standard is a very important priority.

It is simply unacceptable that IFRSs only have a stopgap standard for this very important part of the financial industry.

We need to ensure that each of these standards is as good as it possibly can be, that we have listened and understood the various arguments before determining, with clarity, how to proceed. We will not be able to please everyone, which is why the standard-setting process has to be beyond reproach.

2. Consulting on the post-convergence agenda

Second, we will begin to develop the IASB's post-convergence agenda. Within the next few weeks, we will publish a consultation document that sets out some ideas but more importantly is designed to solicit feedback.

You will notice that we deliberately leave many questions open for comment. What is in urgent need of fixing? How should we best deploy the limited resources at our disposal? At the same time, there are some obvious candidates for the future agenda. Everyone is asking us to complete the conceptual framework, and thereby firm up the philosophical and methodological underpinning of our work.

I also think our future agenda should clearly show that we have a lot of new jurisdictions tied to IFRSs, which includes China. These countries have legitimate requests and are waiting for an answer.

Our consultation document mentions several possible projects that are particularly relevant to this region, including business combinations between entities under common control, foreign currency translation and agriculture.

Many of our stakeholders feel that we need to come up with a much firmer underpinning for Other Comprehensive Income and the related issue of "recycling". I think this is very important as it relates very closely to the endless discussions around volatility in measures of reported profit and equity.

A major complaint during the financial crisis was that accounting standards led to excessive volatility by relying too much on unreliable market information. These critics feel that accounting standard-setters should serve not only transparency, but also stability.

I have always thought this supposed conflict between stability and transparency to be a false contradiction. In my view, transparency is an essential precondition for stability. The crisis was caused by lack of transparency of risks building up in the system. So the main contribution of accounting standards to stability is by providing transparency.

The IASB is sensitive to the issue of avoiding introducing accounting volatility. At the same time, many of us feel that the methodological underpinning of OCI is not firm enough and that it is too often used as the dumping ground for difficult issues.

If we could come up with a sound definition of OCI and therefore also of the P&L, we will have achieved a major feat. I am not sure if we can completely succeed in putting the debate on stability versus transparency to rest, but of one thing I am sure: accounting should not be the source of volatility, but it should never be used to mask volatility.

3. Delivering global standards

Third, we must do all we can to complete the G20-endorsed transition towards global financial reporting standards. There is an enormous amount of support for a single set of global financial reporting standards, from the G20 leaders down. How do we harness this incredible support and goodwill at the highest levels, to help us achieve our goals? This is one of the most important questions for the IFRS Foundation in the coming years and we will be reaching out to others for their help and support.

An important piece of the IFRS jigsaw is encouraging the United States to come on board. IFRSs are already permitted for use by non-US companies listed on US markets. The SEC has indicated that later this year it will make a decision about incorporating IFRSs into the US financial reporting regime for US companies.

The United States is the largest national capital market in the world, with the most developed and sophisticated national accounting standards.

It therefore seems reasonable to me that the SEC has taken its time to make the appropriate transitional arrangements. At the same time, it is understandable that US companies need certainty in the near future, and a decision this year has been promised.

Let us be clear. This is not an easy choice for the US to make. The rationale for European adoption in 2005 was relatively straightforward. You couldn't have a European common market with 25 ways to account for the same transaction.

The United States already has high quality, mature financial reporting standards. In fact, US expertise has been a very positive influence on the development of IFRSs. So objections regarding the cost of transition and perceived loss of sovereignty must be handled in a sensitive manner. I think it is only logical that the United States would have a national endorsement protocol for new and amended IFRSs. Other countries do exactly the same.

Difficult as the decision may be, it is hard to imagine the possibility of the United States not taking a positive decision. US investors invest globally and US companies seek international capital, and it is in the economic interest of the US to adopt IFRSs. As a signatory to G20 communiqués, the US has repeatedly expressed its support for global accounting standards.

But the main thing is this: if you believe in a global language for financial reporting, then IFRSs are the only possibility.

I am convinced that the United States will want to maintain its position of leadership in international financial reporting, and therefore it is hard to fathom a negative decision on the part of the SEC.

For other countries that are "nearly" on board, that are following paths to align national standards with IFRSs but have not yet adopted, our message is equally clear. Come fully on board and help to make this an even more global organisation. The big growth economies should assume the leadership role that their economic strength is calling for.

4. Strengthening institutional relationships

Fourth, we will continue to strengthen the IASB's institutional relationships in a way that respects and enhances the independence of the standard—setting process. By that, I mean to deepen our engagement with those around the world who are impacted by our work, and to ensure that they have a sense of ownership and respect for the product that we are developing for investors globally.

Chinese leadership in financial reporting

Having outlined our priorities, the final topic I would like to discuss today is Chinese leadership in international financial reporting. A topic that is pertinent to all of you in this room.

Since it began its programme of economic reform, China has sought to transition its accounting system from one based on the needs of a planned economy towards international accounting standards based on market economic principles. In 2006, this culminated in the Chinese Ministry of Finance promulgating an entirely new set of new accounting standards principally in line with IFRSs. These new Chinese standards are developed through a process that China calls "continuous convergence" with IFRSs as issued by the IASB. Indeed, while Chinese GAAP is not word-for-word IFRSs, I understand that analysis by the Chinese regulator shows that for companies with dual listings in Shanghai (using Chinese GAAP) and Hong Kong (using IFRSs) the average difference in reported profit is 0.6%. The difference in term of net assets is even as smaller as around 0.2%.

The opportunity for Chinese leadership in financial reporting is significant, and in my opinion, vital. However, I cannot help feeling that China has not received the international recognition it deserves for this herculean effort. Indeed, when broad-brush developments in international financial reporting are discussed, it is the United States, Europe and Japan that seem to be front of mind.

Why is this, when China is the world's second largest national economy and has invested so substantially in high quality financial reporting?

I believe there are three primary reasons.

First, despite evidence to the contrary, there is a lingering suspicion among the broader international financial reporting community about closeness between IFRSs and Chinese accounting standards. In this regard, the term 'principally in line with IFRS' does China no favours. It is for this very reason that Brazil, another country that is on the verge of fulfilling its full economic potential, has decided to fully adopt IFRSs. In its strategy to become the leading regional financial marketplace, Brazil knew it needed the full benefits of the IFRS franchise. Investors in London, New York, Paris, Frankfurt, and Shanghai all understand when a Brazilian company's financial statements are labelled "in conformity with IFRSs".

Let me postulate that we respect any decision that China takes vis-à-vis IFRSs. Only China can decide the steps it wants to take to further its interests in accounting standard-setting. But if the remaining differences between Chinese GAAP and IFRSs are as small as I believe they are, why don't we work together to eliminate them? To paraphrase Neil Armstrong, when he first set foot on the Moon; it would be a small step for China, but a huge step for the accounting world. Small technical differences in the standards should not stand in the way of Chinese leadership in international financial reporting.

Working together to eliminate these small differences will eliminate any doubt about China's commitment to high quality financial reporting, and will ensure that Chinese influence in standard-setting matches its economic might.

The way to achieve this is to deepen cooperation between the IASB and the Chinese authorities. This could include the setting out of a roadmap that describes the steps to address these remaining differences. Importantly, this should not be just one direction of travel. The IASB will ensure that Chinese circumstances are given due consideration as part of the forthcoming agenda consultation to be undertaken by the IASB. Such a two way approach, as I understand, was one of the key ideas from Vice Minister Wang Jun, when he started to lead the transformation of traditional Chinese standards towards internationally accepted ones in 2005.

Second, I believe there is insufficient understanding internationally of China's commitment to IFRSs and the IASB's commitment to China. Collectively, we can do more to draw attention to the extensive cooperation that has been in place for a number of years. Wayne Upton, our Director of International Activities, spends more time in China than in any other country. Chinese interests are well represented on the IASB, the Trustees and our various advisory bodies.

However, more needs to be done.

I will ensure that Chinese interests are given careful consideration in IASB debates, and that China gets the credit it deserves for its commitment to IFRSs. Chinese requirements will form an important input for the forthcoming agenda consultation. In return, we need China to speak up on international accounting matters, in the same way it does on other areas of global economic cooperation and financial regulatory reform.

Third, at a technical level we have not managed to engage sufficiently with Chinese stakeholders as part of our day-to-day standard-setting activities. Using a crude measurement of comment letters received, less than 3% of comment letters received in the last year have come from Chinese stakeholders. More has to be done to encourage Chinese stakeholders to engage in the IASB's standard-setting process, either directly or through the Chinese standard-setter. To address this, we will further increase the amount of outreach the IASB undertakes in China.

The emergence of regional standard-setting groups is also an important development in this regard. The formation of the Asia Oceania Standard-Setters Group, or AOSSG, provides an important vehicle for China and other countries in the region to work together to share experiences and viewpoints when working with the IASB.

China played a leading role in the formation of this group and has been instrumental in strengthening its voice to match the well-coordinated regional voices from elsewhere in the world. I strongly support the work of this group and welcome China's participation in this endeavour.

Conclusion

I am grateful for your attention during my address. The prospect of increasing Chinese buy-in and ownership of IFRSs is an enticing one.

I hope that the four priorities that I have outlined-completing our convergence programme to the highest quality, planning for our post-convergence work programme, addressing the missing pieces of the IFRS jigsaw,

On Global Accounting Standards

and strengthening the IASB's institutional relations, provide the necessary encouragement for you to deepen your involvement in our work.

There is important work to do, to ensure that China receives the international recognition for the substantial work it has already done to embrace IFRSs. The completion of this work is important to ensure that China's influence in international financial reporting matches that of the country as a whole.

Under my Chairmanship, I will do everything I can to make sure this happens.

Accounting Transparency and Financial Crisis[①]

Speech by Hans Hoogervorst at European
Parliament ECON Committee
03 October 2011

Introduction and welcome

Chairwoman Bowles, Members of the ECON Committee, I am grateful for the opportunity to address this committee. It has been a while since I served as a minister in the Dutch government. Being in a Parliamentary setting once again brings back many fond memories.

I am delighted to answer any questions you may have about our work. However, I would like to begin by make some brief opening remarks on two topics.

First, I want to say a few words on the importance of the IASB.s relationship with Europe. Second, I want to provide some observations on the role of accounting standards and the financial crisis.

Europe's relationship with the IASB

The relationship between Europe and the IASB is strategically important to both of us.

Europe invested a great deal of political and financial capital in its decision to adopt International Financial Reporting Standards (IFRSs) in 2005. Europe.s decision placed the IASB firmly on the path to becoming a global standard-setter.

The European Parliament overwhelmingly endorsed[1] IFRS adoption

---

① The title was added by the translator.

On Global Accounting Standards

by a majority of 458 votes. The Parliament also called for IFRSs to become the globally accepted language of financial reporting.

This call has been heeded by many. More and more countries have chosen to follow Europe's lead and adopt IFRSs. In the Americas, almost all of Latin America and Canada are fully on board. In Asia-Oceania, Australia, New Zealand, Korea, Hong Kong and Singapore are, or will be, full adopters. Japan already permits some domestic companies to report using IFRSs, while China is on the path to convergence. South Africa and Israel are fully on board.

In Europe, outside of the EU, Turkey has adopted the standards in full and Russia is in the process of doing so. The majority of the G20 members are IFRS adopters.

The US Securities and Exchange Commission (SEC) will decide shortly whether to incorporate IFRSs into its own financial reporting regime and, if so, how. I am optimistic on the prospects for a positive decision from the SEC. A negative decision would be a tremendous disappointment after so many years of convergence work. Such a decision, however unlikely, would delay our progress, but it would not stop it. The momentum behind adoption of IFRSs is now too powerful, and too important to be rolled back.

This is remarkable progress in less than 10 years. Europe's strategy of providing international leadership in financial reporting has been vindicated. However, that does not mean the IASB can take European support for granted.

That is why the IASB consults widely with European stakeholders in the development of new IFRSs. We have developed strong relationships with the European Financial Reporting Advisory Group (EFRAG) and the Commission. We consult with European national standard-setting organisations across the member states, and we seek input from European investor and preparer representative groups and others as part of our standard-setting activities.

Despite the frequency and intensity of this dialogue, there will be times when we disagree. Europe quite rightly has Europe.s interests at heart, whereas the IASB has to consider input from around the world. Even within Europe there is often disagreement on accounting matters between individual European member states, or between European investors and preparers.

Where disagreement happens, the onus is on the IASB to demonstrate that the choices we have made as part of our standard-setting activities are based on well-informed, sound judgement with appropriate due process and oversight.

We will continue to increase the sense of trust and buy — in among those who have adopted our standards. We will continue to strengthen the institutional relationships between the IASB and Europe, in the same way as we are doing in other parts of the world. That is how we, as an independent standard — setter, must reciprocate your trust. This will continue to be a priority of the IASB as the organisation evolves into a global standard-setting authority.

The financial crisis and accounting standards

The second topic I would like to address is the relationship between accounting standards and the financial crisis.

This is a subject that deserves far more time than is available in these brief opening remarks. But I do believe some context would be helpful before we discuss the more specific aspects of our work.

The crisis was caused by a collapse of business standards and a failure of macro-economic policies. Failures in regulation allowed the resulting huge risks to grow unnoticed until it was too late. In many cases there was insufficient transparency for investors to be fully aware of the risks they were taking.

It is unbelievable that this happened in the first place, and we cannot allow this to happen again. In this regard, financial reporting has an important role to play.

Transparency is what gets us accounting standard-setters out of bed in the morning. The highest levels of transparency allow users of financial statements to peer into the darkest corners of a company.s financial position.

Transparency is the single biggest contribution the accounting profession can make to the long-term stability of financial markets. It is a necessary precondition to long-term financial stability. Without it, measures to provide financial stability offer little more than a fa.ade, allowing risks to grow unnoticed until it is too late to deal with them.

Transparency does not always paint a pretty picture. Much of the current economic volatility is deep-rooted. The CEO of Deutsche Bank recently said "volatility is the new normality". The days of "risk-free assets". are long gone, if ever they existed.

If volatility is indeed the new normality, how should accounting standard—setters respond? Should we artificially shield investors from learning of this underlying economic volatility? Or should accountants try to describe, as accurately as possible and with full transparency, this new normality?

Most people I speak with believe that financial reporting should tell it how it is, rather than how we would like it to be. If the emperor really has no clothes, then it is the responsibility of financial reporting to say so, no matter how unpopular the truth may be.

There is however one important caveat to this. Asking accountants to describe economic volatility is one thing, but we should be careful that in doing so financial information does not become the source of economic volatility. For that reason the IASB has always remained pragmatic about which measurement techniques to adopt. We know there is no one right answer and therefore we have always employed a mixed measurement approach, combining historic cost with fair value. That is why we have recently completed the reform of our fair value measurement standard that provides new guidance on illiquid markets. It is why we are proceeding with caution in the reform of financial instruments accounting. Our upcoming hedge accounting rules will prevent artificial accounting volatility to companies who hedge their risks. Accounting should not mask volatility, but neither should it be the source of it.

Conclusion

Members of the Committee, I am grateful for your attention. We do indeed live in interesting times. We all need to work together to address the many deep-rooted problems facing the global financial system.

My commitment to you is that the IASB will continue to work in close co-operation with European stakeholders, including the Commission and the Parliament. We will seek opportunities to deepen our engagement with you, and to play our part in reinforcing investor confidence in financial markets.

There are many topics that I have not had time to address in these brief opening remarks. I would be delighted to answer any questions you may have.

Thank you.

---

[1] http://www.iasplus.com/resource/euiasreg.pdf.

The Mission and Responsibility of America in the Process of International Convergence of Accounting Standards[①]

Speech by Hans Hoogervorst at IFRS Foundation/AICPA
conference in Boston, USA
05 October 2011

Introduction

This is my first speech in the United States since being appointed as Chair of the International Accounting Standards Board (IASB). So I think it is appropriate to tell you a little about myself.

I have spent the majority of my professional life serving the public interest. As a minister of Health and minister of Finance I served in administrations that concentrated on trimming the bloated Dutch welfare state. My colleagues and I got a lot done and the Netherlands is now, once again, one of the strongest economies in Europe.

So in 2007, I thought it was time for me to leave politics. I went on to chair the Authority for the Financial Markets, the Dutch equivalent of the US Securities and Exchange Commission (SEC). I was happy to leave the hectic world of politics behind me and to enter into what I thought to be the relatively rational world of finance.

Little did I know!

During the financial crisis, it became clear that the banking industry had become just as dependent on the state as the clients of the Dutch welfare state!

The banks had gradually been allowed to operate on the flimsiest of

---

① The title was added by the translator.

capital margins. Only through implicit and explicit government and central bank support could this system be kept afloat.

I wondered why it had taken the markets so long to figure out that this emperor was not wearing any clothes. The obvious answer was lack of transparency. Prior to the crisis, the banks' financial health was measured by the Basel regulatory capital ratios. These were based on a system of risk-weighing assets, which turned out to be completely faulty. A bank could have a seemingly healthy Basel capital ratio of 12%, while it was in effect 50 times leveraged. Many investors were misled by these illusory numbers. If only people had paid more attention to the regular accounting numbers! Then they could have seen that most banks' capital was not higher than 1% or 2% of their balance sheet.

So I thought it was grossly unfair when critics started scapegoating accounting standards during the financial crisis. Fair value accounting was the most frequent target. I believed this view to be wrong. It ignored the basic and flawed economics that the accounting was attempting to describe.

For this reason I joined Harvey Goldschmid to co-chair the Financial Crisis Advisory Group (FCAG), formed to advise the IASB and the FASB on their joint response to the financial crisis. I think the FCAG was able to bring some common sense to the heated discussions about accounting.

The trauma of the financial crisis left me deeply convinced of the need for transparency and investor protection. Transparency and investor protection are indeed two sides of the same coin. Investors need active protection as mis-selling of complex products is unfortunately commonplace in financial markets. For the same reason, increased transparency is the key to investor protection.

High quality financial reporting standards are essential for improving transparency in the markets.

They provide rigor, discipline and comparability to the presentation of the performance of entities. High quality accounting standards are the bedrock of trust in our market economies. For this reason I am very much honoured and deeply motivated to have become the Chair of the IASB.

The importance of global accounting standards

Let me now turn to the importance of having one global financial reporting language.

First of all, I am convinced that you stand a better chance of developing standards that have teeth, if you do so at an international level. If everyone is committed to the same objective, then we can raise the financial reporting bar internationally without fear of disadvantaging those nations that are trying to do the right thing. That was the view of the FCAG, of IOSCO and of securities regulators around the world, and it continues to be the view of the G20 leaders.

There are also good commercial advantages to everyone speaking the same high quality financial reporting language. We will hear later how Ford Motor Company sees IFRSs as an important element of its "One Ford" strategy.

Standardising on IFRSs has the potential to allow Ford to use the same financial reporting language for both internal management reporting and external financial reporting on a worldwide consolidated basis.

One language will eliminate duplication and translation risks across all Ford international subsidiaries. The long-term cost savings could be substantial.

Ford is not alone in identifying such benefits. Archer-Daniels-Midland, the Bank of New York Mellon, Kellogg, Chrysler and United Continental Holdings all joined Ford in signing a recent public letter[1] to the SEC calling for the adoption of IFRSs in the United States. Clearly, this is an important issue to them, as it is to other major preparers that share similar views.

For investors, the benefit of a global financial reporting standard is equally profound. The cause for international accounting standards gained momentum when many investors burned their fingers during the Asian Financial Crisis in the late nineties. Companies that had shown seemingly fantastic results suddenly turned out to be broke. Clearly, financial reporting needed to be improved around the world.

Nowadays, investors are even more dependent on the international capital markets than before.

The US's current share of global market capitalisation[2] now stands at just over 30%, compared to an average of 45% between 1996 and 2006. US financial markets have not shrunk; it's just that other parts of the world-in particular the Asian financial centres-have become global players.

These developments call for the United States to play a key role in developing global standards. The California Public Employees' Retirement System, or CalPERS, the largest public pension fund in the United States, explained in its submission[3] to the SEC why it believes the SEC should move forward with adoption of IFRSs. In closing, CalPERS stated that "the SEC has the opportunity to effectively improve accounting standards, and to regain and increase investors' trust in financial reporting." To me, that says it all.

US investors, preparers and capital market providers recognise the substantial benefits that come from everyone speaking the same financial language, while securities regulators understand that, without it, opportunities for regulatory arbitrage will remain.

That is why I believe that the case for global accounting standards, and with it the case for US adoption of IFRSs, remains compelling.

The SEC consideration of IFRSs

I would now like to turn to the possible SEC decision on incorporation of IFRSs. This is an important decision for the United States, as well as for other parts of the world that have yet to formally commit to IFRSs. There are various arguments for or against incorporation of IFRSs in the US financial reporting regime. Many of these arguments are valid, others I believe less so.

Quality

Let us start with the most important one-the quality of the actual standards. I have often felt that arguing about the relative superiority of IF-

RSs vs. US GAAP is not very productive. Academic studies have concluded that both IFRSs and US GAAP are high quality standards[4]. A decade of joint work to improve and align IFRSs and US GAAP means that both sets of standards have improved and are moving closer together. Each is used within major capital markets. Each has its relative strengths and weaknesses.

While I am not dismissing these differences, I am not convinced by the arguments that one set of standards is clearly superior to the other.

So I could not imagine that concerns about quality would play a major role in the decision to adopt IFRSs.

Actual usage of IFRS

Next, I have heard it argued that few major economies actually use IFRSs. Some even say that Europe does not use IFRSs due to the optionality of nine paragraphs of IAS 39 Financial Instruments. Yet this option is used by less than 30 companies. That is less than 1% of listed companies in Europe. The other 99%, some 8 000 listed European companies, all use full IFRSs.

It is also a fact that the world has moved to IFRSs at an astonishing pace. In the Americas, almost all of Latin America and Canada are going to be fully on board. In Asia-Oceania, Australia, New Zealand, Korea, Hong Kong and Singapore are or will be full adopters. South Africa and Israel are fully on board. In Europe, countries outside the EU, such as Turkey and Russia, are also full adopters. The majority of the G20 members are full adopters of IFRSs.

Application

A more compelling criticism of IFRSs is that inconsistent application of the standards makes international comparison more difficult.

There is certainly some truth in this argument, as we have witnessed with the accounting for Greek sovereign debt. However, the same is true when you have different accounting standards. You can only work towards consistent application if you have one single language. We are very much committed to working with securities regulators and the accounting profession to enhance consistent application around the world. It will take time, but it can be done. If you do not have a single language, international consistency in financial reporting will always remain an illusion.

A major comfort to the United States should be that if you adopt IFRSs the SEC will remain in full control of enforcement. So there is absolutely no danger of importing different enforcement standards from abroad into the United States. Indeed, it is much more likely that international standards of IFRS enforcement will benefit from the SEC's rich experience and active participation.

Preparedness and costs

Many American companies worry about the costs of adopting IFRSs. Let's not beat about the bush; these are real costs.

Therefore it would be reasonable that a relatively long transitional period is provided, particularly for smaller publicly traded companies. An option to allow early adoption of IFRSs also seems sensible for those companies that can already see substantial net benefits of IFRSs.

At the same time, the difficulties of transition should not be exaggerated. Convergence has brought IFRSs and US GAAP much closer together. There is already a lot of IFRS knowledge in the United States. The SEC has built-up a substantial IFRS competence, overseeing the financial statements of a growing number of foreign private issuers listed in the United States. Many large preparers already have IFRS expertise within their organisations through international subsidiaries.

The CFA Institute now teaches IFRS financial statement analysis to all CFA Program students studying in the United States and elsewhere. From this year, students sitting the AICPA's CPA exam will be tested on IFRSs.

These substantial investments will ensure that the United States is well prepared in the event that the SEC decides to proceed with IFRSs. And let's face it, if Brazil and Korea could adopt IFRSs in a short period of time, certainly the United States can do the job.

Sovereignty

Another argument used against US adoption of IFRSs is the perceived loss in sovereignty. The SEC Staff Paper specifically addresses this point. It makes it clear that the FASB and the SEC will continue to have ultimate responsibility for accounting standards regardless of whether the United States moves forward with IFRSs.

Obviously, participation in any international agreement, whether it is the World Trade Organisation or IFRS standards, requires negotiation and cooperation. The United States will continue to have a great deal of input into the standard-setting process. The knowledge base within the FASB is too valuable to the IASB to be excluded.

In addition to the role of the FASB, the United States has, and will continue to have, a great deal of influence within the IASB. Four out of the fifteen board members are American and they certainly play a significant role.

On that note, I want to congratulate Patricia McConnell, my fellow IASB Board member, on being inducted into the Institutional Investor "All America Research Team Hall of Fame". Pat has been rated as the number one accounting analyst in the United States for sixteen years running. Her extensive experience and contacts with the US analyst community is a real asset to the IASB.

American sovereignty will also be protected by the SEC's intention to adopt similar endorsement mechanisms to those used elsewhere in the world. Such endorsement mechanisms provide an important "circuit-breaker" if the IASB produced a standard with fundamental problems for the United States. An endorsement process would also ensure that the FASB continues to play a prominent role. It is important that the IASB and the FASB, along with other standard-setting bodies, continue to work in close co-operation once the convergence project has ended.

Independence of the IASB

The final topic I would like to touch upon is the readiness of the IASB to become a global standard—setter. For some commentators this translates into the due process followed by the IASB and concerns that the IFRS process is too political.

When the IASB was established in 2001 its standard-setting process was largely modelled on that of the FASB. Since then both organisations have continued to enhance our respective due processes.

For the IASB, this has resulted in enhancements to the depth and transparency of its standard-setting and consultation activities, including the introduction of effect analyses and post-implementation reviews for major standards.

I have never worked in an organisation that is so transparent in its activities, and that consults so widely.

As for political pressure: I can only admit that it can be there. But this is not unique to the IASB. In the heat of the financial crisis, both the IASB and the FASB were put under intense pressure to relax our rules. It was not a pretty picture. Pressure on the boards is a fact of life. Our work affects many business interests that often find the willing ears of politicians. But I think that, as the IASB grows and diversifies, it will become much more difficult for special interests to force their issues onto the board.

On a more personal note, I did not leave politics to make accounting political. Quite the opposite; I will use all my political skills to keep accounting as apolitical as possible.

Conclusion

I began my address by touching on the importance of transparency in the context of investor protection. This is a subject that my friend and colleague Harvey Goldschmid will discuss in more detail. I believe that it is important for investor protection in the United States and internationally that the SEC remains at the forefront of determining international financial reporting policymaking. This cannot be done from afar.

It is difficult to imagine that, after a decade of investment in convergence, a negative decision could be a possible outcome, or that the United States would intentionally choose to discard international leadership, in something as fundamental as financial reporting.

It is also not clear what the alternative would be. IFRSs will continue to evolve. A US commitment to maintaining existing levels of convergence with IFRSs would require the FASB to spend most of its time eliminating new differences. Is this the best use of the FASB's considerable talents, expertise and knowledge of the international environment? If the US chooses not to maintain convergence, it would lead to divergence. That is certainly not what policymakers need as they navigate the ongoing financial crisis.

It is for these reasons that I am optimistic about the prospects of a positive decision by the SEC on IFRSs.

I believe the direction of travel for IFRSs is established, the momentum unstoppable and the endpoint is clear. Ultimately, there will be a global language and IFRS is the only candidate.

Ladies and gentlemen, thank you for your time. I wish you a very successful conference.

---

[1] http://www.sec.gov/comments/4-600/4600-39.pdf.
[2] US Committee on Capital Markets Regulation, see www.capmktsreg.org/competitiveness/index.html.
[3] http://www.sec.gov/comments/4-600/4600-137.pdf.
[4] American Accounting Association Financial Accounting Standards Committee, 2008.-Karim Jamal.

Adoption of IFRS to Be the Best Way to Protect Investors in America[①]

Speech by Hans Hoogervorst at AICPA Conference on current
SEC and PCAOB developments in Washington, USA
06 December 2011

Introduction

This is the largest gathering of accounting professionals I have addressed since becoming Chair of the IASB earlier this year. The number of people in the audience and watching via video link demonstrates the deep commitment of this country to reliable financial reporting.

Let me begin by taking a few minutes to introduce myself and to describe how I came to this important role.

I have spent the majority of my professional life serving the public interest. As a Minister of Health and Minister of Finance in The Netherlands I served in administrations that concentrated on trimming the bloated Dutch welfare state. My colleagues and I got a lot done and the Dutch government is now one of the few remaining triple-A rated countries in Europe.

In 2007, I left politics and went to chair the Authority for the Financial Markets—the Dutch equivalent of the US Securities and Exchange Commission (SEC). I thought I was entering the relatively "rational" world of finance.

I could not have imagined what lay ahead! Whatever innocence I had left after a decade in politics, I lost very soon.

---

① The title was added by the translator.

Shortly after the financial crisis began, I was asked to join Harvey Goldschmid, who is well known to many in the room for his time at the SEC, to co-chair a Financial Crisis Advisory Group.

The group was formed to advise the IASB and FASB on their joint response to the financial crisis. Through the traumatic experience of this crisis, I became convinced more than ever that the best protection available to investors is transparency. Indeed, without transparency there cannot be enduring stability.

For these reasons, I was honoured and deeply motivated to become Chairman of the IASB.

My background gives me a passion for the goals of the IASB: to develop and sustain, first and foremost for investors, a single set of globally accepted and high quality accounting standards. These standards must be set independently and then consistently applied and enforced.

These goals may sound familiar. They are almost identical to those of the FASB. When the IASB was established in 2001, our structures and governance were largely modelled on the FASB.

We are a private sector, independent body. Our mission is clear and investor focused. We have three tiers to our governance structure. A thorough and transparent due process is at the heart of our work. These principles, enshrined in the Financial Accounting Foundation (FAF) and the FASB, are deeply embedded in our processes and standards.

I cannot overstate the important role that the United States has had on our operations. The SEC was a key player in establishing the framework that set up the IASB back in 2001. Paul Volcker was the first Chairman of the Trustees.

The Norwalk Agreement of 2002 committed the IASB and FASB to convergence. Bob Herz, a member of the IASB, became Chair of the FASB.

The US is represented by four IASB Board members and five US Trustees. Mary Schapiro represents the SEC as one of five public capital market authorities comprising the Monitoring Board.

When I was elected Chair of the IASB, I said that I have investor protection in my DNA. Clearly, the US is in the DNA of the IASB.

The Case for Global Standards

High quality financial reporting standards are essential for transparency and for the efficient functioning of capital markets.

When the FASB was founded back in 1973, capital markets looked much different than they are today. Market participants on either side of a transaction were mainly located in the same jurisdiction. Investors and preparers could speak the same financial reporting language.

Since then, and especially in the last 20 years, the world's capital markets have integrated and become more interdependent. US investors seek investment returns and diversify risk on an international basis. US companies seek to raise capital on markets around the world, while US capital markets seek to attract international listings.

The emergence of interconnected financial markets explains the momentum gathering behind the move to global accounting standards. Investors need comparable, reliable financial reporting around the world. For global investor protection, we need a global accounting language.

That is why it is appropriate for the SEC to be asking, as it now is, whether the system in the United States should evolve to reflect the new dynamics of capital markets.

Many other countries have asked the same question. Almost all have concluded that adoption of International Financial Reporting Standards (IFRSs) are in their domestic interests and the best way to protect investors. It has taken less than 10 years for IFRSs to be required or permitted for use by companies in more than 100 countries, including the majority of the G20.

IFRSs are no longer just for Europe. In the last five years we have seen IFRS adoption move at an astonishing pace. In the Americas, almost all countries of Latin America are fully on board. So is Canada to the north and Mexico in 2012 to the south. South Africa and Israel are full adopters. In Asia-Oceania, Australia, Hong Kong, Korea, New Zealand and Singapore are also full adopters. Japan already permits some companies to report using full

On Global Accounting Standards

IFRSs and will decide next year whether to mandate a full transition to IFRSs.

For emerging markets, IFRS has become the de facto financial reporting standard. These markets are attracting vast amounts of inward investment from US fund managers looking to spice-up their investment portfolios. Of the so-called BRIC countries, Brazil already is and Russia very soon will be full adopters, while China is very close.

Of course, the countries that still have to make further and final steps towards full IFRS adoption are looking very carefully at what is happening here in the United States.

US Decision

I recognise the challenges and significant pressures facing the SEC in making its decision. The US is the largest and most liquid national capital market in the world. So, transitional concerns have to be carefully considered. The SEC must believe that this is the right decision for the US. From an investor protection and capital formation standpoint, I believe it is.

US investors now seek and should seek investment returns on a global basis. For example, in its submission to the SEC, CalPERS made the point that they currently invest in 47 markets around world. If the SEC is to protect CalPERS in this international environment it must be an active participant in the development and global enforcement of IFRS. For that to happen, the SEC needs skin in the game.

At our IFRS conference in Boston earlier this year the Controller of Ford Motor Company explained why Ford supported US adoption of IFRS.

His video presentation articulated Ford's support for a single set of high quality standards and IFRSs being the most effective means to accomplish that objective.

Ford is not alone. Archer-Daniel-Midland, Bank of New York Mellon, Kellogg, Chrysler, and Ford Motor Credit all joined with Ford in a recent public letter to the SEC (http://www.sec.gov/comments/4-600/4600-39.pdf) calling for the use of IFRSs by US companies.

Companies like these have been leading the way in terms of consolidating and coordinating their international financial reporting. I think providing a limited number of such US companies with the option to use IFRSs for their US consolidated financial reporting would offer a good test of IFRSs.

I know that there are inevitable concerns about having two GAAPs in the US marketplace. However, if the major competitors of such companies are using IFRSs, comparability will actually increase. Comparability could be further assured if those competitors were foreign private issuers in the US, already subject to SEC review.

From a global perspective, such a limited and early option to use IFRSs would provide a clear signal of a US commitment to IFRSs.

Now I understand that legitimate concerns regarding the introduction of IFRSs in the United States exist. One of these concerns is consistency of application. The SEC Staff recently published a study on this. It looked at how well IFRSs are being applied by Fortune 500 companies.

While the study concluded that the financial statements generally complied with IFRSs, there were inconsistencies observed-mainly due to a lack of disclosure of accounting policies and how individual standards had been applied.

However common such findings about inconsistent application around the world may be, these concerns cannot be dismissed. Standard-setters and securities regulators know that we have to do all we can to improve consistency of application.

Consistency will be improved by working in close cooperation amongst national and regional standard-setting bodies, securities regulators coordinated by IOSCO and the accounting profession.

However, the important point is this. We can only work towards consistent application if we have one single accounting language. If there is no global standard, consistency will always remain an illusion.

By the way, if IFRSs were adopted here in the US, the SEC should and undoubtedly will retain all of the powers that it already has. This includes the area of enforcement. IFRSs pose absolutely no danger of importing different enforcement standards from abroad into the United States. Rather, the example of US enforcement of IFRSs in the US will raise the international bar.

Let me give an IASB perspective on the role of the FASB. The SEC Staff paper rightly addresses the issue of sovereignty in emphasising the FASB's role to endorse IFRSs for use in the US.

Endorsement is the model that is used in most other parts of the world, including Australia, Brazil, Canada, Europe and Korea.

Through this mechanism, the FASB and the SEC retain ultimate responsibility for and control over US accounting standards. It will also ensure a strong role for the FASB in our global system. If we would not have a deep engagement with the FASB, the IASB would obviously run serious risks of non-endorsement.

At the same time, the key to making this model work is setting an appropriately high threshold for non-endorsement. This ensures that any deviations are extremely rare. If we end up with non-endorsements and carve-outs left and right, the gains of adopting IFRSs will remain elusive.

Using full due process, we at the IASB have to make sure that we work in full coordination with national standard—setters, to make sure these deviations do not proliferate.

One way to reduce the temptation to deviate from full IFRS as adopted by the IASB is to engage national and regional standard-setting authorities, including the FASB, in all stages of our work.

The recent FAF comment letter to the SEC (regarding the SEC Staff Paper: Exploring a possible method of incorporation, November 2011) rightly raised the role of national standard-setters. The SEC staff paper sets out a good model for working with such standard-setters. National and regional standard-setting authorities must be the eyes and ears of the IASB. We must consult with them on a very active basis.

Furthermore, I am becoming increasingly convinced that in the future we may have to go beyond pure consultation. A more institutional arrangement for engaging national standard-setters and regional bodies concerned with accounting standards is needed. The FAF comment letter suggested several options that are worth thinking about.

Finally, I would like to make some comments about convergence.

Our convergence history with FASB has been extremely useful in getting us to a point where IFRS and US GAAP are much improved and closer together.

So, it's tempting to just maintain the status quo. But for the long-term, the status quo is an unstable way of decision making that inevitably leads to diverged solutions or sub-optimal outcomes.

For example, let's look at just one part of the Financial Instruments project-Offsetting. We began in alignment with the FASB, but we've ended up in different places. To investors, the balance sheet of many US banks, which are allowed to net derivatives, will look much smaller than that of Asian and European banks, which have to present them gross.

Through disclosures we will try to bridge the gap, but I doubt that investors in the US or elsewhere will see it as a satisfactory outcome. At the same time, we at the IASB believe that our conclusion is right for investors. I am sure that Leslie would believe the same for the FASB.

The simple truth is that when you have two boards of independently thinking professionals, sometimes they will simply reach different conclusions.

The same would be true if I were to split my Board in two and ask them to consider 10 projects. I doubt each smaller Board would reach identical conclusions on all 10 projects.

I'm sure the SEC realises that the outcome of its decision cannot be convergence by another name. Obviously, it is up to the SEC which decision it wants to make. It will be equally obvious that we at the IASB and stakeholders in the US in support of global standards would like this decision to be a clear and positive one.

Conclusion

I began by stressing the importance to investors of transparency and comparability. In a global economy, investors need a global accounting language and IFRSs are the only candidate. This concept underpins the approach advocated by the FAF in their comment letter that calls for the gradual introduction of IFRSs.

Much of that letter is consistent with the SEC staff paper published earlier this year (SEC Staff Paper: Exploring a possible method of incorporation of IFRS, May 2011 www.sec.gov). Indeed, as suggested before, I think that an endorsement approach makes sense.

At the same time, it is important that any such approach has a couple of key characteristics for us to reach our shared goal of a single set of high quality global standards.

There should be a clear timeline for the completion of the initial "endorsement process". There should also be a presumption that-given full due process and extensive involvement of the national standard-setter-non-endorsement would be very rare indeed. Once the initial process of endorsement is completed, US companies should be able to assert compliance with both US GAAP and IFRSs.

Finally, as my own festive season request, I hope that the SEC gives serious consideration to the merits of an early adoption option to use IFRS for a number of US companies.

All of us here today-whether we write accounting standards, prepare financial statements, verify the integrity of financial statements or study the numbers to understand the performance of a commercial enterprise-are part of a global effort that underlies free trade and free-flowing capital. The entire IASB take our responsibilities in this endeavour extremely seriously.

It is important for investor protection in the US and internationally that the SEC remains at the forefront of determining financial reporting policy. This cannot be done from afar. We need the United States to remain on board. We count on your commitment and you can count on ours.

Ladies and gentlemen, thank you for your time. I wish you a very successful conference.

On Revenue Recognition, Lease and Financial Instruments[①]

Speech by Hans Hoogervorst at Ernst & Young IFRS seminar in Moscow, Russia
23 January 2012

Introduction

This is my first visit to Russia. I have always been fascinated by this country—by its people, by its history and by its culture.

As the sixth largest economy in the world and a member of the so-called "BRIC" economies currently driving global growth, it is only logical that Russia would like to be home to a major financial centre. This is not yet fully the case.

Many large Russian companies raise capital in London or New York, while few international companies are listed on the Moscow Stock Exchange. I know that this is an area that Russia is now seeking to address, by putting into place the building blocks required to construct an international financial centre.

One of the most important of these building blocks is Russia's commitment to adopt International financial Reporting Standards (IFRSs) in full from 2012. It is important to note that Russia is doing this properly. No amendments to IFRSs. No additions. No omissions. Full IFRSs, as issued by the IASB and required for all publicly listed companies. This really is very impressive. Russia should be congratulated for its full and unambiguous commitment to global accounting standards.

---

① The title was added by the translator.

As a result of this commitment, international companies using IFRSs will now be able to raise capital in Russia, while international investors will be entirely familiar with a set of Russian financial statements.

Reflecting this commitment to IFRSs, the IASB is fully committed to working in close cooperation with Russian stakeholders throughout the standard-setting process.

I will now like to turn to the business of today, and in particular the three topics that I will touch upon during my talk with you.

First of all I will bring you up to speed on the IFRS work programme-what's on our plate right now and how we see the future mapped out.

Second, I will offer my outlook on the prospects for global standards.

Third, I will say a few words on what we are doing to address the specific challenges faced by emerging economies such as Russia when applying IFRSs.

IFRS roadmap

Let's begin with the current work programme, which right now means completing the remaining elements of the convergence programme to the highest possible standard.

The IASB and the FASB set out on the convergence path back in 2002 with the signing of the Norwalk Agreement. This programme was further refined in 2006 when the two boards agreed a Memorandum of Understanding (MoU) to improve and align IFRSs and US GAAP.

Standard-setters have a reputation for moving at glacial speed. Yet, in just five years the boards have completed most of these projects, leaving just three MoU projects to complete: Financial Instruments, Revenue Recognition and Leasing, as well as one project that was not listed in the MoU, Insurance.

The good news is that we appear to be making progress on all of these fronts.

The first of these projects is revenue recognition. Revenue is the top line number and is important to every business. It is all the more important that we get this standard right. Because the topic is so important we have taken a very careful and conservative approach in developing this standard. We have published a second exposure draft and the consultation period runs a full 120 days until March 2012.

The new standard will replace US requirements that are generally considered to be too detailed and international requirements that are not detailed enough. We need your input to make sure we have got the balance about right.

Next is lease accounting. This is a difficult area, but one where improvements are needed.

For many companies, lease obligations represent their greatest area of off balance sheet financing.

Despite what you may hear, we have not set out to kill the leasing industry. Leasing provides many important economic benefits to companies and that will not change.

All we ask is that these transactions are accounted for in a way that is transparent to investors. It seems odd to me that investors must guess what a company's liabilities from leasing are, even though management has this information at its fingertips. These obligations can be substantial.

The boards are finalising the revised proposals and we expect to publish a further exposure draft for public comment shortly. Once again, your input will be important to achieving a high quality outcome.

The final MoU project is financial instruments. This project was always going to be difficult. It took more than 10 years to develop IAS 39, the existing financial instruments standard. Doing it midway through the worst financial crisis in 80 years has made it even harder.

We and the FASB have been pulled in different directions. We've each tried to respond as best we can, but that has made achieving convergence very challenging.

We now have some difficult choices to make, beginning with classification and measurement.

We set out to replace IAS 39 with an entirely new standard.

We completed the first part of this work in less than a year, issuing IFRS 9 at the end of 2009. It is a very good standard. We reduced the complexity associated with IAS 39. We addressed the "own credit" issue.

Our outreach efforts were widely praised. We sought input and revised our proposals in real time.

Meanwhile, the FASB has been refining its own approach on classification and measurement.

They responded to feedback on their exposure draft and moved from a full fair value approach to a mixed measurement model. There are still differences in our positions, but we're not a million miles apart.

At the same time, as our work on the insurance standard progressed, it became increasingly clear that we had problems with its interaction with IFRS 9. We gradually came to the conclusion that we could make a lot of progress on both these issues-insurance and convergence-by revising IFRS 9 in a limited way. And that is what we have now set out to do.

It is one thing to say these changes are going to be limited, but in practice there will undoubtedly be pressure for wider adjustments. Nevertheless, the potential gains are clear. We will proceed with caution and limit any changes to those that are absolutely necessary.

On impairment, after exploring a number of alternative approaches, the IASB and FASB are finally on the same page with a workable model. We have recently agreed on an approach that divides expected loan losses into three categories-referred to by our staff as "The Good, The Bad and The Ugly."

I am hopeful that we are now in a position to move quickly to the exposure draft stage. Again, we need to get this one right.

All being well, the boards should finalise this phase of the project before the end of the year.

On hedging, we have come up with a general model that has been very well received. We will soon publish on our website a staff draft of our model to make sure, that, in this case as well, we have got everything absolutely right.

It will also give the FASB additional time to take a closer look at our proposals. We are convinced that our hedging model gives investors a more reliable view on the economic reality of modern business practices. By redressing accounting mismatches it gives investors a much better view of the way in which companies hedge their economic risks. This work will also establish the underlying principles for macro hedging, that will be subject to a separate exposure draft.

Finally, let me address the insurance project. This is another tough one.

When the IASB began its work in 2001 it knew the industry needed guidance while the Board took the time to develop a new standard. And so, the Board recommended the continued use of local accounting practices for insurance transactions.

As a result, there continues to be a great deal of diversity and complexity in how insurance companies report their numbers.

Investors often talk about insurance accounting being a "black box". This lack of transparency can lead to insurance companies to trade at a discount relative to their peers in other areas of financial services.

The project is challenging because different financial reporting practices have become embedded in different parts of the world. We are working with the FASB to develop a model that lifts financial reporting for insurance contracts to a common and improved level. We are committed to completing this project in a timely fashion.

That brings you up to date on our current work programme.

But what next?

Well, in July last year we published a consultation document on the IASB's post-convergence agenda. We asked very open questions. What is in urgent need of fixing? How should we best deploy the limited resources at our disposal?

There are some obvious candidates for the future agenda.

Everyone is asking us to complete the conceptual framework — the philosophical and methodological underpinning of our work. We will take a serious look at this.

We are also hearing loudly and consistently that we should look at performance reporting and Other Comprehensive Income. However, views on how we should go about this work are mixed.

Some advocate the elimination of Other Comprehensive Income. Others want to retain it, but argue for a stronger underpinning of the concept.

Whether to recycle OCI or not also remains at the top of the list for many people.

Our future agenda consultation recognises that many new jurisdictions such as Russia have their own legitimate requests-including foreign currency translation, business combinations under common control, agriculture and many more. We will have to make a judicious choice here, being mindful that we do not overload our agenda.

The most common request is for a period of calm. In some cases this request is followed by "apart from this one very specific project". The difficulty is that the "very specific project" varies in different parts of the world, so difficult choices will have to be made if the period of calm is to become a reality.

However, I suspect that after the somewhat frenetic period of the last few years, a slowing down in the pace of change would be welcomed by most if not all of our constituents.

Prospects for global standards

The second topic I would like to discuss is the prospects for global accounting standards.

As I have already observed, we have made remarkable progress in ten years. Before the IASB was established everyone did their own thing, which made international comparability very difficult.

Since then, progress has been truly remarkable. IFRSs are now required or permitted for use by companies in more than 100 countries.

The move towards global accounting standards is seen as an essential part of the global financial reform agenda, providing the transparency on which to build a better, more resilient global financial infrastructure.

On Revenue Recognition, Lease and Financial Instruments

The majority of G20 members now require the use of IFRSs. With Russia joining Brazil in fully adopting our standards, the BRICs are more than half-way there. Real progress is also underway in China and India.

China has come a very long way in a very short period of time. Chinese accounting standards are now closely aligned with IFRSs.

To come fully on board, China just has to take some small steps. I am convinced that a country that is used to making great strides forward will make this very small step too.

Indian authorities are in the process of substantially revising their accounting standards. India still has obstacles to overcome on the way to full adoption. However, I was in India last week and I sensed a real desire for them to come fully on board.

Regarding Japan, the IASB and the Accounting Standards Board of Japan (ASBJ) have worked together for many years to bring about convergence of IFRSs and Japanese GAAP.

In recognition of this work, Japan now allows large international Japanese companies to report using IFRSs.

Several Japanese companies have already done so and I believe that many more are planning to follow suit.

Furthermore, Japan is expected to decide this year whether to mandate a national transition from Japanese GAAP to IFRSs, and if so, when. There has been some debate about the transition period if Japan were to decide to fully commit itself to IFRSs, but this is secondary to the actual decision to switch.

That leaves the United States.

Wherever I go in the world I am asked one question more than any other. Will the US come on board with IFRSs, and if so, when and how?

I have no privileged insight regarding the SEC's internal decision making. However, the SEC's Chief Accountant said in public recently that the SEC will make a decision on IFRS in the coming months.

This is not an easy decision to make. The US already has developed a sophisticated set of financial reporting standards over many decades. Transitional concerns have to be carefully considered.

That is why I have supported the general approach for the endorsement of IFRSs described by the SEC staff's work plan. It is also important to note that the US is committed to supporting global accounting standards. It is SEC policy, it is US Government policy and it is the policy of the G20, in which the US is a key player.

There are many practical challenges facing the SEC in making the decision. I don't deny that they are real. However, both I and my counterpart at the FASB have made it clear that a continued programme of convergence by another name is not an acceptable way forward. I do believe that the US will ultimately come on board. Quite simply, they need us and we need them.

Support for emerging economies

The third and final topic I want to touch upon is what we are doing to support Russia and other emerging economies that have adopted IFRSs.

International financial markets may be closely coupled, but not all markets are the same. In the United States, Japan and many parts of Europe you see mature capital markets that are both deep and highly liquid. In other parts of the world, such as Russia, you see markets that are growing at an astounding rate but from a much lower base, so applying market-based pricing, to pick one example, can be challenging. A single set of global accounting standards must be able to be applied, on a consistent basis, across all different types of financial markets within both developed and emerging economies.

Consistent with requests from the G20, we have taken a number of steps to ensure that the needs of emerging economies feed into the standard-setting process.

First, we have established an Emerging Economies Group (EEG), of which Russia is a founding member.

The EEG is chaired by the IASB with the secretariat provided by the Chinese Ministry of Finance. The group has met twice and the prospects are encouraging.

Second, the constitution of the IFRS Foundation has been amended to take account of a broad range of stakeholders, both by type and location. As a result, emerging economies have the opportunity to be well represented among the Trustees, on the Board and in our various advisory bodies.

Third, we have significantly expanded the amount of outreach we do outside the established financial centres of London, New York and Tokyo.

This conference, supported by the IFRS Foundation, is a good example of this programme of work. Wayne Upton, our Director of International Activities, continues to prioritise outreach in emerging economies and has visited 16 countries in the last year.

Finally, we consult with emerging economies on IFRS policy matters. In June last year, the IFRS Foundation held its second IFRS International Policy Forum in Indonesia. Representatives from standard-setters, central banks, regulators and governments from more than 20 countries attended the event.

Conclusion

Ladies and gentlemen, I am grateful for your attention. We have a lot on our plate right now. We will complete the remaining convergence projects to a very high standard. At the same time, we will carefully consider our future agenda and play close attention to the needs of our newer members, such as Russia.

We are closer than ever to moving from "international" financial reporting standards to "global" financial reporting standards.

You have committed yourselves to using our standards in full. My commitment to you is that we will support you every step of the way.

Thank you for your time. I wish you a very successful conference.

Building a Stronger International Accounting Standard Board[①]

Speech by Hans Hoogervorst at the Consejo Mexicano de Normas de Información Financiera (CINIF) in Mexico City, Mexico

07 March 2012

Introduction

One of the benefits of being Chairman of the International Accounting Standards Board (IASB) is that I get to spend time in some pretty amazing places. Mexico is one of those places.

When studying for my Masters' degree I majored in Latin American studies, so visiting Mexico has always been a pleasure and never a chore.

Of course, Mexico is far more than a destination for tourists. With Free Trade Agreements with more than 40 countries, Mexico is one of the most open countries in the world to international trade. As an export-oriented economy, Mexico has benefited hugely from globalisation. Mexico has become the destination of choice for multinational companies looking to tap into a business—friendly environment, with a highly skilled workforce.

Being fully wired into the global economy, Mexico's decision to adopt International Financial Reporting Standards (IFRSs) in full from 2012 for listed companies made perfect sense. Business is more efficient when recognised industry standards are adopted. The same is true of financial reporting. By adopting IFRSs in full and without modification, Mexico will become fully compliant with financial reporting norms used by more than 100 countries, including two-thirds of G20 members.

---

① The title was added by the translator.

From this year, international investors will be entirely familiar with Mexican financial statements.

A great deal of the credit for these achievements must go to the Consejo Mexicano para la Investigación y Desarrollo de Normas de Información Financiera, or CINIF The CINIF is an important partner to the IASB and we appreciate greatly your continued support.

Let us now move on to the business of the day.

As you may know, the IASB is approaching the completion of its convergence programme with the US Financial Accounting Standards Board (FASB). It is ten years since the boards set out on this path, and a great deal has been achieved. We have four remaining convergence projects to complete and I am hopeful that we can complete this work in relatively short order. Amaro Gomes, my friend and fellow Board member will provide you with an update on these projects later in the programme.

So, what then? What do the next few years look like for the IASB? What will our priorities be, and how should we use the limited resources at our disposal?

In the last year or so, the IASB, as well as our Trustees, have been giving serious consideration to these questions.

The Trustees have recently completed their strategy review and the IASB is nearing the completion of its first comprehensive review of its future work plan.

If you want to know what the future holds for international financial reporting, there is no better place to look than these two reviews. That is why I will spend the remainder of this talk describing what I believe are their most important elements.

Agenda consultation

Let us begin with the agenda consultation.

Sir David Tweedie, my predecessor as Chairman of the IASB, often used to say that the IASB had little control over its agenda.

This certainly used to be the case. The IASB spent its first five years improving IFRSs in time for adoption by Europe and other countries. The following five years were largely dominated by its convergence work with the FASB.

Both of these events have delivered substantial improvements to the quality of financial reporting but they also predetermined the IASB's work programme.

This work is largely now behind us. For the first time in the history of the IASB, we will have a relatively clean slate.

I say "relatively", because the IASB has a constitutional commitment to complete post-implementation reviews two years after each new IFRS or major amendment has been implemented. Doing these reviews properly, and on a timely basis, will take up some time and resources of the Board.

Everything else is up for grabs. That is why the IASB has conducted a thorough and comprehensive consultation on its future agenda. In 2011 we published for public comment a consultation document that set out some ideas, but more importantly solicited feedback on the agenda. In parallel, the Board and staff have held numerous meetings, round-table discussions, webcasts and other outreach activities. For instance, a discussion forum will take place here in Mexico City next Friday at the Mexican Institute of Public Accountants.

We have made a particular effort to seek the views of the worldwide investor community.

We all know how difficult it can be to encourage investors to comment on a particular feature of an accounting standard that may not come into effect for another five years.

Undeterred, we held meetings with buy and sell-side analysts, heads of research and fund managers across the world. We held international webcasts and conducted online surveys with investor representative groups such as the CFA Institute.

I am pleased to say that as a direct result of this work we received more investor feedback on the agenda consultation than on any other IASB activity to date.

The consultation is ongoing, and while I do not want to prejudge the outcome there are some common themes that are easy to spot.

The most common feedback is a request for a period of stability. This is quite understandable. Ten years ago no major economies used IFRSs. Now, more than 100 do. At the same time, many of our standards have been re-written. That is ten years of unprecedented change. It is not surprising that our friends around the world want some time for the dust to settle.

Now we have most of the world on board, even a small change to a standard can be like dropping a pebble into still water. The changes will ripple-out and affect tens of thousands of preparers. Investors must become familiar with the new rules. Auditors must learn how to audit them and regulators will need to enforce them.

It's not just the final standard that must be digested. Every call for feedback on our proposals, in the form of discussion papers, exposure drafts and so on must be considered and in many cases responded to.

This is a responsibility that we take very seriously. That is why determining the IASB's future work programme will involve cherry-picking the most important areas where change is required. Let's fix what needs fixing, and no more.

So what does that mean for our post—convergence work programme? Well, many of these areas fall naturally out of the feedback from the consultation.

First, there is almost universal support for completing revisions to our conceptual framework. This framework serves as a point of reference for the IASB's decision-making. Where choices are not clear-cut, the framework serves to encourage the IASB to make decisions that are consistent across the standards.

The framework is also an important reference for companies when applying principle-based standards.

We already have a framework that works reasonably well. However, feedback from the consultation indicates that we should prioritise the completion of this work. Areas such as Measurement are just too important to ignore.

Second, it has become increasingly clear that we are suffering from disclosure overload. This is not entirely due to financial reporting. The plain fact is that businesses have become more complex. It is the job of financial reporting to describe this complexity, not to mask it.

Not all disclosures provide useful information to investors. Standard boilerplate responses are more about ticking boxes than helping investors really understand what is going on under the hood of the business. This is an issue that preparers, auditors, regulators and standard—setters will have to tackle together.

For our part, we need to make sure that disclosure requirements are appropriate. Bottom up; each individual disclosure requirement may have made sense when the standard was first introduced.

However, from a top-down perspective do the disclosures in totality improve the clarity of financial reporting, or do they make it more difficult to really see what is going on?

I suspect that there will be few quick wins. One investor's disclosure clutter is another investor's golden nugget of information. Taking information away is never easy. Nevertheless, feedback from the agenda consultation indicates that this is an important area for many respondents-particularly smaller listed companies, many of whom believe that the disclosure overload falls disproportionately on their shoulders.

Thankfully, we are not starting from scratch and some excellent preparatory work has already been completed in this area.

The Scottish and New Zealand accounting institutes, the French Autorité des Normes Comptables, the European Financial Reporting Advisory Group (EFRAG), the UK Financial Reporting Council (FRC) and the FASB have all conducted independent research on current disclosure requirements. We will continue to work closely with them and with other colleagues as part of a project to develop a new IFRS disclosure framework.

Next, we must decide what to do with Other Comprehensive Income (OCI).

OCI is increasingly used as a home for income of a less than certain nature. It is true that income reported in OCI should come with a health warning, yet investors ignore OCI at their peril.

Providing a clearer conceptual definition of OCI will help to address the endless debates about volatility and financial reporting, as well as tackling the thorny issue of recycling. There are no easy or clear answers, but this is a project that I am very much looking forward to getting my teeth in to.

Finally, there are a few other, less ambitious projects that the Board may well consider taking on. These include agriculture, business combinations under common control, hyperinflation and rate-regulated industries.

We have a few further round-table discussions planned, but I think it is fair to say that our direction of travel is becoming clear.

I am not ruling out other projects for consideration by the IASB, but if we are to provide a period of relative calm then difficult choices will have to be made.

Strategy review

This brings me on to the Trustees' strategy review.

As you may know, the Trustees have recently concluded a far-reaching review of the strategy and vision of the organisation.

The review was conducted in parallel with a separate governance review by the IFRS Foundation Monitoring Board, which oversees the work of the Trustees. Both reviews are well worth reading.

In their report, the Trustees made a number of excellent recommendations.

These include improvements to oversight of the IASB's due process and the establishment of a dedicated research function.

However, I believe the most important recommendation was the need for the IASB to strengthen and formalise its relationships with standard-setters, regulators and the accounting profession.

The development of IFRSs involves close cooperation with national and regional standard-setting bodies. Once issued, the standards are endorsed for use in jurisdictions around the world. Auditors then attest compliance with the standards while securities regulators enforce their use.

Up until now we have achieved great things through informal dialogue with other participants in this supply chain. However, it is now time to move from this loose affiliation to a more integrated supply chain based on strengthened and more formalised relationships.

An integrated supply chain means that you are better able to guarantee the quality of the product.

I see two important benefits to this work.

First, the formalisation of this network will greatly assist our global standard-setting activities by binding — in national and regional standard-setting bodies more closely and earlier on in the standard-setting process.

Doing so will allow the IASB, in a more inclusive way, to share the "heavy lifting" involved in research, field testing and outreach activities. It will allow the IASB to tap-in to a broader pool of talent when considering difficult issues. It will also provide a more formal mechanism for this input to feed into our standard-setting process.

This network has the potential to improve the quality of the standards, to reduce duplication of effort between the IASB and other standard-setting bodies and to reduce the risk of non-endorsement of a particular standard.

That is why the formation of the Group of Latin American Standard-Setters, or GLASS, is so important to the IASB. The GLASS has the potential to provide a regional forum for national authorities to exchange views. We are very keen for this initiative to be a success.

Second, the network will provide a mechanism for all participants in this financial reporting supply chain to work together to encourage greater consistency in the implementation of IFRSs.

A single set of standards provides the baseline. However, the standards need to be endorsed, implemented, audited and enforced on a globally consistent basis. This network will provide a forum for securities and audit regulators, the profession and the IASB to discuss ways to improve consistency, and to address areas of divergence.

In many ways, this is the missing piece of the jigsaw of global accounting standards.

The construction of such a network is not without its challenges.

What should the membership criteria be? Most people understand what we mean when we referring to "national accounting standard-setters".

Yet, such organisations look very different in different countries. Some, like the FASB or the CINIF, are fully independent boards while others are an extension of the Ministry of Finance or the Central Bank.

How do we balance input from national standard-setting bodies such as CINIF and regional standard-setting bodies such as GLASS? What about organisations such as EFRAG, which is not a standard-setter but which obviously plays an important role in endorsement of IFRSs in Europe?

How should the network interface to the IASB? Should it be in the form of a technical advisory council, structured along similar lines to the existing IFRS Advisory Council or do we need to create some other mechanism?

These are challenges that we will begin to work through in the coming months. However, I am convinced that establishing this fully integrated supply chain of financial reporting is essential if the promise of global financial reporting standards is to be achieved.

Conclusion

Ladies and gentlemen, I am grateful for your attention. We have important work to do, and Mexico's support, as the current Chair of the G20, is very important to us.

I have shared with you today what I believe are the most important objectives and challenges for the IASB in the coming years. Our future agenda is becoming clearer. I fully expect that forging closer and stronger links between members of the financial reporting supply chain will help us to deliver high quality and more globally consistent standards of financial reporting.

Thank you for your time. I wish you a very successful conference.

The Prospects of International Accounting Standard Board[①]

Speech by Hans Hoogervorst at the KASB/Korea
Accounting Institute Seminar in Seoul, Korea
04 April 2012

Introduction

Ladies and gentlemen, honourable guests, I would like to thank you for the opportunity to address such a distinguished audience.

I am grateful to Duck-Koo Chung, Trustee of the IFRS Foundation, and to OuHyung Kwon, President of the Korean Institute of Certified Public Accountants for your encouraging opening remarks.

I am also grateful to Chungwoo Suh for his comments. Of course, Chungwoo is a newly appointed member of the IASB, so his job is to say nice things about our organisation!

This is my 2nd visit to Korea and my 5th trip to Asia since becoming Chairman of the IASB nine months ago. In the last six months I have visited Asia more times than any other region, including the United States. I believe this also true for most of our Board and senior staff.

There is nothing surprising about this. The IASB is firmly on the path to becoming the global accounting standard-setter. That means making sure we consult with every part of the world in equal measure. Asia is home to many of the world's fastest growing economies, and we need to make sure our standards meet your needs.

There are various ways we go about this work.

---

① The title was added by the translator.

First, at a national level we work in very close cooperation with local organisations such as the Korea Accounting Standards Board (KASB) and the Korean Institute of Certified Public Accountants (KICPA). This cooperation will deepen further with the appointment of Chungwoo Suh to the IASB.

Second, we are working at a regional level with the Asia Oceania Standard-Setters Group (AOSSG), to understand the collective views of the region as a whole. The AOSSG has been up and running for several years and serves as a very helpful sounding board for the IASB. Later this year, the IASB will open its first office outside of London. The office, located in Tokyo, will be fully staffed and will serve the needs of the entire Asia-Oceania region.

Third, we have established an Emerging Economies Group (EEG), of which Korea is a founding member.

The EEG is led by Wayne Upton — the IASB's Director of International Activities, who is with me today. This is a very important group. It provides an excellent forum to understand the challenges emerging economies can have when applying certain aspects of IFRSs such as fair value measurement. Taken as a whole, Korean interests are well represented at all levels of our organisation.

Let us now move on to the business of the day. As you may know, the IASB is approaching the completion of its convergence programme with the FASB. It is ten years since the boards set out on this path, and a great deal has been achieved. We have four remaining convergence projects to complete—leases, revenue recognition, financial instruments and insurance accounting.

I am hopeful that we can complete this work in relatively short order, although I have learned that in accounting, short can be rather long.

I believe a timely decision by the SEC about US adoption of IFRSs will serve to speed up the remainder of convergence. Needless to say, I am looking forward to that moment.

So, what then? What do the next few years look like for the IASB? What will our priorities be, and how should we use the limited resources at our disposal?

In the last year or so, the IASB, as well as our Trustees, have been giving serious consideration to these questions.

The Trustees have recently completed their strategy review and the IASB is nearing the completion of its first public consultation on our future agenda.

Today I would like to focus on the likely outcome of that consultation.

IASB future agenda

In 2011 we published for public comment a consultation document that set out some ideas, but more importantly solicited feedback on the IASB's future agenda.

In parallel, the Board and staff have held numerous meetings, round-table discussions, webcasts and other outreach activities. The consultation has yet to conclude, but there are some common themes that are easy to spot.

The most common feedback is a request for a period of stability. I do not think we will get it, but the request for a period of calm is understandable. Ten years ago few economies used international standards. Now, more than 100 do. At the same time, many of our standards have been re-written. That is ten years of unprecedented change. It is not surprising that our friends around the world want some time for the dust to settle.

That is why determining the IASB's future work programme will involve cherry-picking the most important areas where change is required. Let's fix what needs fixing, and no more.

So what does that mean for our post-convergence work programme? Well, many of these areas fall naturally out of the feedback from the consultation.

First, there is almost universal support for completing revisions to our conceptual framework. This framework serves as a point of reference for the IASB's decision-making. Where choices are not clear-cut, the framework serves to encourage the IASB to make decisions that are consistent across the standards. The framework is also an important reference for companies when applying principle-based standards.

We already have a framework that works reasonably well. However, areas such as Measurement are still less than perfect, to put it mildly. It is easy to understand why this is the case. After all, measurement is the most judgmental, difficult and politicised part of accounting.

We need to bring more rigor and clarity here, but it will be an extremely arduous task which will require a lot of brainpower and courage.

Second, many of our constituents are complaining of disclosure overload. This is not entirely due to financial reporting.

The plain fact is that businesses have become more complex. It is the job of financial reporting to describe this complexity, not to mask it.

Not all disclosures provide useful information to investors. Standard boilerplate responses are more about ticking boxes than helping investors really understand what is going on. This is an issue that preparers, auditors, regulators and standard-setters will have to tackle together.

For our part, we need to make sure that disclosure requirements are appropriate. Bottom up; each individual disclosure requirement may have made sense when the standard was first introduced. However, from a top-down perspective do the disclosures in totality improve the clarity of financial reporting, or do they make it more difficult to really see what is going on?

During the last extremely fruitful meeting of the Advisory Council there was a surprising consensus on this issue. Almost everybody agreed there will not be many quick wins.

One investor's disclosure clutter is another investor's golden nugget of information. Taking information away is never easy. Nevertheless, feedback from the agenda consultation indicates that this is an important area for many respondents-particularly smaller listed companies, many of whom believe that the disclosure overload falls disproportionately on their shoulders.

Thankfully, we are not starting from scratch. Some excellent preparatory work has already been completed by a number of accounting standard-setting bodies around the world. This work will help us as we review our approach to disclosure.

Next, we must decide what to do with Other Comprehensive Income (OCI). Everybody is asking us to shed more light on it. What is the meaning of OCI? What should be in it? How does it relate to Profit or Loss (P&L)? Should we allow recycling?

In the past year I have witnessed many heated discussions on this subject. It struck me that those who are the biggest fans of the P&L, often want to put as much as possible in OCI.

That is, as long as it can be recycled to earnings in due time, of course. It is impossible for me to anticipate at this time what the outcome of these deliberations will be. All I can say at this time is that the juxtaposition of the P&L and OCI often seems counterproductive to me.

I do not think it is right to regard OCI as a largely irrelevant number which should preferably be buried in the notes. True, Other Comprehensive Income is often of a less certain nature than Profit or Loss.

But that does not make OCI meaningless. Especially for financial institutions with large balance sheets, OCI can contain very important information. It can give indications of the quality of the balance sheet.

It is very important for investors to know what gains or losses are sitting in the balance sheet, even if they have not been realised. OCI can give information on duration mismatches between assets and liabilities; it can signal sensitivity to interest rate fluctuations.

Since controlling the volatility of the balance sheet is a core task of the management of financial institutions, OCI can indeed be a very important performance indicator.

While providing a clearer conceptual definition of OCI we will also have to tackle the thorny issue of recycling. Around the world there are many supporters of recycling. The main argument for recycling of OCI is that it ensures that the total amount of profit or loss will ultimately be equal to the total amount of cash flows.

It is a pretty powerful argument. Still, the IASB has never been very enthusiastic about recycling. One of the main reasons for our reluctance is the scope for earnings management in the timing of realising gains and losses. That is why investors often demand to see profit or loss before recycling where recycling is permitted. They know recycling has the potential of clouding the true performance of an entity.

I am sure we will have many interesting and fierce discussions on this topic in the coming years.

This is a topic very close to my heart and I am very much looking forward to beginning work on this project. If we succeed in delivering a firmer theoretical underpinning of OCI, I am sure its usefulness to investors as a performance indicator will be enhanced.

Apart from these grand themes, we will probably take on board some smaller projects, such as agriculture, business combinations under common control, hyperinflation and rate-regulated industries.

We have to draw the line somewhere. The experience of the last few years should remind us of the perils of trying to do too much at one time. At the same time, we cannot simply put on ice for three years issues that are causing problems in different parts of the world. For example, I am well aware of Korea's desire for the IASB to update our standard on foreign currency translation.

That is why we have decided to introduce a new research phase to our work programme under the leadership of Alan Teixeira, the IASB's Senior Director of Technical Activities. The research phase of our agenda will become the place to incubate projects before they are considered as candidates for the IASB's work programme.

However, we have no plans to establish an IFRS university on 30 Cannon Street. We have neither the means nor the ambition to do so. What we can do is to define the parameters of the research work, but we will invite other accounting standard-setting bodies to work with us to do the research and report back their findings.

Foreign currency translation is a good example of a project that may come onto the IASB's research agenda. The KASB has already done a great deal of excellent research on this topic, as has the Emerging Economies Group. However, I am also aware that views are mixed on how we should proceed with this project.

We will look to the KASB and others to further develop this research under the auspices of the IASB's research agenda. In effect, we would ask the KASB to do the heavy lifting that normally takes place during the discussion paper phase of our standard-setting work. It will enable us to understand national and industry perspectives earlier in the process.

In turn, this will reduce the development time for a new IFRS should the project migrate onto the IASB's work programme but in a way that does not overload the Board.

The introduction of a research phase to our work stream, delivered by other accounting standard-setting bodies within the parameters set by the IASB, is an excellent example of our desire to formalise and strengthen our relationships with other organisations such as the KASB.

Conclusion

Ladies and gentlemen, I am grateful for your attention. We have important work to do and your support is very important to us.

Thank you for your time. I wish you a very successful conference.

On Accounting Transparency and Financial Stability[①]

Speech by Hans Hoogervorst at 3rd ECB Conference on Accounting, Financial Reporting and Corporate Governance for Central Banks in Frankfurt

04 June 2012

In debates on accounting, one particular issue keeps on popping up. This hotly debated question is whether the primary purpose of financial reporting should be to provide transparency, or if it should also serve the goal of stability.

In this debate, transparency and stability are often juxtaposed as if they were conflicting goals. I think that this is essentially a false and counterproductive contradiction. In my view, it is clear that transparency is a necessary precondition of stability. Indeed, a lack of transparency significantly contributed to the credit crisis. Huge risks were allowed to build up both on and off balance sheets without being noticed. Without proper transparency about risks, stability is bound to collapse in the end.

In short, stability is not the same as transparency, but there can be no durable stability without transparency. So accounting standards/financial reporting can contribute to stability by enhancing transparency. Before I make clear how we intend to do so, let me make also perfectly clear what we cannot do.

Stability should be a consequence of greater transparency, but stability cannot be a primary goal of accounting standard-setters. It is not our remit and we simply lack the tools for fostering stability. For example, we cannot set capital requirements for the banking industry. This instrument belongs

---

① The title was added by the translator.

to the prudential regulators and central banks which do have stability as their main mission.

What accounting standard setters can also not do is to develop standards that make items appear to be stable when they are not. And, quite frankly, we are sometimes suspicious that we are being asked to put a veneer of stability on instruments that are inherently volatile in value. Our standards should not create volatility that is not already there economically. But, if volatility exists, our standards should certainly not mask it.

That being said, there are plenty of ways in which we are trying to make a contribution to greater transparency in the financial industry, often in close consultation with the prudential community and regulators, such as the Basel Committee and the Financial Stability Board.

First, the accounting standard-setters have improved consolidation requirements to prevent undesirable off-balance-sheet financing. In particular, US GAAP was tightened up in this respect. While the broad consolidation principles of IFRS held up reasonably well during the financial crisis, in the United States off-balance-sheet financing through special purpose vehicles and repo transactions was more of a problem. With tighter consolidation requirements and better disclosures, we can reasonably hope that this problem will now be a matter of the past.

The use of fair value accounting has been the biggest bone of contention between accounting standard-setters on the one hand and prudential and central banking authorities on the other hand. Opponents of fair value accounting state that too much reliance on market prices exacerbates the economic cycle in both upturns and downturns. These critics believe that fair value accounting strengthens pro-cyclicality and thus leads to artificial volatility, which threatens stability.

This line of reasoning was greatly reinforced by the fact that the efficient market hypothesis was heavily discredited by the financial crisis. The ECB and the Basel Committee asked that we limit the use of fair value to address this pro-cyclicality.

As a former Minister of Finance, as well as a former regulator, I have always been sceptical of the efficient market hypothesis. Too often, I have witnessed that markets can go very crazy indeed, especially in the short run. However, if you operate in a market environment, you had better be prepared for markets to go loony every now and then. I have always been amazed by bankers telling me that market information cannot be relied upon, while they themselves are major players in that very market, or even market-makers!

Moreover, it is hard to imagine an industry that is as prone to volatility as the financial sector. Both sides of a bank's balance sheet are vulnerable. Its assets can be very sensitive to the economic cycle, whether they are derivatives or loans backed by bricks and mortar. Even gold-plated, triple-A government bonds can turn sour very quickly, as we have seen in the case of Ireland.

The banking industry's liability side is also notoriously vulnerable. Funding, whether it is wholesale or retail, can evaporate with the speed of a mouse-click. As if this is not risky enough, the banking industry has been allowed to operate on the flimsiest of capital margins. The capital cushion of the banking industry has shrunk dramatically in the last century. Just before the crisis, tangible common equity of many banks was negligible. It was generally only 1 to 3 percent of the balance sheet, and sometimes even below that.

In conclusion, the recent volatility was inherent to the financial sector's business model. If accounting requirements had a role to play, that role was at most only as a minor actor. Indeed, many independent studies have concluded that fair value accounting played at most a very minor part in the turmoil of the financial crisis. That conclusion was only to be expected, given that the bulk of traditional banking assets (e.g. loans) are still valued at amortised cost.

The IASB has decided to continue with a mixed measurement model in IFRS 9. In IFRS 9, financial instruments that have basic loan features and that are managed on a contractual yield basis are measured at amortised cost. For such instruments, amortised cost is deemed to provide more relevant information than short-term market fluctuations.

The IASB is currently reconsidering limited parts of IFRS9.

We recently decided to re-establish a fair value through OCI category for debt instruments that are managed with the objective of both collecting the contractual cash flows and selling the assets. This can be the case for assets that are held for liquidity management. But assets that are solely held to collect contractual cash flows-among which vanilla debt instruments-will continue to be measured at amortized cost. In this respect there is no fundamental difference from our previous proposals.

The last area of transparency I would like to discuss today relates to impairment. A well-functioning impairment model is of paramount importance for an amortised cost measurement to be reliable and credible. After the outbreak of the crisis, our current impairment model, which was based on incurred losses, was criticised for being too little, too late.

We think that this criticism was partially justified. The fact that the market capitalisation of many banks is far below their book value is an indication that market participants do not believe that their current level of provisions reflect economic reality.

I say partially justified, because I am convinced that the incurred loss model could have been applied much more vigorously in the last couple of years. In current circumstances, I do not think that there is a lack of triggers to start writing off certain assets. There has been simply too much hesitancy to do so or political pressure not to do so.

The very late write-downs of Greek government bonds are a case in point. Despite severe market dislocation, repeated downgrading and steep discounts of Greek debt, most banks only started provisioning when a restructuring decision had been taken. And even then, some banks thought an allowance of 21 percent was enough. In sum, we are convinced that even the current impairment rules allow for much more decisive measures.

Nonetheless, both the IASB and the FASB are convinced that we need a more forward-looking impairment model. In fact we are well on our way to completing an expected loss model.

The basic principles of this model are as follows. From day 1, for all new financial assets, an allowance balance needs to be built up that captures the expected losses in the next 12 months. If credit quality deteriorates subsequently to such an extent that it becomes at least reasonably possible that contractual cash flows may not be recoverable, lifetime losses need to be recognised. We will not try to define exactly what "reasonably possible" means, but it primarily refers to the inflection point when the likelihood of cash shortfalls begins to increase at an accelerated rate as an asset deteriorates.

To some degree, this expected loss model will rely on judgement, because it is not possible to predict with precision when the probability of default starts to accelerate. To arrive at this judgement, market indicators can and should play an important role. So even for assets that are measured at amortised cost, fair value can contain very important information.

Take the example of sovereign debt securities. If a sovereign's debt is faced with clear sustainability issues, sinks below investment grade and suffers from double-digit market discounts, clearly there is a serious possibility that contractual cash flows will not be paid in full. A lifetime loss will probably need to be recognised, even if the securities in question are still being serviced. One just has to look at current market conditions to realize this model would lead to a much more timely recognition of losses than is currently the case.

I know that many prudential regulators hope that an expected loss model can serve to dampen the cycle of credit booms and busts. As a showcase, they have often pointed at the dynamic provisioning model that Spanish banks were using before the crisis broke out. While dynamic provisioning contained some elements of an expected loss model, it clearly was not able to adequately counter the cycle.

For the following reasons, I believe we have to keep our expectations realistic about the anti-cyclical effects of accounting rules. First of all, accounting standards are not an instrument of economic policy; they merely serve to depict financial and economic reality as reliably as possible. Dampening the economic cycle is neither our task nor within our area of expertise.

Secondly, as I said before, the expected loss model relies to some extent on judgement. Before the present crisis, many banks and their supervisors obviously were not able to perfectly anticipate risk. Even where the writing that warned of a full-fledged credit orgy was clearly on the wall, the magnitude of problems to come was not predicted.

Given the fact that economic history is littered with credit bubbles and busts, there is no guarantee that future bankers will do a much better job of anticipating risk than current bankers. So it is not likely that all the risks that are building up during an economic boom will be recognised in time. Even with an expected loss model, many losses will only become apparent when the economic downturn sets in.

Once a credit bust erupts, risks tend to crystallise on a massive scale. The current situation in Spain is a case in point. Since the outbreak of the crisis, Spanish banks have written off assets to the amount of some 18 percent of GDP. Some think that more is still to come. The dynamic provisioning of the Spanish banks was completely overwhelmed by the magnitude of these losses.

The lesson is that economic cyclicality can be too powerful to be dented significantly by mere accounting. Nevertheless, I am convinced that the introduction of our expected loss model will be a major improvement.

First, it should lead to provisions being made in a more timely and realistic fashion and a heightened, more forward-looking risk awareness in the financial industry. Secondly, a timely clean-up of the banking system should free up resources to viable sectors of the economy instead of exercising forbearance on essentially defunct companies.

Thirdly and perhaps most importantly, there is nothing more damaging to the credibility of the financial sector than serial underestimation of the true magnitude of problematic assets. Partial recognition of inevitable losses may buy time in the short run, but in the end leads to round after round of "definitive" rescue programmes and a gradual erosion of confidence in the markets.

It is obvious that for a rigorous and adequate application of the expected loss model, banks need to be properly capitalised. Whether the recent reforms of the Basel regime for capital requirements go far enough in this respect is open to debate.

It is well documented how, before the crisis, the Basel capital ratios had been gamed to increase leverage by exploitation of the risk weights. Banks with a seemingly sound Tier-1 ratio of 10 percent could in fact be leveraged 40, 50 or 60 times! Instead of being a source of transparency, the Basel ratios had been abused as a scheme for hiding leverage.

Basel III will undoubtedly be a great improvement, because it enhances the capital requirements both quantitatively and qualitatively. Moreover, the introduction of a leverage ratio will give more insight in what the true gearing of a bank is. Yet, under Basel III, a bank is still allowed to be leveraged 33 times. I am not a prudential regulator, but I truly wonder if a bank with leverage of even just 20 times can accommodate a crisis of Spanish or Irish proportions.

In addition, the system of risk weighting of assets is still fraught with risk. It allows banks to assume that sovereign debt has little or no risk, which by now we should know is highly doubtful. Both Spain and Ireland had very low levels of public debt and still they lost their triple-A rating almost overnight.

Not only the risk weighting, but also the absence of a large exposure regime for highly rated sovereigns, greatly encourage banks to load up on sovereign risk. Once a sovereign enters the danger zone, the needs for provisioning may explode dramatically. This is of course not an accounting problem, but a real prudential problem. With an expected loss model, this prudential vulnerability will be exposed sooner than is currently the case. That is in itself a good thing, but banking supervisors had better be prepared.

In conclusion, I believe that the introduction of an expected loss model can lead to a much more timely recognition of losses than is currently the case. The incurred loss model provides too much leeway for procrastination and has to go. But an expected loss model in itself should not be expected to significantly dent the pro-cyclicality of the credit cycle.

Unless bankers and their supervisors become a lot better at containing credit booms and their risks, busts with massive losses will periodically take place. Even then, an expected loss model is preferable to an incurred loss model. But for an expected loss model to be applied rigorously, it is essential that banks are well capitalised. If such is not the case, even law-abiding banking supervisors might be tempted to buy time by condoning some stretching of accounting rules. Obviously, that is a temptation to which nobody should be exposed.

The Imprecise World of Accounting

**Speech by Hans Hoogervorst at the International Association for
Accounting Education & Research (IAAER) conference in Amsterdam, Netherlands
20 June 2012**

Accounting should be the most straightforward of topics for policy-makers to deal with. Accounting is mainly about describing the past-to reflect faithfully what has already happened. This should be dull business, better left to "bean-counters". Surely counting beans cannot cause too many problems?

Yet, over the years, many securities regulators have told me of their surprise upon finding out that accounting policy is one of the most difficult and controversial topics to deal with. It is the same around the world. Just ask the Japanese FSA, the US SEC or the European Commission.

So, why is it that accounting is the source of such heated debates?

Of course, there are many reasons why this is the case. Sir David Tweedie, my predecessor as Chairman of the IASB, used to say that it was the job of accounting to keep capitalism honest. It is no wonder that accounting standard setters come under so much pressure! Some business models can thrive off a lack of transparency. Just think of the pre-crisis Special Purpose Vehicles in the banking industry.

There is second reason why accounting can be so controversial, and that is the inescapable judgement and subjectivity of accounting methods. Put simply, there is a lot to disagree about.

When I became Chairman of the IASB in July last year, I knew enough about accounting to know that I was not entering a world that was governed by the iron rules of science. I knew that Accounting has the same problems as its sibling Economics: you need maths to exercise it, but you should not count on outcomes with mathematical precision. In short, I did not have naive expectations of accounting. Or so I thought.

One year later, however, now that I am well ahead on a steep learning curve, I must admit that I may have been a bit naive after all. Let me give you a couple of examples that served to open my eyes.

First of all, I was struck by the multitude of measurement techniques that both IFRSs and US GAAP prescribe, from historic cost, through value-in-use, to fair value and many shades in between. In all, our standards employ about 20 variants based on historic cost or current value. Because the differences between these techniques are often small, the significance of this apparently large number should not be over dramatised.

Still, the multitude of measurement techniques indicates that accounting standard-setters often struggle to find a clear answer to the question of how an asset or liability should be valued.

It is also remarkable that our standards can cause one and the same asset to have two different measurement outcomes, depending on the business model according to which it is held. For example, a debt security has to be measured at market value when it is held for trading purposes, but it is reported at historic cost if it is held to maturity. In this case, the business model approach certainly provides a plausible answer. Still, some may find it counterintuitive that a government bond that is held to maturity would be valued at a higher price than the same bond held in a trading portfolio, where it may be subject to a discount. In the exact sciences, such a dual outcome would certainly not be acceptable.

One of the biggest measurement dilemmas relates to intangible assets. We know that they are there. While the value of Facebook's tangible assets is relatively limited, its business concept is immensely valuable (although 25% less immense than a month ago).

Likewise, the money-making potential of pharmaceutical patents is often quite substantial. However, both types of intangible assets go unrecorded (or under-recorded) on the balance sheet. Under strict conditions, IAS 38 Intangible Assets allows for limited capitalisation of Development expenditures, but we know the standard is rudimentary because it is based on historical cost, which may not reflect the true value of the intangible asset.

The fact is that it is simply very difficult to identify or measure intangible assets. High market-to-book ratios may provide indications of their existence and value. However, after the excesses of the dot.com bubble, there is understandable reluctance to record them on the balance sheet.

Although our accounting standards do not permit the recognition of internally generated goodwill, our standards do require companies to record the premium they pay in a business acquisition as goodwill. This goodwill is a mix of many things, including the internally generated goodwill of the acquired company and the synergy that is expected from the business combination. Most elements of goodwill are highly uncertain and subjective and they often turn out to be illusory.

The acquired goodwill is subsequently subject to an annual impairment test. In practice, these impairment tests do not always seem to be done with sufficient rigour. Often, share prices reflect the impairment before the company records it on the balance sheet. In other words, the impairment test comes too late. All in all, it might be a good idea if we took another look at goodwill in the context of the post-implementation review of IFRS 3 Business Combinations.

It is not only the balance sheet that is fraught with imprecision and uncertainty. We also have a problem defining what income is and how to measure it. We report three main components of income: the traditional profit or loss or net income, other comprehensive income and total comprehensive income. Total comprehensive income is the easy part; it is simply the sum of net income and other comprehensive income, or "OCI". Not too many people seem to be paying attention to it, even if they should.

The distinction between net income and OCI, however, lacks a well-defined foundation. While the P&L is the traditional performance indicator on which many remuneration and dividend schemes are based, the meaning of

OCI is unclear. It started as a vehicle to keep certain effects of foreign currency translation outside net income and gradually developed into a parking space for "unwanted" fluctuations in the balance sheet. There is a vague notion that OCI serves for recording unrealised gains or losses, but a clear definition of its purpose and meaning is lacking.

But that does not make OCI meaningless. Especially for financial institutions with large balance sheets, OCI can contain very important information. It can give indications of the quality of the balance sheet. It is very important for investors to know what gains or losses are "sitting" in the balance sheet, even if they have not been realised.

In the future, OCI will most certainly be an important source of information about insurance contracts. A couple of weeks ago, both the FASB and the IASB proposed that changes in the insurance liability due to fluctuations in the discount rate would be reported in OCI. Many of our constituents requested us to do so.

Both preparers and users wanted to prevent underwriting results being snowed under by balance sheet fluctuations. As a result, OCI will become bigger and will contain meaningful information, such as indications of duration mismatches between assets and liabilities.

This decision for the use of OCI was not easy to make. Our fellow board member Stephen Cooper showed us in a razor-sharp analysis that in this presentation, both Net Income and OCI-if seen in isolation-might give confusing information. We will try to tackle some of these problems with presentational improvements. But it is also clear that a full picture of an insurer's performance can only be gained by considering all components of total comprehensive income. We will point this out explicitly in the Basis for Conclusions of the new standard.

More fundamentally, we will look at the distinction between net income and OCI during the upcoming revision of the Conceptual Framework. All of our constituents have asked us to provide a firm theoretical underpinning for the meaning of OCI and we will endeavour to do so. For now, while we may not always know how important OCI exactly is, we can be sure that net income is not a very precise performance indicator either. Both need to be used with judgement, especially in the financial industry.

What is the reason for all this ambiguity and lack of precision in accounting? Well, to a great extent it is simply the nature of the beast. Valuation is as much of an art as a science and we are fully aware of that. Our Conceptual Framework says: "General purpose financial reports are not designed to show the value of a reporting entity; but they provide information to help users to estimate the value of the reporting entity." Value is ultimately in the eye of the beholder. There is often not a clear cut answer to the question as to which measurement technique is most appropriate to capture it.

These comments about the imperfections of accounting should not be interpreted as a sign of wary relativism about the significance of our standards. Quite the opposite: I am deeply convinced that our accounting standards are an essential ingredient of trust in our market economy. In an economic system in which so many parties are working with other people's money, high quality accounting standards that provide transparency to the market are of paramount importance.

IFRS as a global standard has had a tremendously beneficial impact for global investors, who lacked all comparability in the pre-IFRS days. Several academic studies have shown that the introduction of IFRS has contributed to lowering the cost of capital.

Moreover, financial reporting does not need to be mathematically exact to be useful. It is a tool to help investors on their way. Warren Buffett is known to use financial reports as a rough-and-ready checklist: more than five or six questions marks are enough for him to decide against making an investment.

One has only to look at the insurance industry to see how essential proper accounting standards are. Currently, IFRS does not have a full-blown standard for insurance. As a result, financial reporting by the industry is riddled with non GAAP measures and there is a serious lack of comparability. Because the industry's reporting lacks the underlying rigour of uniform accounting, investors demand a higher price for capital to make up for the lack of transparency.

Public sector accounting also demonstrates the primitive anarchy that results without the discipline and transparency that good financial reporting provides. While the IPSASB has created good standards for the public sector, based on IFRS, they are used only haphazardly. Around the world, governments give very incomplete information about the huge, unfunded social security liabilities they have incurred. Many executives in the private sector would end up in jail if they reported like Ministers of Finance, and rightly so.

So there can be no question about the relevance and importance of our standards. As the convergence programme comes to a close and the IASB is ready to take on a new agenda, we should concentrate on further improving the quality of our standards. Although we know that some of the imprecision and ambiguity I mentioned before is inevitable, it is our job to push back the grey areas in accounting as far as possible.

So how should we go about it? I believe we should be guided by the following three terms: Principles, Pragmatism and Persistence.

Principles: for the very reason that accounting is not an exact science, principle-based standard setting remains the right way forward. If the use of judgement is inescapable, it should be guided by clear principles and not by detailed, pseudo-exact rules.

We will strengthen our basic principles by finishing the review of the Conceptual Framework and by tackling thorny issues such as measurement, performance indicators, OCI and recycling.

While I am not so naive to think that a new Conceptual Framework will solve all our problems, I think it can serve to give us firmer ground under our feet. Even if precise answers are not always available, a completed Conceptual Framework should give us more guidance on the recognition of assets and liabilities, measurement techniques and performance indicators.

Pragmatism. If we know that there is not always a precise answer to every question, our work needs to be grounded in pragmatism and common sense. As Keynes said, it is better to be roughly right than to be precisely wrong. We should avoid trying to get companies to achieve precision without accuracy.

Pragmatism also means we need to look very carefully at any possible undesirable use of our standards. Whenever we are confronted with a high degree of uncertainty, we should act with great caution. I just gave the example of intangible assets. We know they are there, but measurement is a big problem. If our standards were to provide too much room for recognition of intangible assets, the potential for mistakes or abuse would be immense.

In such circumstances, it is better for our standards to require more qualitative reporting than pseudo-exact quantitative reporting.

By the way, people always tell us we should not set our standards from an anti-abuse perspective. I think that is nonsense. If we see ample scope for abuse in a standard, we had better do something about it. There are sufficient temptations and incentives for creative accounting as it is.

Pragmatism is important, but it should not be confused with opportunism. That is why we need Persistence, too. In the face of the pressures we are continually facing, persistence is an important quality for standard setters. Accounting standard setting should be sensitive to legitimate business concerns, but should also be firm and independent in the face of special interests. Many times, doomsayers have predicted their business would come to an end as a result of our standards. Just as often, the industry in question miraculously seemed able to survive our rules very well indeed. We always need to listen, but we have to take decisions, too.

For the IASB to persist on a steady course, it would be hugely beneficial if the investor's view was heard more loudly and clearly than currently is the case. While investors are our prime audience, their voice is too often drowned out by vociferous business interests. In the coming years, we are determined to further invest our relationship with investors, to ensure we get more balanced feedback on our proposals than currently is the case. We are especially interested in strengthening our relations with what I would like to call our "end-users".

On Global Accounting Standards

With this term I refer to true investors, in the sense that they actually own assets, such as institutional investors. The support of the investor community will make it easier for us to stay our course.

So it is with principles, pragmatism and persistence that the IASB will take on its new agenda. We should use the coming years to strengthen the underlying principles of our work. We should improve the significance of the quantitative outcome of our standards where possible. Where this is impossible, we should make this clear and put more emphasis on qualitative information.

This is all much easier said than done, but my Board looks forward to taking up this challenge with our highly motivated staff. Whatever the coming years may bring: a period of calm they will not be.

The Concept of Prudence: Dead or Alive?

Speech by Hans Hoogervorst at FEE Conference
on Corporate Reporting of the Future in Brussels, Belgium
18 September 2012

Ladies and gentlemen, I am grateful to the Federation of European Accountants for the opportunity to participate in today's conference. As has often been said, Europe kick-started the move towards global accounting standards when it and others adopted IFRSs from 2005. The accounting profession in Europe played a vital role in the success of this project. I and my fellow members of the IASB are extremely grateful to FEE and its membership for leading this important work.

The theme of today's conference is corporate reporting of the future. There could be no better time to consider such a topic. In the last ten years we have seen nothing short of a revolution in financial reporting. Ten years ago, no one used international standards. Today, companies in more than 100 countries do so, including almost three quarters of the G20. Against any measure, this has been quite an achievement.

So, after the revolution, what comes next? What is the future of corporate reporting? There are various initiatives trying to address this question. One of the most important is the work to take a more holistic view of corporate reporting, known as integrated reporting. The goal of integrated reporting is to bring together many reporting requirements including sustainability, the environment, social issues as well as of course financial reporting. These topics are becoming more inter-dependent, and many investors want to understand the interplay between them. I also think for investors to properly understand financial statements, they are in need of non-financial key performance indicators. For example, a company might decide to cut back sharply on training and education of its employees. This decision might make its next quarterly statement look good, but it could be disastrous for long-term profitability. For all these reasons, I support this important initiative and am I happy to serve on the governing council of the IIRC.

While financial reporting is much further developed than integrated reporting, we are still struggling with very fundamental questions. Our Conceptual Framework has definitions of assets and liabilities, but we still do not find them completely satisfactory. While you would expect accountants — of all people — to be able to make a clear distinction between mine and thine, we are still not quite sure how to distinguish equity from liabilities. Measuring the performance of an entity is also very hard. We measure Net Income, but then there is also Other Comprehensive Income, which keeps on growing without us being sure what it means.

These are all the thorny issues that we need to resolve in the next phase of the revision of our Conceptual Framework. We are planning to write new chapters on elements, measurement and presentation, including a solid disclosure framework. This is perhaps the most important work we can undertake. Get the underlying concepts right, and you have sound and consistent reference points for the rest of our standard-setting work.

The significance of this work is underlined by the fact that up to this day, the existing Conceptual Framework is still the subject of intense controversy. I am referring specifically to the Concept of Prudence. When the IASB revised the first chapters of the Conceptual Framework in September 2010, it replaced the concept of Prudence by Neutrality. Ever since, IFRSs have been periodically criticized for actually being imprudent, allegedly leading to overstated profits and/or understated liabilities. For example, critics blame the incurred loss model for understating losses on bad loans and the use of fair value accounting for inappropriately recognizing unrealised profits.

This criticism needs to be taken seriously. In previous speeches, I have spoken about the fact that financial reporting is far from an exact science and that it is highly dependent on judgement. If these judgements will systematically err on the side of optimism, obviously the investor will be very poorly served. Exaggerated profits inevitably lead to overpriced investments.

But before I examine the question whether IFRSs lead to imprudent financial reporting or not, let us first try to determine what Prudence actually means. The previous version of our Conceptual Framework listed Prudence as a characteristic of Reliability (which is now called Faithful Representation). The Framework said that Prudence was the inclusion of a degree of caution in the exercise of the judgements needed in making the estimates required under conditions of uncertainty, such that assets or income are not overstated and liabilities or expenses are not understated.

You might very well ask what the heck was wrong with this definition of Prudence? My answer would be: absolutely nothing. The definition basically says that if you are in doubt about the value of an asset or a liability it is better to exercise caution. This is plain common sense which we all should try to apply in our daily life.

While cautioning against overly rosy assumptions, the old definition of Prudence also contained a clear warning against creating hidden reserves and excessive provisioning. This warning was basically designed to prevent cookie jar accounting and income smoothing. Again, I agree 100 percent.

There are two problems with excessive conservatism. First of all, during an economic upturn, profits are artificially depressed and investors might miss out on a good investment opportunity. But the biggest problem kicks in during the downswing of the economic cycle. In those circumstances, hidden reserves can be used to artificially increase an entity's earnings. Profits are overstated, masking the deterioration of the entity's performance. Again, the casualty is transparency. The investor is likely to be misled and might be induced to hold on too long to his investments.

More generally, cookie jar accounting undermines confidence in the reliability of financial reporting. In 1993, Daimler Chrysler of Germany acquired a secondary listing in the United States. In its conversion to US GAAP, voluminous hidden reserves became transparent in Daimler's financial statements. Although Daimler's financial position was much better than previously reported, it led many to wonder how the lack of transparency provided by the then German GAAP affected other German companies. People know that hidden reserves can easily turn into hidden losses.

So I think that the old definition of Prudence, stressing caution while warning against cookie jar accounting, was spot on. Why then did we remove it?

One reason was convergence with US GAAP, which did not have a definition of Prudence. More generally, many felt that in practice the concept of Prudence was often used as a pretext for cookie jar accounting. In this respect, it is important to realise that the incentives for earnings management are huge. Remuneration and reputations are very much dependent on steadily rising earnings figures. Accordingly, the ability to smooth earnings is highly prized by executives.

Even analysts are often (wittingly or unwittingly) sympathetic to accounting techniques that allow for some earnings management. Predicting earnings is the bread and butter of analysts and too much volatility makes that very hard to do! Given all these temptations, both the IASB and FASB felt it was important to stress the neutrality of financial reporting, by leaving out the concept of Prudence. In this context, I find this a defensible decision.

It is also easy for me to accept the revised Conceptual Framework since the old concept of Prudence—if in doubt, be cautious—is still very much engrained in our standards. Let me just give you a few examples:

- While fair values are often seen to be synonymous with exuberance, in IFRS 13 we actually require risk adjustments when fair values are measured using mark-to-model techniques.
- Our standards require liabilities to be recorded for guarantees or warranties, even when they have not yet been called in.
- Inventory is typically carried at lower of cost or net realisable value; again a prime example of exercising caution.
- Impairment tests are required to ensure that the carrying amount in

the statement of financial position is not greater than the recoverable amount of the asset.
- ○ IFRSs also have very strict rules governing the balance sheet presentation, giving little room for off-balance sheet financing.
- ○ As is well known, our standards are quite restrictive in terms of the netting of derivatives. The difference with entities reporting under US GAAP can be as big as 30% or 40% of the balance sheet. We believe derivatives are too important-and their net positions too volatile-to be relegated to the notes.
- ○ The upcoming leasing standard is another effort to make off-balance sheet financing more transparent. Analysts around the world routinely adjust the balance sheet for leases that they perceive to be off-balance sheet financing. It is highly prudent that we are going to enshrine this in our standards.
- ○ Equally, our consolidation rules, based on the principle of control are very strict. Rather than choosing for a bright line, we opted for a qualitative principle which may require consolidation, even if a company's interest is less than 50%.

Given all these examples, it is not surprising that the British government recently stated that it "does not accept that IFRS has led to a loss of prudence", saying "the concept of prudence continues to permeate accounting standards". I believe this to be an appropriate conclusion.

Having said so, I think there is further room for improvement of our standards with the old concept of Prudence in mind. In a previous speech, I have mentioned the risks associated with intangible assets. They are undeniably there, but measuring them is often a huge challenge.

In this respect, I have specifically mentioned my concerns about goodwill resulting from business combinations. This goodwill is a mix of many things, including the internally generated goodwill of the acquired company and the synergy that is expected from the business combination. Usually, there is real value there, but nobody knows exactly how much. Most elements of goodwill are highly uncertain and subjective and they often turn out to be illusory.

Given its subjectivity, the treatment of goodwill is vulnerable to manipulation of the balance sheet and the P&L. In normal circumstances, you would expect at least part of the goodwill to be written off gradually, as the expected synergies for which goodwill was paid are being realized. But in practice, entities might be hesitant to impair goodwill, so as to avoid giving the impression that they made a bad investment decision. Newly appointed CEO's, on the other hand, have a strong incentive to recognize hefty impairments on their predecessor's acquisitions. Starting with a clean slate, they can more or less ensure a steady flow of earnings in the future. The question is if our current rules provide sufficient rigor to these decisions.

There is no simple solution to these problems. It might be worthwhile to take a fresh look at the impairment rules during our upcoming post-implementation review of IFRS 3 *Business Combinations*, but I am the first to acknowledge this will be very challenging indeed.

I mentioned before that a frequent criticism of fair value accounting is that it would lead to inappropriate recognition of unrealised profits. I believe this criticism is mostly unfounded. It should be noted that fair value measurement is often much quicker in picking up deterioration than amortised cost; just look at recent write-downs of Greek debt. Nevertheless, I am sure that the treatment of unrealized versus realised earnings will be an important issue in our future work on the new Measurement chapter of the Conceptual Framework.

A final example of our efforts to build sufficient caution into our standards is our work on an expected loss model for financial instruments. After the outbreak of the financial crisis, our current impairment model, which was based on incurred losses, was criticised for being too little, too late. Both the IASB and the FASB have indeed come to the conclusion that we need a more forward-looking impairment model. In the past 18 months we have worked hard to come to a converged solution.

As you know, the FASB recently developed second thoughts about the model we had jointly developed and a converged solution now seems unlikely. Whatever the final outcome of our deliberations, though, both approaches will be based on expected losses and both should be more responsive to changes in credit expectations than what we have now.

Both models will also share the main drawback of any expected loss model: namely, increased subjectivity. Obviously, estimation of expected losses will require more judgement than measuring incurred losses. Reliability can be a real issue.

To the IASB, it is important that the expected loss model meets two conditions: first, it should reflect economic reality as closely as possible and second, it should keep leeway for earnings management as small as possible. Let me expound a little bit on both issues.

If the expected loss model is to reflect economic reality, it should keep recognition of losses on day-1 to a minimum. Obviously, when a loan is made on market terms, at inception a loss is not suffered. To recognise lifetime losses on day 1 could bring the book value of a loan (significantly) below its economic value. For non-investment grade loans to small and medium-sized companies, which are quite common, these day-1 losses could be quite substantial. Investors would rightly be very suspicious of such numbers.

A model that leads to day-1 expected losses across the board, could also have serious, unintended consequences. When earnings are depressed, cutting back on new lending (and thus avoiding day-1 losses) would be a very easy way for banks to boost their profits. Bank lending might become even more pro-cyclical than already is the case!

Moreover, a model that is based on expected lifetime losses on day 1 will necessarily be highly subjective, even if they are based on historical statistics. Such statistics can indeed be very treacherous, as both the American and Spanish mortgage markets have shown. Minor tweaks in lifetime expected losses can have a very big impact on earnings. The temptations of earnings management will be hard to resist.

Again, while steep provisioning might be conservative on day 1, they might serve to mask a deteriorating performance on day 2. For this reason, the Financial Crisis Advisory Group concluded in its final report of June 2009 that, although an expected loss model seems more prudent than the incurred loss model, the Boards must take care to avoid fostering earnings management which would decrease transparency. Given the fact that I was co-Chair of the FCAG, you will not be surprised that I wholeheartedly support this conclusion.

For these reasons, our model requires recognition of full lifetime losses only after a loan has suffered deterioration. In the jargon of our proposal: a loan is impaired when it has experienced a more than insignificant deterioration and when it has become reasonably possible that contractual cash flow will not be fully collected. This threshold is much lower than in the current incurred loss model, but it avoids the pitfalls of full lifetime losses on day 1. We acknowledge that our model also requires the use of judgement and will not be completely free of subjectivity. We are still working hard to develop proper application guidance so as to keep the room for subjectivity as limited as possible.

Let me try to come to a conclusion. I think I made it clear in this speech that I think it is absolutely vital that our standards result in information that is as neutral as possible. A systemic bias towards conservatism undermines the value of earnings as a performance indicator. I have also shown my understanding for the fact that IASB felt a need to be completely unambiguous about this issue by removing the Concept of Prudence from our Conceptual Framework.

Yet, I have also demonstrated that the basic tenets of the Concept of Prudence are still vital for our work. Indeed, the exercise of caution is visible in many of our standards and is also an important issue in the development of new standards. Indeed, one might very well conclude that the old Concept is not dead, but alive and kicking indeed. From what I have said, it will be clear that I have absolutely no problem with that. As the old Gospel says: "old time religion, it's good enough for me."

Ladies and gentlemen, thank you for your time. I wish you a very successful conference.

Accounting Harmonisation and Global Economic Consequences

Speech by Hans Hoogervorst at the London School of Economics
06 November 2012

Welcome and introduction

I am delighted to join you this evening to tell you about the work of the International Accounting Standards Board. At the end of my speech, I hope I will have convinced you that developing international accounting standards is of vital interest to the global economy. Our work is important, very challenging and can even be fun!

If you know a bit about my career, you will understand why accounting is challenging to me. I am not a trained accountant. Instead, I read History at the University of Amsterdam before going on to study International Relations at Johns Hopkins University in the United States. After a brief spell working for a US bank, I saw the light and decided to commit myself to serving the public interest. I returned to the Netherlands to enter the world of politics. I became parliamentarian and moved on to become minister at the departments of finance, social affairs, and health. In all these roles I worked with my colleagues to reform the Dutch welfare state. It was a very rewarding period, as we saw the Dutch economy regain its former strength.

After leaving politics, I spent several years as Chairman of the Authority for the Financial Markets, a Dutch financial regulator. The AFM is an across-the-board conduct of business regulator, almost identical to its British counterpart, the Financial Conduct Authority. My job was to make sure that the financial industry was transparent and that it treated its customers fairly. As I assumed my position just after the outbreak of the financial crisis, this was a challenging task and that's putting it very mildly!

The AFM was also responsible for overseeing financial reporting. This was my first exposure to financial reporting and much to my surprise I found it a fascinating area. As the crisis started to unfold, many people in the financial industry started to blame accounting rules for the volatility in the financial system. I found this criticism very suspicious as it was a typical case of blaming the messenger.

I made the mistake of using a couple of speeches to speak out on this topic.

Those speeches came to the attention of the IASB, and I was asked to co-lead an advisory group that advised the IASB and its US counterpart on their joint response to the financial crisis. And a few years later I was asked to become Chairman of the IASB, which I did in July 2011.

The moral of the story? Be careful what you say in speeches!

So, why was I interested in chairing the IASB, when I am not a chartered accountant? Believe me, in the year since I was appointed, I have asked myself that question several times. Especially, when we are mid-way through a five-day Board meeting discussing 8 alternatives to accrete interest on the insurance liability, or some other piece of accounting rocket science!

Joking aside, the fact is that accounting really matters. David Tweedie, my predecessor as Chairman of the IASB, used to say that the job of accounting is to keep capitalism honest.

I couldn't agree more. In our public capital markets, many people are working with other people's money.

The relationship between investor and investee is usually anonymous. This relationship is highly based on trust in economic standards, markets and institutions.

The financial crisis has demonstrated how incredibly weak the checks and balances in the public capital markets can be. The banking system was allowed to get horribly risky and leveraged on the back of implicit and explicit state guarantees. We are living in the biggest credit bubble in history and five years after the outbreak of the crisis a global economic catastrophe is still a very real possibility.

The many excesses in corporate remuneration are also indicative of the poor way investor's interests are represented in public capital markets. Since executive pay is more often than not linked to earnings, corporate management has an enormous interest in accounting rules that allows them to present those earnings in a favourable way. Many breakthroughs in accounting were hard-won victories over vested interests; I will give you a couple of concrete examples later on in my speech.

You will start to understand that even accounting is political and why they asked a former politician to lead the IASB. It takes a thief to catch a thief!

High quality financial information is the lifeblood of market-based economies. If the blood is of poor quality then the body shuts down and the patient dies. It is the same with financial reporting. If investors cannot trust the numbers, then financial markets stop working. For market-based economies, that is really bad news. It is an essential public good for market-based economies.

Financial reporting, market economies and globalisation

I would now like to turn to the relationship between the globalization of the world economy and surge in the use of the standards as produced by the IASB. In the world of financial reporting, the most startling development of the last 10 years has been decisions by most of the world's economies—developed and emerging —to embrace International Financial Reporting Standards, or IFRSs as issued by my organisation, the IASB.

There are many reasons why this has come about, but the main one has been the globally interconnected nature of today's financial markets. Capital no longer respects national borders. Investors seek diversification and investment opportunities on a global basis. Multinational corporations want to maintain one set of books across all of their international activities, while regulators and policymakers want a level playing field for financial reporting.

In such a globalised environment it makes no sense to maintain national accounting standards.

They introduce friction to global financial markets, confuse investors and add unnecessary cost to companies. That is why repeated G20 communiques have supported the work of the IASB and called for a rapid move towards global accounting standards.

The good news is that, in the last 10 years, we have made remarkable progress in this area. From pretty much a standing start in 2001, we now have more than 100 countries using IFRSs, including more than 2/3rds of the G20. Half of all Fortune Global 500 companies now report using IFRS.

To understand the scale of this achievement, just look at Europe. In 2002, the European Union decided to switch to IFRS from 2005. The 25 member states at that time had less than three years to prepare. On 1 January 2005, around 8 000 companies simultaneously switched from more than 20 different national accounting regimes to IFRS. That is a truly remarkable achievement.

Where Europe led, others have followed. Look at an IFRS map of the world and you will see all of South America is now on board, Mexico and Canada in North America, the Caribbean, Australasia, vast swathes of Asia, most of Africa and of course Europe, including non-EU countries such as Russia and Turkey.

The growth economies such as China, Korea and Brazil are very supportive of our work. They see IFRS as an opportunity to secure a seat at the top table of global financial reporting. For example, China provides the secretariat for the IASB's emerging economies group. Recognising the growing economic importance of the Asia-Oceania region, next week we will open our first ever regional office, located in Tokyo.

This is quite remarkable progress in little more than 10 years. In my view, the momentum for IFRS becoming global standards has now become unstoppable.

Of course, we cannot overlook the fact that the United States has yet to decide whether and how to adopt IFRS.

As the world's largest national economy, we would very much like the US to be a fully paid-up member of the IFRS community. The US Securities and Exchange Commission, or SEC has been a long-term supporter of our work. The SEC has already determined that IFRS is of high quality by permitting its use by non-US companies listed on US markets. It is estimated that over 500 companies-many of which are European—are now listed in the United States using IFRS.

The SEC had intended to make a decision on IFRS during 2011, but announced in July that it would postpone this decision. We hope that 2013 will bring better news. For the call of the G20 for a single set of global accounting standards to remain credible, it is important that progress is made soon.

The IASB has also acquired a firm position in the governance of the world economy.

The IASB is a member of the Financial Stability Board and works in close cooperation with other international organisations with responsibility for the global financial system. In this role, we have an opportunity to help shape the global regulatory reform agenda.

Why financial reporting is so controversial

The second question that I want to discuss is why financial reporting can be so controversial. There are several reasons for this. It is fair to say that we do not always help ourselves. Many say that the extensive disclosure requirements of both US GAAP and IFRS need some pruning. Sometimes our standards do not seem to make a lot of sense. Allowing banks that have suffered a ratings downgrade to recognise a gain due to a decrease in value of their own debt is politely described as "counter-intuitive". In each of these cases, we have either fixed the problem or are in the process of doing so, but these examples do not help our cause.

In other areas, controversy looms because we are trying to shine a light into some dark corners of the financial system. Some historic examples of this are the expensing of stock options and getting pension liabilities on the balance sheet, while a current example is the battle to bring leases onto the balance sheet.

Some time ago, the IASB and the FASB had the mother of all battles against vested interests to record the granting of stock options as an expense. Up to then, companies could grant these options at seemingly no cost, while these stock options obviously diluted the holdings of existing shareowners. There was a huge lobbying campaign led in part by the technology sector, to keep it that way. But there was one question that this lobby never could answer: if these stock options really cost nothing, why not give them to everybody? Even legendary US investor Warren Buffett waded into the ferocious debate.

Writing in the 1998 Berkshire Hathaway annual report[1], he said:

> "A distressing number of both CEOs and auditors have in recent years bitterly fought FASB's attempts to replace option fiction with truth and virtually none have spoken out in support of FASB. Its opponents even enlisted Congress in the fight, pushing the case that inflated figures were in the national interest."

More than 70 Million dollars was spent[2] lobbying the US Congress and other policymakers that the end of the world was nigh, but on that occasion the standard-setters ultimately won. It was the IASB that led the way, paving the way for the FASB to follow suit.

Almost ten years later and very few people question to logic of recording stock options as an expense. It is simply regarded as good business practice.

The same is true with pensions and other post-employment benefits. Many years ago, companies were able to keep off the balance sheet information related to these liabilities.

As is often the case, what is not measured is not managed. As a result, the management of some companies were able to literally give away the value of the company without shareholders knowing anything about it.

At the time, bringing pensions liabilities on balance sheet was hugely controversial. To some degree, it still is. However, such liabilities are now routinely discussed in the boardroom and with investors. This is especially true as many pension schemes are in trouble, and the company is on the hook if things go wrong.

Today, we have a similar battle with leasing. The vast majority of lease contracts are not recorded on the balance sheet, even though they usually contain a heavy element of financing. For many companies, such as airlines and railway companies, the off-balance sheet financing numbers can be quite substantial.

What's more, the companies providing the financing are more often than not banks or subsidiaries of banks. If this financing were in the form of a loan to purchase an asset, then it would be recorded. Call it a lease and miraculously it does not show up in your books. In my book, if it looks like a duck, swims like a duck, and quacks like a duck, then it probably is a duck. So is the case with debt-leasing or otherwise.

Right now, most analysts take an educated guess on what the real but hidden leverage of leasing is by using the basic information that is disclosed and by applying a rule-of-thumb multiple. It seems odd to expect an analyst to guess the liabilities associated with leases when management already has this information at its fingertips. That is why it is urgent the IASB creates a new standard on leasing and that is exactly what we are doing, in close cooperation with the FASB.

Companies tend to love off-balance sheet financing, as it masks the true extent of their leverage and many of those that make extensive use of leasing for this purpose are not happy.

Furthermore, the leasing industry itself is fighting its own battle. Members of the US congress, heavily lobbied by the industry, are writing letters to our colleagues at the FASB. A recent report in the United States claimed that our joint efforts with the FASB to record leases on balance sheet will lead to 190 000 jobs being lost in the US alone. I seem to remember similar claims being made when the IASB and the FASB required stock options to be expensed.

We should not be surprised by this lobbying. The SEC predicted it would happen. In June 2005, the SEC submitted a report to Congress regarding the use of off-balance sheet arrangements[3]. Arguing for a change in lease accounting, the report said, and I quote:

> "The fact that lease structuring based on the accounting guidance has become so prevalent will likely mean that there will be strong resistance to significant changes to the leasing guidance, both from preparers who have become accustomed to designing leases that achieve various reporting goals, and from other parties that assist those preparers."

These words turned out to be quite prophetic. As the financial crisis was caused by excessive leverage, our efforts to shed light on hidden leverage should be warmly welcomed around the world. The fact is that we are still facing an uphill battle. We will need all of the help we can get, to ensure that we do not get lobbied off course. We need national accounting standard-setters, regulators such as the SEC, investors and others to stand by their beliefs and help us to bring much-needed transparency to this important area. We really need their vocal support to counter what is a well-funded and well-resourced lobbying campaign.

Accounting as an economic science

Thus far, I have told you about the public interest of accounting and the reasons why it tends to be so controversial. The third reason why I think accounting is fun, is the fact that it is intellectually challenging and interesting. Basically, accounting is an economic science.

That means that, just like economics, it is as much of an art as a science (no offence meant). Like other forms of economic science, there is an awful lot of judgement that goes into preparing financial statements. Accounting has the same problems as its sibling Economics: you need maths to exercise it, but you should not count on outcomes with mathematical precision.

For example, accounting has multiple ways of measuring the same asset or liability, depending on the business model according to which it is held. The measurement of intangible assets is fraught with difficulties, such as how to value the brand of an acquired company.

The application of professional judgement is an essential characteristic of financial reporting, but we should also not forget that in many cases, judgement is little more than an educated guess.

That is why we intend to devote a lot of time revising our Conceptual Framework. The Conceptual Framework is the theoretical foundation of our standards.

It deals with very basic questions, such as: what is an asset; what is the difference between a liability and equity; how do we measure income? Seemingly very simple questions, but I assure you we can make the answers very difficult!

There is almost universal support for completing revisions to our conceptual framework, and on a timely basis. This framework serves as a point of reference for the IASB's decision-making. Where choices are not clear-cut, the framework serves to encourage the IASB to make decisions that are consistent across the standards. The framework is also an important reference for companies when applying principle-based standards.

We already have a framework that works reasonably well. However, areas such as Measurement are still less than perfect, to put it mildly. It is easy to understand why this is the case. After all, measurement is the most judgmental, difficult and politicised part of accounting. We need to bring more rigor and clarity here, but it will be an extremely arduous task which will require a lot of brainpower and courage.

Whatever the outcome, it is most unlikely to receive universal acclaim. Just imagine a group of the world's leading economists sitting together to create the Conceptual Framework of macro-economics. The only certain outcome would be bitter fights, bruised egos and no Framework! The Nobel Prize for economics would automatically fall to the sole surviving economist. Since accountants are very polite human beings, I am sure that we will manage to keep it civilized, but universal praise we will never get.

Conclusion

Ladies and gentlemen, it has indeed been a pleasure to share my thoughts with you today. To summarise, I do believe that IFRSs will become global standards. I also believe that standard-setters will continue to remain unpopular, because change is rarely popular—even if it is change for the better. There are just too many people that profit from status quo.

Thank you for your time. Given that this is the London School of Economics, I look forward to some very challenging questions. Please do not disappoint me!

---

[1] Berkshire Hathaway Inc. 1998 Annual Report. www.berkshirehathaway.com.

[2] Warren McGregor. Personal Reflections on Ten Years of the IASB. *Australian Accounting Review*, Sept 2012.

[3] Report and Recommendations Pursuant to Section 401(c) of the Sarbanes-Oxley Act of 2002 On Arrangements with Off-Balance Sheet Implications, Special Purpose Entities, and Transparency of Filings by Issuers, June 2005, www.sec.gov.

Dispelling Myths about IFRS

Introductory remarks by Hans Hoogervorst
15 November 2012

    Minister Nakatsuka, President Hagiwara, distinguished guests. It is a great honour to be here today on this momentous occasion for the IASB. Today we are opening our first office outside of London, and the Asia-Oceania region is the perfect place for this facility. That is why I am delighted to be here today. To thank the Japanese Financial Accounting Standards Foundation for their support in helping to establish this office, and to assure you of my commitment to making sure that it is a remarkable success.

    First of all, Asia-Oceania is the most dynamic economic region of the world. For the IASB it is a privilege that so many jurisdictions and companies in this region want to use our accounting language to speak with investors around the world. The IASB needs a presence here to ensure that the financial reporting standards we are developing are fully compatible with the needs of this important region.

    Second, in the field of financial reporting, Asia-Oceania has some really smart thinkers. We at the IASB always look forward to comment letters and other input received from this part of the world. We can rely on this input to be of very high quality, expressing some very clear thinking. We need to tap better into this thinking through this office.

    Across the Asia-Oceania region you have a rich diversity of 25 independent voices. The great work of the Asia-Oceania Standard-Setters Group is helping to synthesise these national views and where possible, trying to express an Asia-Oceania view to the IASB. We truly hope that this office will contribute to further deepen cooperation and communication in this region. We also need to be here to make sure Asia is fully plumbed into the IASB's day-to-day activities.

The Asia-Oceania office will also help the IASB to make itself better understood in this region. As a relatively young organisation we still have a lot to do in this respect. In my frequent travels around the world, I have noticed that there are still quite a few misconceptions about the IASB that need to be put to rest. Now that I am here, let me take this opportunity to dispel just a few of these myths.

One persistent myth about the IASB is that we (perhaps secretly) would only be interested in fair value. The truth is that we have always been proponents of a mixed measurement model. While our colleagues at the FASB at one time proposed a full fair value model for financial instruments, the IASB decided from the outset that a mixed attribute model would be more appropriate. We understand full well that while fair value measurement is very relevant for actively traded financial instruments, for a manufacturing company it does normally not make a lot of sense to fair value its Property, Plant and Equipment.

Currently, we are reviewing the measurement chapter of the Conceptual Framework. We will try to develop clear principles on which measurement technique to use in what circumstances. We have some very tough nuts to crack and the outcome of this exercise is far from clear. However, it is most unlikely that it will result in a choice for fair value as the single measurement technique. So the fair value myth can be put to rest.

The second myth I would like to briefly touch upon is that the IASB is only interested in the balance sheet, and that we aim to replace net income with comprehensive income. Again, I see no evidence of such bias. We do not designate one type of information, about balance sheet or about profit and loss, as the primary focus of financial reporting. Both are indeed complementary. We also view net income as an important performance indicator. We know comprehensive income contains many different items that users need to analyse separately.

Having said that, we are also aware that we do need to clarify the basis upon which different gains and losses are reported in different ways. Other Comprehensive Income has become a very crowded parking spot for sensitive accounting problems. The fact is that nobody knows what OCI really means. It is our duty to tidy things up and to make income presentation more meaningful. In the review of the Conceptual Framework we will try to do so. Wish us luck!

In the meantime, rest assured that we have no plans to eliminate profit or loss as a measure of performance or to make comprehensive income the only measure of performance. So, once again fact is somewhat different from fiction.

The two preceding misconceptions have led to a third persistent myth, namely that IFRSs are only of use to the financial whizz-kids in London and Wall Street. This myth holds that our standards are incompatible with the culture of countries with a strong manufacturing tradition. Again, this is not true. Around the world, the vast majority of companies using IFRS are normal businesses involved in normal business activities such as manufacturing, retail and the services sector. Since the global financial crisis first broke out in 2007, media coverage of IFRS has been dominated by what it means for financial institutions. Media coverage is one thing, but the reality is that IFRSs are used day in, day out by businesses in the "real economy".

The fourth and final myth I want to touch upon is that the IASB is sometimes perceived to be an ivory tower, dominated by Anglo Saxons in far-away London. Fortunately, this criticism seems to abate as we are strengthening our efforts to engage with our constituents around the world.

Indeed, the IASB is not a foreign organisation but a truly international one. We have staff and board members from around the world, who are deeply committed to the public interest. We only have one mission: to develop high quality accounting standards that serve our constituents around the world. We rely heavily on input from jurisdictions around the world when setting our standards. Our relationship with national standard setters and regional bodies such as the AOSSG will soon be deepened by the creation of an Accounting Standards Advisory Forum.

The opening of the Asia-Oceania office is another moment of huge symbolic significance. It demonstrates the commitment of the IASB to be a truly global organization.

You can count on our continued commitment to this very important region and its constituents. In closing, I would like to thank once again Japanese authorities and the Japanese Financial Accounting Standards Foundation for making this office possible.

The Search for Consistency in Financial Reporting

Speech by Hans Hoogervorst at Cass Business School invited by E&Y
17 January 2013

Good afternoon and thank you for inviting me here today. As you may know, we have been doing quite a bit of work to develop a research capability at the IASB. An important thread of this work is to encourage independent research that complements our own activities. So I am really encouraged by the type of work that Professor Pope and his team have undertaken.

This is impressive research, carried out in a thorough and systematic manner. The main conclusion of the report is that there is considerable variation in compliance with some impairment disclosure requirements across countries in Europe, suggesting uneven application of IFRS. Although consistent application of the standards is not the primary responsibility of the IASB, we of course take great interest in these findings.

In many ways, Europe's decision to adopt IFRS in 2005 was a leap into the unknown.

No one had tried to apply the same, word-for-word set of accounting standards across such a diverse range of economies and cultures. The rest of the world looked on with interest.

One year after adoption, a study sponsored by the European Commission[1] found that adoption of IFRS had been challenging but ultimately successful. The study concluded that "there was widespread agreement that IFRS has made financial statements easier to compare across countries, across competitors within the same industry sector and across industry sectors".

However, to get the most out of comparability the standards also need to be applied, audited and enforced on a consistent basis. That is some challenge across a union of 27 highly diverse member states with different cultures of enforcement. Especially when you consider that the economy of the largest state is more than 400 times that of the smallest.

I am not surprised that the research presented today has identifiedvariationsin the extent to which IFRSs are applied and enforced across the European Union, or that higher quality reporting is more likely in member states with a stronger regulatory environment.

Even a strong regulatory environment is not a guarantee for consistent application. The recent SEC staff report on IFRS[2] noted that during 2010, the SEC conducted reviews of around 4 500 existing issuers, resulting in restatements by around 15% of those issuers. This goes to show that in an economy as sophisticated as the United States, using a deeply entrenched national GAAP, you still see challenges with consistent application of the standards.

Critics of IFRS like to state that as long as there is uneven application and enforcement around the world, there is no point in adopting IFRS. This argument is, of course, nonsense. The truth is that even an unevenly applied global standard provides much more global comparability than an equally unevenly applied multitude of diverging national standards.

Without a global standard, there is absolutely no chance you will ever arrive at global comparability. IFRS vastly improves the opportunities to improve application around the world.

A uniform accounting language makes it much easier to detect inconsistency of application and to do something about it. This very report could not have been written in the absence of a single accounting language in Europe. Thanks to IFRS, this report is able to clearly identifyindications of application problems in specific jurisdictions. These results could, and I am sure will be used by ESMA to encourage further improvements in the consistent application of IFRS.

It is primarily the task of regulators and auditors to take the leadin tacklingchallengeswithconsistent applicationofour standards. But we also recognise that the IASB has an important role to play in this work. I will spend a few minutes updating you on five areas that we are taking the lead on.

As an accounting standard-setter, our most obvious contribution is to develop principle-based standards that are capable of being applied, audited and enforced on an internationally consistent basis.

Over the last few years we have improved the quality control of our work during the development of new standards.

We have deepened our cooperation with national and regional standard-setting bodies such as the AOSSG and EFRAG and we have announced a new platform to coordinate this interaction with the standard-setting community, known as the Accounting Standards Advisory Forum, or ASAF.

The ASAF will be up and running in the next few months. In the same way as car manufacturers test their development models in different terrains, the ASAF will play an important part in helpingusto road-test new-standards, thushelpingus to understand how the standards function in a community as diverse as the European Union.

Second, as a result of enhancement to our due process, we now complete a post implementation review of major standards and interpretations two years after they have come into effect.

This review provides an important safety net, to identify and rectify unforeseen difficultiesin areas such as consistency, that only come to light once the standard is used in practice.

We are close to completing the first of these reviews looking at our standard on segment reporting, with business combinations being the next standardsubject to review.

Third, we recently completed a two-year review of the IFRS Interpretations Committee. As a result of this review, the Committee has a much wider array of tools at its disposal to address diversity in practice and will be more responsive to requests for help.

As well as developing interpretations the Interpretations Committee helps the Board develop narrow scope improvements to Standards.

Fourth, we are stepping up production of educational material. In December last year we published educational guidance on Fair Value Measurement and we are mid

-way through developing similar educational guidance for Joint Arrangements.

Finally, we have significantly increased our cooperation with securities regulators, at an international level under the auspices of IOSCO, and at a regional level with ESMA.

The fact that both Michel Prada, the Chairman of our Trustees and myself have been securities regulators in the past is indicative of the natural affinity between our organisations.

Dialogue between our respective organisations is truly excellent and we are discussing ways to expand this cooperation, possibly through some form of MoU or other formal agreement.

So in summary, our contribution to tackling the challenge of consistency is better wording, more support, being more responsive to requests for help and working with others to deliver stronger enforcement.

At the same time, we should not forget how far we have come. Less than 10 years ago, the European Union had 25 entirely different ways to account for the same transaction. Today, we have one. That is some achievement, of which Europe should be proud.

As I said beforehand, addressing the challenge of consistency requires coordinated action by standard-setters, auditors, regulators and others. The large accounting firms have a particular important role to play.

They are the only organisations that have the global reach, with offices in both the largest and the smallest countries of the European Union, and for that matter, the world.

As this research is sponsored by Ernst and Young, I am very interested to hear your own plans to help tackle the ever-present challenge of consistency in financial reporting.

Ladies and gentlemen, thank you for your time.

---

[1] EU Implementation of IFRS and the Fair Value Directive, a report for the European Commission, www.icaew.com.

[2] SEC WorkPlanfor the Considerationof IncorporatingIFRS intothe Financial ReportingRegime for US Issuers, p31, July2012, www.sec.gov.

Accounting and Long-Term Investment
—"Buy and Hold" Should not Mean "Buy and Hope"

Speech by Hans Hoogervorst in London
09 April 2013

As a former politician, I am all too familiar with the pitfalls of short-termism. Harold Wilson once famously said that a week is a long time in politics. He made that comment well before the age of the internet and the 24-hours news-cycle. Unfortunately, short-termism is a big issue in the economy as well. Two, related factors are conducive to short-termism. First, in our modern market economy, more than ever before, people work with other people's money. Secondly, with the increasing complexity of the economy, the distance between investor and investee has increased dramatically as well.

Corporate governance and regulation have been struggling to keep up with the complexity of financial intermediation and its many temptations. Not many investors are capable of keeping a close eye on the managers they have entrusted their money to. In addition, conflicts of interest are rife. Investment companies who should be holding their investee's management to account, might also be interested in managing their pension fund. How critical are these investors going to be?

All this is an ideal backdrop for short-termism. Money managers have huge incentives for making momentum-driven investment decisions. Indeed, recent research has confirmed it to be a very profitable exercise[1]. In the short run, going with the flow is often the safest bet, no matter how irrational this flow may be. As long as the going is good, the money manager does not face criticism; when the music stops, he can blame it on the markets.

On top of that, macro-economic policies are currently not particularly helpful for investors who want to take a long-term view. Central banks around the world are employing highly expansionary policies to make sure there is still an economy tomorrow. What these policies will bring for the day after tomorrow is highly uncertain, but they might very well end in tears.

Many observers are worried that the prevalence of short-term horizons in the financial markets is detrimental to long-term investment and economic growth. Recently, the Financial Stability Board, Group of Thirty and the European Commission have published reports on this issue[2]. While accounting standards are not a central theme, some of these reports do contain suggestions that, some believe, could make accounting standards more helpful to investors with a long-term horizon.

What is the role of the IASB in promoting healthy, long-term investment? I would say it is an essential part of our job. The purpose of accounting standards is to keep capitalism honest, as my predecessor, David Tweedie, used to say. Financial reporting forces management to show how they have discharged their responsibilities to make efficient and effective use of the company's resources. This is the principle of stewardship. In essence, it means accountability.

A couple of years ago, we removed the term "Stewardship" from the Conceptual Framework. Some critics regret this removal of the word stewardship. Some see it as an indication that the IASB would no longer attach sufficient importance to the interests of the long-term investor. To these critics, we usually answer that the word Stewardship was only removed because it was so difficult to translate in other languages. We also point out that the essence of the principle is still covered by the Conceptual Framework. Close-reading the Conceptual Framework reveals this is true. Yet I can imagine that some might find the essence of the Stewardship principle a bit hard to find.

There can be no mistake that holding management to account remains a very important purpose of financial reporting. Management must tell investors what resources the company acquired, why it acquired them, and how it used those resources. Management must tell what obligations the company incurred, why it incurred them, and how it satisfied those obligations. Information of this kind is not only useful for buy, hold and sell decisions, it also helps investors decide how to vote on management's actions. If Stewardship is impossible to translate, perhaps we could replace it by a better word, such as accountability.

Whatever we call it, there should be no ambivalence about Stewardship being a central goal of financial reporting. Apart from our general principles, are there other ways in which our standards could affect long-term investors? It is often said that IFRSs discourage long-term investment by relying excessively on fair value or other forms of current measurement. Excessive use of fair value would, supposedly, encourage financial engineering and short-term profit taking.

So what are the facts? The truth is that, outside the financial industry, most companies have little to do with fair value accounting. The bulk of their assets and liabilities are measured on a cost basis. Those who follow our discussions on the Conceptual Framework know this is not likely to change. Even in the financial industry amortized cost is still an important measurement base. Most of a bank's traditional assets, such as loans, are measured at amortized cost, now and in the future. It is no surprise, that most academic research shows that fair value accounting was not a major driver of volatility during the financial crisis.

Still, in the financial industry current measurement techniques play a bigger role than in other parts of the economy. As many financial instruments are traded around the clock in active markets, market value often gives the most relevant information. Where fair value was used during the crisis, it often gave much more timely information on the poisonous instruments that had been injected into the system. Preparers and investors who paid attention to fair value signals were often much better at limiting damage than those who chose to ignore them. The use of current measurement techniques in the financial industry will be substantially increased by our upcoming insurance standard. As you probably know, the IASB is close to finalising an exposure draft on insurance contracts. The proposed standard will prescribe current measurement of the insurance liability, while many insurers currently still use historic cost. The public discussions on this standard provide a microcosm of the debate on long term investment versus short-termism.

Many in the insurance industry are concerned about what is coming. They criticize the new standards for creating too much volatility. They claim that this volatility will discourage them from making long-term investments and from providing products with guaranteed results. So what is fact and what is fiction? Let me start out by saying that the insurance industry is a hugely important investor. In Europe alone, the insurance industry has a 5.4 trillion euro investment portfolio. Life insurance is a long-term liability business, so the industry potentially has an enormous appetite for solid long-term investments.

Unfortunately, current monetary policies make life very difficult for the insurance industry. EIOPA, the European Insurance regulator recently raised the alarm bell about the effects of persistent low interest rates on the industry. On the liability-side, low interest rates increase an insurer's obligations in today's terms, while the return on assets is depressed. Said differently, if low interest rates persist, insurers may find that their assets do not generate the cash flows needed to pay policyholders' claims.

EIOPA is concerned that a considerable number of insurance companies will not be able to meet their capital requirements. EIOPA refers to Japan, where persistent low interest rates caused some insurers to fail, while others had to lower the returns they had promised to their customers.[3] If the insurance industry is a victim of the crisis, it has been a rather silent victim thus far. Part of the reason why it has not made more headlines is that the problems cannot be seen for lack of a proper accounting standard.

In many jurisdictions, insurance companies measure their insurance liabilities at cost. They still show reasonable results, but these results might be based on completely outdated interest rates from, say, 10 years ago. EIOPA says about these firms: "the fact that the effects of low interest rates are slow to emerge in balance sheet terms does not mean the problem is not there and there is a real risk that firms could build up hidden problems."

Our new standard will bring these problems to light because it requires measurement of the liability using current interest rates. This will allow investors to gain a much more reliable view on the true performance of the industry. Markets will gain much more insight into how effective insurers are in matching their liabilities with assets. Critics say that interest rates and other market fluctuations go all over the place and that our standard will lead to unnecessary short-term volatility.

We have not turned a blind eye to these criticisms. Indeed, our exposure draft will contain a host of proposals to reduce accounting volatility. But we have rejected proposals that reduce volatility in an artificial way. Some insurers have brought forward proposals which are echoed in the report of the Group of Thirty which I mentioned earlier. One proposal is that the measurement of the insurance liability should be based on the expected return on the assets held by the insurer. While some in the insurance industry are enthusiastic about this idea, we have our doubts. We call this "hope-and-wish"-accounting. We do not think it is prudent to base the measurement of a liability on an uncertain yield of assets. "Buy-and-hold" should not turn into "buy-and-hope".

The appendix to the report of the Group of Thirty contains a yet more radical idea to eliminate short-term fluctuations, the so-called "target-date accounting approach". In this approach, a diversified portfolio of equities would be put in a "target-date fund" with a binding commitment to hold them for a long horizon. The fund would then be valued at a time-weighted average of cost and market value with the objective of smoothing out short-term volatility.

This proposal is fraught with difficulties as well. If the books of a company were based on averages that are different from market values at the reporting date, trust in financial reporting might be seriously jeopardized. Market participants will react by simply converting the whole target-date fund back to market values. I think we should save them the trouble. We remain convinced that a model based on current measurement gives the best insight in the financial position of an insurance company. Our new standard will be a huge improvement in that respect. Where it leads to more volatility, it is probably a reflection of real economic risks. Only adequate levels of capital can deal with this risk; accounting standards should not serve to cover it up.

Finally, I would like to stress that even long-term investors cannot afford to ignore short-term fluctuations, if only because you never know how short the short-term will be. Central bankers call current interest rates "exceptionally low". The fact is that exceptionally low interest rates have been around for almost 15 years in Japan! In the West we have been going at it for more than five years and nobody knows when interest rates will revert to normal levels.

It is estimated that an airplane flying from London to New York will only spend 10% of the time pointing in the right direction. The direction of the plane is not determined by the pilot alone, but also by external factors such a wind speed and direction.

The pilot needs to make continuous short-term corrections in order to achieve the long-term goal-to arrive safely in New York. Business is no different. The renowned Swedish long-term investor Boerje Ekholm recently said that while his company always has a long-term objective, "we'll be terriers in the short term on how you run the business". He stressed that in reaching your long-term objective, you have to evaluate every day[4]. If you do not adjust your business in time, the risk of a much larger correction further down the line grows exponentially.

So, beware of people who tell you that they only care about the long term and who do not want to be bothered by market values. For a company to take a long term view, it has to be able to withstand the inevitable short-term fickleness of the market place. The real problem is that we allowed a historically unprecedented build-up of leverage to take place in our economies. Extreme leverage has brought large parts of the financial industry very close to the edge. Even after Basel 3, banks will be able to finance 97% of their assets with debt. How this level of indebtedness can be conducive to long term growth, is a mystery to me. Now even insurance companies are treading hazardous territory. They flee into the bond market, not because of accounting, but because they do not have enough capital left to sustain the risks of equity investments.

The IASB cannot contribute to a solution of these problems by pretending these risks are not there. Our standards would not be right if they tell the pilot he is flying to New York, while is plane is actually blown off track. Those who care about the long term, should also know where they stand today. Our job is to provide maximum transparency both for the short and the long term. Our contribution is to provide the long term investor with the best information he needs at all times.

---

[1] A market strategy that keeps on rolling, Financial Times, 8 March 2013.

[2] FSB: Financial regulatory factors affecting the availability of long-term investment finance, 8 February 2008, Group of 30: Long-term Finance and Economic Growth, European Commission, Long-Term Financing of the European Economy, 25 March 2013, http://www.ft.com/cms/s/0/077de35e-93bc-11e2-b528-00144feabdc0.html#axzz2OUkkNNrf.

[3] EIPOA: Supervisory Response to a Prolonged Low Interest Rate Environment, 28 February 2013.

[4] Scandinavia: Model Management, Financial Times, March 21 2013.

IFRS and Indonesian Accounting Standards 2013 and Beyond

Speech by Hans Hoogervorst at IAI-AFA
International Seminar in Jakarta, Indonesia
06 March 2013

This is not my first visit to Indonesia. I first visited your wonderful country in the late nineties, in my then capacity as junior Minister for Social Affairs in the Dutch Government. Visiting this dynamic city of Jakarta, I remember being struck by the huge potential of this country. Indonesia is the fourth most populous nation in the world and has a wealth of natural resources. It was immediately clear to me that Indonesia possessed the raw ingredients to enjoy many decades of strong economic growth.

However, at the time of my visit, Indonesia was not in a very optimistic mood. Indeed, your nation was one of the countries that were most affected by the severe financial crisis that plagued the Asian region at the time. Like many countries around you, Indonesia went through a period of serious economic and political difficulties.

I returned to Indonesia in 2007, this time as a tourist. I thoroughly enjoyed the beauty of your country and the friendliness of your people. As a Dutchman I have been exposed to your culture (and to your food) since I was a child and I was very happy to get even better acquainted with both. Unfortunately my touristic visit to your country was far too short. But it was long enough to see that already in 2007 Indonesia was doing a lot better. Your financial system had been rebuilt. Your economy was moving again.

I am now visiting your country in circumstances that are yet again very different. Again there is a very serious financial and economic crisis. Yet this time, it did not start in Asia, but in the West. This time, Asia had learned the lessons from the crisis in the nineties. Thus far, most Asian countries weathered the storm pretty well.

This time, the West forgot the lessons it had taught Asia in the past. The doctor did not follow the treatment it gave to his patients and now he is getting a taste of his own medicine. This time, it is the Western banking system that is broken and Western public finances that are in disarray. The industrialized world is struggling to show any growth at all.

And what is it that the IMF has to say about Indonesia this time? I quote a report from 2012: "A fundamental reform of the policy framework over the past decade left Indonesia in a strong position when the global economy turned sour after 2007." It continued: "The strong policy framework ensured that Indonesia came out of the 2008 global financial crisis much better that its Asian peers". A ringing endorsement of Indonesia by the IMF, who could have imagined that 15 years ago?

So Indonesia now seems to be well on its way to fulfilling its potential. In 2005, Goldman Sachs included Indonesia in a list of the "Next 11" economies that would come to serve as the engines of global growth. They forecast that Indonesia will experience outsized growth compared to the rest of the world. By 2050, Goldman Sachs expects the Indonesian economy to be larger than either Germany or indeed the United Kingdom.

Of course, it is difficult to predict what the world will look like in 40 years' time. But what cannot be dismissed is that Indonesia has the potential to achieve that goal. I am here to tell you that I firmly believe IFRS can be an important tool for your country in its quest to fully unlock its potential. I am convinced that full adoption of IFRS can really help Indonesia to sustain its economic development.

But before I explain how Indonesia can benefit from IFRS, let me begin by telling you about how IFRS is close to becoming the global language of financial reporting.

Ten years ago very few countries of the world used IFRSs. Now more

On Global Accounting Standards

than 100 countries require or permit the use of IFRS, including three quarters of the G20. In the America's, almost all of Latin America and Canada are using IFRS. The United States still has to make up its mind, but it allows more than 500 foreign issuers to list using IFRS. All of Europe uses IFRS. In Asia-Oceania countries like Korea, Malaysia, Australia, New Zealand and Hong Kong are full adopters and many others are on the way. China uses standards that are substantially converged and in Japan the number of companies that are using IFRS is expected to increase significantly. Half of all fortune Global 500 companies now report using IFRS. Every year, new jurisdictions decide to adopt IFRSs, most recently Russia and Taiwan.

How could this happen in such a short time? Why have so many jurisdictions, large and small, moved from the familiarity of local accounting standards to IFRS? Well, each jurisdiction has its own reasons.

Europe needed to create a common economic market. For that, it needed a common financial reporting language. At the beginning of the century, the member states of the European Union spoke many different accounting languages. In Germany, the accounting system was very closely aligned to their tax system, while at the other end of the spectrum the UK's accounting system was not dissimilar to the United States. This multitude of accounting dialects was impossible to understand.

In 2002, the EU decided to adopt IFRSs and it completed the task in just three years. In 2005, more than 7 000 companies across 25 countries simultaneously switched to IFRSs. Various reports have concluded that the move to IFRS was a remarkable success. It led to increased transparency and greater comparability. Investors acquired more trust in the numbers and the cost of capital went down. It goes to show that with IFRS, where there is a will, there is a way.

If the introduction of IFRS brought economic benefits to Europe, imagine the benefits that emerging economies can draw from the use of IFRS. In fact, the Asian crisis of the nineties was an important driving factor for the development and spread of IFRS. Too many investors, who had just begun to invest on a global scale, had burned their fingers during the Asian crisis.

They wanted to see financial statements that were the same as the statements they saw at home. IFRS provides the global language that investors want. It gives added credibility to your capital market and brings down the cost of capital.

For many emerging economies, adoption of IFRS has become an important statement of ambition—an international commitment to adhere to the highest possible standards of financial reporting. For example, an investor in London, New York or Hong Kong can pick up a Korean set of IFRS-compliant financial statements and be entirely familiar with that company's financial performance.

In a country like Korea the move to IFRS has helped to reduce the so-called "Korean discount" that international investors would charge, in part due to the unfamiliarity with the previous Korean accounting rules. Today, those same international investors are able to compare and contrast a company with its international peers in more than 100 countries around the world.

It is important to understand that the full benefits of using the IFRS-brand can only be enjoyed if you adopt it fully. For foreign investors it is very difficult for investors to discern small differences from big ones. If a jurisdiction cannot state that it has fully adopted IFRS, investors are likely to think that the differences are much bigger than they really are. If you have gone through all the trouble to adopt 95% of IFRSs, please make sure you also do the last 5%. Otherwise, you have all the pain of transition without the full gain of international recognition of that achievement.

Almost all jurisdictions that adopt our standards experience some challenges with adjusting domestic accounting practices to IFRS. That is to be expected. Often these problems can be resolved, sometimes it is more difficult, such as is the case with the issue of land rights in Indonesia.

Most jurisdictions have concluded that the credibility bonus of full adoption of IFRS outweighs the temptation to tinker with the standard to address local problems. Chances are that other jurisdictions are also having the same problems, so it is much better that we work together, to fix the problem centrally so that all IFRS adopters can benefit from such improvements.

I am delighted to see that Indonesia is well along the path to IFRS adoption. The DSAK has made huge progress under the firm leadership of Rosita Uli Sinaga. At the same time, the road to full adoption still needs to be completed. Completing that transition is an important step in order to convince international investors that Indonesia is serious about unlocking the potential I referred to earlier.

I am here today to offer the full assistance of my organisation. To help you make the small remaining steps in order to reap the large premium that comes with full adoption of IFRS. I am confident that the few remaining obstacles to full adoption can be overcome.

The relationship between the IASB and the DSAK is already very strong. Our respective staffs work very well together. But I also believe that there is an opportunity to further deepen that cooperation.

The IASB has already invested heavily in supporting economies in this important part of the world. We have recently opened an Asia-Oceania office in Tokyo, to better support Indonesia and other important jurisdictions across the region. Our Director of the Asia-Oceania office, my good friend and colleague Mitsuhiro Takemura, is here with me today, to learn more about Indonesia's plans and to understand better what we can do to help you.

We have also established an Emerging Economies Group, headed by Wayne Upton, Chairman of the IFRS Interpretations Committee. The purpose of this group is to understand better the challenges of applying IFRS in jurisdictions with less developed capital markets. I am glad to see Indonesia participating actively in the Emerging Economies Group.

Furthermore, we continue to work in very close cooperation with the Asia Oceania Standard-Setters Group, or AOSSG, which provides an important mechanism to coordinate views on our work across this diverse region. Rosita is a member of the AOSSG and has used it very effectively to present Indonesian issues in a very eloquent way. The AOSSG is likely to be represented in the Accounting Standards Advisory Forum, or ASAF, that we have created to deepen our cooperation with standard-setters across the world.

All of these initiatives provide wonderful opportunities for strong Indonesian participation in financial reporting. The door is open for you, and there are several ways that you can take advantage of this opportunity-as other jurisdictions continue to do so.

You could help us in the researching of areas of accounting—particularly those where Indonesia has highly relevant experience. I also encourage you to continue acting as a vocal member of the AOSSG. Europe, the United States and other likely members of the ASAF will most likely be highly vocal in our discussions. It is essential that the AOSSG can also express itself clearly, ideally with one voice.

I will now move on to describe our current work programme as well as our plans for the future.

Current programme

Our main priority is to complete the remaining elements of convergence projects with the FASB. We have four major projects awaiting completion. Let me begin with the two standards where we were able to stay completely converged with the United States.

Revenue Recognition

The first of these projects is revenue recognition. Revenue is the top line number and is important to every business. It is also an area that perhaps sees the most divergence in practice. This makes it all the more important that we get this standard right.

We published a revised exposure draft in November 2011 and expect to issue a full standard in the first half of this year. The new standard will replace US requirements that are generally considered to be too detailed and international requirements that are not detailed enough.

The new revenue recognition standard should address some of the concerns regarding the "percentage of completion" method of accounting utilised in IFRS. We are aware that this has been a particular point of concern for the commercial real estate and construction sectors here in Indonesia.

Historically there was some diversity in the way companies recognised revenue from the construction of residential real estate. As a result, the IFRS Interpretations Committee issued IFRIC 15 in 2007. However, in practice, that additional guidance has proved difficult to interpret and apply in some places. In the new revenue recognition standard, the IASB has tried to solve these problems.

The new standard will contain a clear principle as to when revenue should be recognised, namely as goods and services are transferred to the customer. It will also provide supporting guidance that has will provide more clarity as to how to recognize revenue from residential real estate construction contracts. We think the new standard will address most of the current interpretation problems here in Indonesia.

As I mentioned above, Revenue is a key performance indicator for every business and I see this project as being one of the resounding successes of the convergence programme.

Leasing

Second is lease accounting. This is a difficult area, but also one where improvements are needed. The vast majority of lease contracts are not recorded on the balance sheet, even though they usually contain a heavy element of financing. For many companies, such as airlines and railway companies, the off-balance sheet financing numbers can be quite substantial.

What's more, the companies providing the financing are more often than not banks or subsidiaries of banks. If this financing were in the form of a loan to purchase an asset, then it would be recorded. Call it a lease and miraculously it does not show up in your books.

Despite what you may hear, reports that the rule changes will lead to the death of the leasing industry are greatly exaggerated. Leasing provides many important economic benefits to companies and that will not change. All we ask is that these transactions are accounted for in a way that is transparent to investors.

At present, most analysts take an educated guess on what the real but hidden leverage of leasing is by using the basic information that is disclosed and by applying a rule-of-thumb multiple. It seems odd to expect an analyst to guess the liabilities associated with leases when management already has this information at its fingertips.

That is why it is urgent the IASB creates a new standard on leasing and that is exactly what we are doing, in close cooperation with the FASB. The boards are finalising the revised proposals and we expect to publish a final exposure draft for public comment very soon. Your input will be important to achieving a high quality outcome.

Financial Instruments

Phase I : Classification and Measurement

As I'm sure you know, our reform of the accounting rules concerning financial instruments has been conducted in different phases. The first of these is classification and measurement. The IASB and FASB started from two completely different perspectives. The FASB initially favoured a full fair value approach while the IASB chose mixed measurement. I consider it a success that we managed to bring our approaches much closer together.

In early 2012 the IASB and the FASB jointly agreed on amendments to our respective models. For IFRS 9 these included clarifying the amortised cost business model and introducing a Fair Value through Other Comprehensive Income measurement category. At the same time, the FASB has moved to a mixed measurement approach which is very similar to ours. We published our proposals in November 2012 and welcome any comments you might want to make.

Phase II : Impairment

The most challenging part of the revision of IAS 39 has turned out to be impairment. Currently, both IFRS and US GAAP use incurred loss impairment models. Many have voiced concerns that these models result in loan losses being recognised too little and too late. Both boards concluded we had to replace the incurred loss model by an expected loss model.

After several false starts, we will publish our third and hopefully final Exposure Draft in the next few days. We believe our new expected loss model will result in more timely recognition of credit losses. Banks will be required to create a loss allowance for all loans based on a 12-month probability of default. If the credit quality of a loan has significantly deteriorated, banks will have to recognise the full expected lifetime loss.

Our new model is a simplified version of an approach we had developed jointly with the FASB. In July last year, the FASB decided to develop its own model which requires entities recognise full lifetime expected losses on initial recognition of the related assets.

In the coming months, both boards will receive feedback on our respective models. We will keep lines of communication open during the comment period and will consider comments on both models during re-deliberations in 2013. Hopefully we might be able to come to a more converged solution, but this is far from certain.

Phase III: Hedge Accounting

The IASB had received feedback that the hedge accounting requirements in IAS 39 were seen as arbitrary, rules-based and detached from risk management. We therefore proposed a fundamental overhaul of hedge accounting requirements to better reflect risk management activities. Also, we wanted to make hedge accounting more accessible for non-financial institutions. We are almost ready to publish the final standard which we believe to be a vast improvement over current practice.

Insurance

Of the remaining convergence projects, insurance is the one that keeps me awake at night. At this time, we do not have a proper IFRS for insurance and the American standard is in need of updating. As a result, there is huge diversity and complexity in how insurance companies report their numbers under IFRSs. Investors often talk about insurance accounting being a "black box". This lack of transparency comes with a corresponding risk premium, which can lead to insurance companies trading at a discount to their peers in other areas of financial services.

The project is challenging because different financial reporting practices have become embedded in different parts of the world. Many insurance companies are using out-dated assumptions in their measurement. This is particularly concerning because it is very likely that insurance companies are likely to be suffering in the current low-interest environment. Without a proper standard, investors cannot see properly how big these financial risks are.

We have been working with the FASB to develop a model that lifts financial reporting for insurance contracts to a common and improved level. Our standards will not be completely converged, but they will both be based on current measurement. As a result they will vastly improve transparency in the insurance industry. An exposure draft is targeted in the first half of this year.

New Agenda

Clearly there is still some important work to be done in all of these projects, but we have made some substantial progress and are well on the way towards completion. As this chapter in our history draws to a close, we have already begun to put in place arrangements for a new programme of work.

Implementation and maintenance

The IASB is responsible for developing enforceable Standards and will give greater emphasis to addressing implementation concerns. Many respondents to last year's agenda consultation suggested that we should give greater emphasis on maintaining the portfolio of existing IFRS requirements rather than creating new requirements. By maintenance, we mean Interpretations, narrow-scope improvements (including Annual Improvements) and education.

The respondents made a good point. After a period dominated by joint projects focused on convergence, now is the time for the IASB, and the Interpretations Committee, to be more active in addressing matters related to the practical application of IFRS.

Conceptual Framework

In May 2012, we decided to restart the Conceptual Framework project. This is perhaps the most important work we can undertake and we have widespread support from constituents in addressing it. We know that if we get the underlying concepts right, then we will have sound and consistent reference points for the rest of our standard-setting work.

Our current Framework has definitions of assets and liabilities, but we still do not find them completely satisfactory. While you would expect accountants-of all people-to be able to make a clear distinction between mine and thine, we are still not quite sure how to distinguish equity from liabilities.

Measuring the performance of an entity is also very hard. We measure Net Income, but then there is also Other Comprehensive Income, which keeps on growing without us being entirely clear what it means. These are all the thorny issues that we need to resolve in the next phase of the revision of our Conceptual Framework.

We want to move as quickly as possible to set in place this important framework, which will shape future work. We have therefore set an ambitious target, aiming to finalise the new sections of the Conceptual Framework by September 2015. The first major milestone is a Discussion Paper, which we expect to finalise in June 2013.

Standard Level projects

One of the most common responses we received following the agenda consultation was a call for a period of calm. This is wholly unsurprising given the level of change we have seen in reposting over the last decade. Whilst a period of complete quiet is not quite achievable, consistent with these calls we have made plans to begin work on only a small number of standard level topics.

These include Agriculture-where we will pay particular attention to the status of so-called bearer biological Assets. These include cash crops, such as palm oil trees and grape vines, which having reached biological maturity are used to produce grow agricultural produce over several years until the end of their useful lives.

This is of particular importance to countries such as Indonesia with a significant agricultural sector. Under current rules, assets such as palm trees are measured at fair value. Under our new proposals, they will be treated more like property, plant and equipment and measured at cost. The revised standard will be less costly to apply and will remove artificial volatility from net income.

Conclusion

Ladies and gentlemen, I am grateful for your time. I hope that from hearing about these initiatives, you get a sense of our commitment to this region and to emerging economies such as Indonesia. Although the office of the IASB is located very close to the Tower of London, my organisation itself is certainly not an ivory tower. We have a dynamic, highly motivated staff recruited from all over the world. We are open to views from all over the world. We need you, just as much as you need us. As the world moves to global accounting standards, the G20 has encouraged us to pay special attention to the needs of emerging economies. You have a wonderful opportunity to help shape the future of global financial reporting.

I am here today, to extend the hand of friendship and to encourage you to come fully on board with IFRS. I wish you a very successful conference.

Are We There Yet?
Charting the World's Progress towards Global Accounting Standards

Speech by Hans Hoogervorst in Hong Kong
05 June 2013

  The term "globalisation" was introduced into the business lexicon by Harvard Professor Theodore Levitt in 1983. He then said that "The Earth is round but, for most purposes, it's sensible to treat it as flat[1]". If Levitt thought that the economic world was flat back in 1983, imagine what he would make of it today, some 30 years later.

  Unfortunately, the regulatory system that underpins this global market has failed to keep up. Indeed, the global economic crisis showed how international regulatory arbitrage was rife. Since the crisis broke, many have been working hard to upgrade this global regulatory infrastructure, to make it fit for purpose for the 21 century.

  In the area of financial reporting, progress had been made a lot earlier. The shocks of the Asian financial crisis, the Enron and WorldCom scandals, and Europe's creation of a common financial market: all these developments helped build consensus for global accounting standards. Every relevant international organisation has expressed its support for our work to develop a global language for financial reporting.

  The G20 Leaders, the IMF, the World Bank, the Financial Stability Board, the IOSCO and the Basel Committee on Banking Supervision: all are on record with their support for this important project.

  So, how are we doing? Who is using our standards and how are they being adopted? Thus far, we have formed estimates of progress based on our own knowledge and the experiences of the large accounting firms. Still, up to now, our knowledge has not been very precise. As a result people often doubt whether progress has really been as great as we think. Some believe that many countries have adopted locally modified versions of IFRS. They claim that the use of unmodified IFRS is actually relatively limited.

For these reasons, we felt it necessary to get a clearer understanding of which jurisdictions have adopted our standards and how. So, in 2012 the Trustees strategy review recommended that we come up with a more precise assessment of progress towards IFRS as the global standard.

For the last nine months our staff, led by former IASB Board member Paul Pacter, has been working to compile this information. We began by conducting a survey among the accounting standard-setters around the world. We then supplemented the survey results with information drawn from other sources, including securities regulators and the large accounting firms.

Finally, we asked the relevant authority within each country or jurisdiction to validate our conclusions.

Today, we are publishing the first batch of 66 jurisdictional profiles on the IFRS website. This first batch includes all members of the G20 and a further 46 jurisdictions that responded to our initial survey request. We are beginning work on a further 50 to 60 jurisdictional profiles, including the 13 EU member states that did not respond to our first survey. We hope to end up with a comprehensive picture of the IFRS-world.

These initial results are both fascinating and very encouraging. Although this is a qualitative assessment, there are some obvious conclusions to be drawn.

First of all, there is almost universal support for IFRS as the single set of global accounting standards. 95% of the 66 jurisdictions have made a public commitment of support for a single set of high quality global accounting standards. Furthermore, with the exception of Switzerland, every jurisdiction stated a belief that IFRS should be that single set of global accounting standards. This includes those jurisdictions that have yet to make a decision on adopting IFRS, such as the United States.

Second, 55 jurisdictions, or more than 80% of the profiles, report IFRS adoption for all (or in five cases almost all) public companies. Most of the remaining 11 non-adopters have made significant progress towards IFRS adoption.

This is a remarkable achievement when you consider that this shift has occurred in little more than 10 years.

Third, those jurisdictions that have adopted IFRS have made very few modifications to IFRS. Most of these modifications have been very limited. For example, the European carve-out from IAS 39 has been used by fewer than two dozen out of 8 000 listed companies in the European Union.

Moreover, where such modifications have occurred they are meant to be temporary arrangements in the migration from national GAAP to IFRS or have little effect in practice. In almost all of these cases, we have active projects on our agenda that address these issues, including agriculture, loan-loss provisioning, macro hedge accounting, separate financial statements and revenue recognition. The end result will be that most of these modifications will likely disappear.

The results also show an impressive uptake for the IFRS for Small and Medium-sized Entities, or IFRS for SMEs.

More than half of the 66 jurisdictions have already adopted the IFRS for SMEs or are planning to do so in the near future. This is all the more remarkable when you consider that the SME Standard is less than four years old.

This is only a subset of the information provided by this first batch of profiles and there is no reason to believe the remaining profiles to be published will tell a very different story. I strongly encourage you to take some time to browse through the extensive information on the use of IFRS that is now available to access from our website.

Compared with other global standards, such as the Basel capital requirements for banks, the use of local adaptations is very limited. The fact that most IFRS adopters seem to be able to resist the temptation to tinker with our standards is truly remarkable. Why would this be the case? This is the question I would like to answer in the next part of my presentation.

First of all, I think that most jurisdictions draw comfort from our highly developed due process. Never before in my long career in public policymaking have I worked in such a transparent environment. All our board papers and all our board meetings are accessible to the public.

We have comprehensive requirements for comment periods and outreach, so we are unlikely to overlook issues raised around the world. A standard that has benefitted from such elaborate due process is far more likely to be high quality and to stand the test of time. Through the creation of the Accounting Standards Advisory Forum, we are further ensuring the inclusiveness of our standard setting. Through ASAF we hope to get timely and insightful input to our standard setting. This should further mitigate the risk of non-endorsement of our standards.

Secondly, the governance of the IFRS Foundation has improved markedly over time. The establishment of a Monitoring Board gave the IFRS Foundation a firm public setting. Our accountability to the Monitoring Board gives additional assurances that the IASB is not a free-floating ivory tower, which we, of course, never were. At the same time, this multilateral body of securities regulators has reinforced the independence of the IASB from undue lobbying from any single jurisdiction.

Thirdly, most constituents also draw comfort from the fact that they have an endorsement mechanism in place. In almost all jurisdictions these endorsement mechanisms are a simple yes-or-no decision to accept a standard. Rarely do they involve a process that is likely to lead to detailed adaptation of IFRS to perceived local needs.

Yet these endorsement mechanisms are very effective in two ways: they create a safeguard as they leave ultimate sovereignty in standard setting in local hands. Secondly, the possibility of non-endorsement ensures that the IASB will have to listen very carefully to its constituents. The fact that so few jurisdictions fail to endorse our standards as issued hopefully reflects the fact that we do listen well and make changes where they will

On Global Accounting Standards

lead to a better standard.

Finally, I believe that it is the technical nature of accounting standards that makes them relatively easy to accept. IFRS aims to achieve a neutral description of economic reality rather than to shape economic reality, such as the capital norms for banks as prescribed by the Basel Committee.

True, accounting standards are not free from judgement and they can be subject to fierce controversy. Sometimes accounting standards can even become politicized, especially when they shed light on risks or practices that people would rather keep in the dark. Yet most accept that accounting standards are essentially technical rather than political. For this reason, most jurisdictions accept that the standard setting is best done by an independent board, provided that proper procedures for due process and accountability are in place.

Despite these safeguards, there are some who believe that rather than having a single, global language of financial reporting, we should switch to a Basel-style of global principles, which should then be adapted and formalized in local standards. I think that would be a recipe for disaster. In fact, this approach has been tried in accounting before, to no success.

The IASB's predecessor body, the IASC, developed accounting standards that were intended to serve as the basis of national accounting rules. All that happened was that countries took those international standards they liked and altered those they did not. The end result was that after decades of trying, the international community had to admit defeat, which led to the formation of the IASB with a new mission of a single set of global accounting standards.

Even when our constituents disagree with part of our standards, they almost always resist the temptation to alter them. Local adjustments are viewed with suspicion by investors, so most jurisdictions will simply take IFRS in full. Also, most of our constituents accept that if local adaptations were to become rife, the benefits of having a global standard would be undermined.

The financial crisis has demonstrated the need for rigorous economic standards that provide maximum transparency. The country profiles show that IFRS has come a long way to provide transparency to investors around the world. They are a cause for celebration about what has been achieved, as well as a yard stick on the work that we yet have to do.

So what is left to do? For a start, it is clear that some large and important economies have not yet (fully) adopted IFRS. But even in such countries more progress is being made than many people are aware of.

Japan already permits the use of IFRS. Currently, 17 of Japan's largest multinationals are using IFRS for domestic reporting. The Japanese Business Association, the Keidanren, has estimated that in the very near future that number will increase to 60 Japanese companies reporting using IFRS, representing around 20% of total market capitalisation of the Japanese Stock Exchange. Contrary to what many think, the dynamics of IFRS in Japan are still quite strong.

In the United States, the SEC's 2007 decision to permit non-US companies to report using IFRS while listing in the United States was a major game-changer. Today, more than 450 Foreign Private Issuers reporting using IFRSs as issued by the IASB, representing trillions of dollars in market capitalisation. So the use of IFRS in the United States is far from marginal.

This, and the fact that US investors increasingly invest in the IFRS—part of the world, explains why the American SEC remains very interested in progress being made by the IASB.

China is different. It has chosen a strategy of convergence of its standards with IFRS for all listed companies. China has already made great progress and has reached substantial convergence with IFRS.

There is still work left to do, but we have to acknowledge that the Chinese had a lot of catching up to do. The Chinese government remains firmly committed to the ultimate goal of full convergence with IFRS.

Despite the enormous progress in adoption of IFRS around the world, we understand that adoption in itself is not enough. Obviously, proper application of the standards is just as important. Proper application is primarily the responsibility of preparers, auditors and regulators. Our role is secondary, but we do to help these parties in promoting proper application around the world.

At the same time, it is clear that the risk of improper application around the world can never be a reason to not pursue global accounting standards. Even an unevenly applied global standard provides much more global comparability than an equally unevenly applied multitude of diverging national standards.

Indeed, the existence of a common language helps bringing problems to light. For example, in 2013 Cass Business School published an analysis of how well asset impairment under IFRS was applied across the European Union[2]. The report concluded that while compliance was generally good, there was scope for improvement.

However, this very report could not have been written in the absence of a single accounting language in Europe. Thanks to IFRS, the report was able to clearly identify indications of application problems in specific jurisdictions.

Taken as a whole, the commitments of the G20 and the international organisations identify a clear end point of a single set of high quality, global accounting standards. The profiles published today provide an indication of the remarkable progress made towards this end point. They also show that deviation from IFRS is rare, while such arrangements are considered to be transitional with almost all of these topics being addressed by our new agenda.

At the same time, these hard-fought gains must be protected. History would not thank us if we allowed a reversal of the progress made in the last 12 years.

The support of the G20 and the broader international community must continue to be harnessed in order to complete our work, for the benefit of investors, to deliver a global language of financial reporting.

I thank you for your time.

---

[1] Theodore Levitt. Globalisation of Markets. *Harvard Business Review*, May 1983.
[2] Cass Business School. Accounting for asset impairment: a test for IFRS compliance across Europe. www.cass.city.ac.uk.

Breaking the Boilerplate

Speech by Hans Hoogervorst at IFRS
foundation conference in Amsterdam, Netherlands
27 June 2013

Today, we have a great deal of ground to cover in a relatively short period of time. Later in the programme, my fellow members of the IASB and our senior staff will provide you with a comprehensive update on our current work programme as well as on our plans for the future.

This morning, I intend to focus my remarks on three topics. First, I will talk about progress towards the G20-endorsed goal of global accounting standards. Second, I will talk briefly about three important parts of our current work programme, namely loan-loss provisioning, insurance and the Conceptual Framework. Finally, the main topic of my speech will be disclosures. I will share with you a ten-point plan to make disclosures more effective.

Global standards

First of all, global standards. How much progress are we making towards the goal of one single set of global accounting standards?

To answer this question, we are undertaking a major piece of research. As you may know, earlier this month, we published the first results on the IFRS website.

The survey offers a very encouraging insight into IFRS adoption. First of all, there is almost universal support for IFRS as the single set of global accounting standards. 95 per cent of the jurisdictions have made a public commitment to the concept of a single set of high quality global accounting standards. Furthermore, almost every jurisdiction confirmed that this single set should be IFRS. This includes those jurisdictions that have yet to make a decision on adopting IFRS, such as the United States.

Second, more than 80 percent of the jurisdictions report IFRS—adoption for all (or in five cases almost all) public companies. Most of the remaining 11 non-adopters have made significant progress towards IFRS adoption. This is a remarkable achievement when you consider that this shift has occurred in little more than 10 years.

Third, those jurisdictions that have adopted IFRSs have made very few modifications to IFRSs. Indeed, more than 40 percent of the IFRS adopters do so automatically, without an endorsement process. Moreover, where modifications have occurred, they are regarded as temporary arrangements to assist in the migration from national GAAP to IFRSs. We expect that most of these transitional adjustments will ultimately disappear.

Of course we know that a few large and important economies have not yet (fully) adopted IFRS. But even in such countries, more progress is being made than many people are aware of.

Japan already permits the use of full IFRS and has recently widened the scope of companies that are allowed to adopt.

The Japanese Keidanren expects that in the near future about 60 big Japanese companies will be using IFRS, representing about 20% of the total market capitalisation of the Tokyo Stock Exchange. Furthermore, the governing LDP party has asked the Japanese FSA to develop a roadmap that will result in around 300 companies using IFRS by 2016.

Contrary to what many think, the dynamics for IFRS in Japan are still very strong.

In the United States, the SEC's 2007 decision to permit non-US companies to use IFRS for their American listings was a major game—changer. Today, more than 450 Foreign Private Issuers are reporting using IFRSs, which represents trillions of dollars in market capitalisation. So the use of IFRS in the United States is far from marginal, which explains why the American SEC remains very interested in progress being made by the IASB. So, all in all, we can conclude that amazing progress has been made around the world in terms of the use of IFRS, although there is clearly more to do.

Current work programme

Let us now turn to the second topic of my speech, namely our current work programme.

First of all, impairment. As you know, both the IASB and the FASB have developed proposals to replace the incurred loss model by an expected loss model.

During the financial crisis it has become clear that the incurred loss model has some serious drawbacks. It simply gave too much room for banks not recognise losses, even when it became increasingly clear that those losses were close to becoming inevitable. Moreover, although the objective of the incurred loss model was to limit the room for earnings management, there are strong indications of wide divergence in practice.

Earlier this year, we published for public comment a simplified version of our expected loss model that we had jointly developed with the FASB. We believe that this model will lead to more timely recognition of credit losses than the existing, incurred loss model. We think our model will faithfully reflect the economics of the underlying transaction. At the same time, the FASB has now developed another variant of an expected loss approach — one that recognises full lifetime expected losses on initial recognition of the related assets.

While this divergence in views between the IASB and the FASB is undesirable, all is not lost. Our respective proposals have overlapping comment periods and both boards are keen to hear views on each approach.

Both boards are well aware of the need to do all that we can to achieve convergence or at least more convergence in this very important area. I am sure that Central Bank Governor Klaas Knot will remind us of the importance of this work later today.

The second area I want to discuss is insurance contract accounting. The insurance industry is a hugely complex and important one, with a collective investment measured in the trillions. There can be no doubt about the systemic importance of the insurance industry.

Given this, it is unacceptable that we do not yet have a proper standard to account for insurance contracts. As a result, there is huge diversity and complexity in how insurance companies report their numbers around the world. Investors talk about insurance accounting being a "black box".

Many insurance companies rely on out-dated assumptions when measuring their liabilities. Indeed, some use interest rates from many years ago, while we know that the current low-interest environment makes life very difficult for the industry.

In Japan, low interest rates caused some insurance companies to go bankrupt, while others had to lower the returns they had promised to their customers.

Many insurance companies also link the accounting for their liabilities to the assets that they hold, or intend to hold. This means that the measurement of their liabilities is affected by their assets, even when they are in fact completely disconnected. This is another source of deficient comparability and transparency in the insurance industry.

Fortunately, the end to this unacceptable situation is in sight. Last week we released our second and final exposure draft for a new insurance standard. In our proposals, we require measurement of liability using current interest rates relevant to the liability. This will allow investors to gain a much more realistic view on the true performance of the industry. Markets will gain much more insight into how effective insurers are in matching their liabilities with assets.

Where our proposals lead to more volatility, it is probably a reflection of real economic risks. At the same time, we have worked very hard to ensure that the new Standard minimises, to the extent possible, non-economic, accounting-related volatility. Our revised proposals go a long way to addressing concerns in this respect about our first exposure draft. We do acknowledge, however, that there has been a trade-off of increased complexity. We think that we have got the balance about right, but we are keen to hear views before moving to finalise the standard during 2014.

Last and not least, a major project for us is the further development of our Conceptual Framework. We will shortly publish for public comment a Discussion Paper. It sets out our preliminary views on some fundamental accounting topics, such as measurement and the use of Other Comprehensive Income. We do not pretend that this Discussion Paper will give a definitive answer to all accounting problems. Even if we took ten years and a thousand pages this could not be done.

We decided to discipline ourselves both in terms of time and scope. Thus far, we have been able to meet our deadlines even though they were very ambitious. Despite these tight deadlines, I think we were able to produce a Discussion Paper that is both readable and thought-provoking. I trust it will serve as a solid basis for a profound public debate.

Hopefully we will be able to shed more light on some of the most difficult issues that have confounded standard-setters for many years. Our Board is looking forward to engaging with our constituents and we are confident we can make progress.

Breaking the boilerplate, behavioural change in financial disclosures

The third and final topic I would like to discuss is the need to improve financial reporting disclosures. For many companies, the size of their annual report is ballooning. The amount of useful information contained within those disclosures has not necessarily been increasing at the same rate. The risk is that annual reports become simply compliance documents, rather than instruments of communication.

In January this year we got regulators, preparers, auditors, users and standard-setters in the same room and refused to let them out until we had all understood the various perspectives of this problem. A common conclusion was that many aspects of the disclosure problem have to do with behavioural factors.

For example, many preparers will err on the side of caution and throw everything into the disclosures. They do not want to risk being asked by the regulator to restate their financials. After all, no CFO has ever been sacked for producing voluminous disclosures, while restatements may be career—limiting. Moreover, excessive disclosures can even be very handy for burying unpleasant, yet very relevant information! And sometimes it's just easier to follow a checklist, rather than put in the effort to make the information more helpful and understandable.

In summary, understandable risk—aversion on the part of preparers, auditors and regulators leads to a ticking—the-box mentality. The communicative value of financial statements suffers as a result. So what can we do to change this culture? What can we do to break the boilerplate?

Well, first of all, we decided to give a good example ourselves. We managed to reduce the size of our 2012 Annual Report and the accompanying disclosures by 25 percent compared to the previous year. At the same time, we actually increased the amount of useful information in the report and made it easier to read.

It took some intensive discussions internally and with our auditors; but I assure you, it can be done!

More importantly, we recently published a feedback statement that set out the key messages everything that we had heard during the disclosure event I just mentioned. On the basis of this document, today I would like to set out a ten-point plan to deliver tangible improvements to disclosures in financial reporting.

Let me start with eight possible measures that could lead to tangible results in the short run. None of these points is particularly revolutionary. Most are even very simple. However, in my experience in government, the simplest solutions are usually the most effective at tackling seemingly intractable problems.

 1. We should clarify in IAS 1 that the materiality principle does not only mean that material items should be included, but also that it can be better to exclude nonmaterial disclosures. Too much detail can make the material information more difficult to understand— so companies should proac-

tively reduce the clutter! In other words, less is often more.

2. We should clarify that a materiality assessment applies to the whole of the financial statements, including the notes. Many think that items that do not make it onto the face of primary financial statements as a line item need to be disclosed in the notes, just to be sure. We will have to make clear that this is not the case. If an item is not material, it does not need to be disclosed anywhere at all in the financial statements.

3. We should clarify that if a Standard is relevant to the financial statements of an entity, it does not automatically follow that every disclosure requirement in that Standard will provide material information. Instead, each disclosure will have to be judged individually for materiality.

4. We will remove language from IAS 1 that has been interpreted as prescribing the order of the notes to the financial statements. This should make it easier for entities to communicate their information in a more logical and holistic fashion.

5. We could make sure IAS1 gives companies flexibility about where they disclose accounting policies in the financial statements. Important accounting policies should be given greater prominence in financial statements. Less important accounting policies could be relegated to the back of the financial statements.

6. At the request of many users around the world, we will consider adding a net-debt reconciliation requirement. Not only would this provide users with clarity around what the company is calling "net debt" but it also consolidates and links the clutter of scattered debt disclosures through the financial statements.

7. We will look into the creation of either general application guidance or educational material on materiality. Doing so should provide auditors, preparers and regulators with a much clearer, more uniform view of what constitutes material information. We want to work with the IAASB and IOSCO on this important matter.

8. When developing new Standards, we will also seek to use less prescriptive wordings for disclosure requirements. Instead, we will focus on disclosure objectives and examples of disclosures that meet that objective. In recent Standards we have already started doing this, creating more explicit room for judgement on materiality.

Finally, we will begin work on two pieces of work to deliver improvements in the medium term.

9. During the second half of 2013, we will begin a research project to undertake a more fundamental review of IAS 1, IAS 7 and IAS 8. This project will revisit some of the work we already did in the Financial Statement Presentation project. The goal will be to replace those Standards, in essence creating a new disclosure framework.

10. Finally, once the review of these Standards has been completed, we will then undertake a general review of disclosure requirements in existing Standards.

I am convinced these measures have great potential. Even the eight quick wins I just mentioned can have a big impact. Taken together, they remove most excuses for boilerplate disclosures. They will certainly help to ignite the much-needed change in mind set of preparers, auditors and regulators that is so sorely needed. The IASB will continue to engage with these constituents and also, very importantly, with users, for the joint effort that is needed to make disclosures less indiscriminate and more meaningful.

Conclusion

Ladies and gentlemen, I am grateful for your attention. We have covered a great deal of ground during my opening remarks. I have talked about how the IFRS profiles provide strong evidence of the success of IFRSs. I have talked about the major projects we are working on, and I have set out a ten-point plan to improve financial disclosures.

We have a wonderful programme for the rest of this event, and I look forward to what will no doubt be a thought-provoking day.

Thank you.

Europe and the Path towards Global Accounting Standards

Speech by Hans Hoogervorst at 2013 Ernst & Young IFRS Congress in Berlin, Germany
09 September 2013

Sehr geehrte Damen und Herren,

Ich bin kein Berliner, aber ich moechte doch am Anfang meines Vortrags einige Worte auf Deutsch sagen. Es ist immer eine Freude nach Berlin zu kommen und ich moechte mich erst einmal rechtherzlich bei Ernst & Young fuer die Einladung bedanken.

Als Europa's groesste Volkswirtschaft, ist Deutschland ein wichtiger Partner in der Zusammenarbeit mit dem IASB. Wie ich spaeter drauf eingehen werde, hat das IASB eine sehr wichtige and arbeitsreiche Phase vor sich. Deutschland's Sichtweise spielt dabei eine wichtige Rolle. Ich bin heute nicht nur gekommen, um ueber das IASB und seine Arbeit zu sprechen, sondern auch um zuzuhoeren und ich bin dabei sehr auf ihre Meinung gespannt.

Being here in the very heart of Europe, I would like to take this opportunity to begin my speech with some general observations on the relationship between the European Union, the IASB and IFRS.

As you may know, EU Commissioner Michel Barnier has asked Philippe Maystadt, former President of the European Investment Bank, to develop proposals to reinforce the EU's contribution to IFRSs. We are grateful to Mr Maystadt for having had the opportunity to contribute to his research and we look forward to the publication of his final report later this year.

Obviously, it is up to the European Union how to organise itself and I do not wish to speculate in any way on the final recommendations that Mr

Maystadt will produce. Instead, I will limit myself to pointing out some important facts that govern the relationship between Europe and the IASB.

First of all, it is no exaggeration to say that the success story of IFRS is a success story for the European Union. Europe's decision to adopt IFRS from 2005 gave IFRS the credibility and critical mass it needed to become the single set of global accounting standards. It was a decisive factor for many jurisdictions in their decision to adopt IFRS or to start a convergence process. Currently, over 100 jurisdictions around the world require or permit the use of IFRS. Without the leadership of the European Union, it is doubtful whether this would have happened.

Equally, there can be little doubt that the replacement of Europe's myriad of accounting languages by IFRS was highly beneficial to the European capital market. It is important not to forget that Europe adopted IFRS in part to overcome more than 20 years of difficulties in achieving a high quality set of European accounting standards.

The introduction of IFRS not only provided Europe with an off-the-shelf solution to this problem, but also greatly increased transparency and led to a lowering of the cost of capital for listed companies. The adoption of IFRS has also proved a tremendous boost to improved enforcement in the European capital markets. The introduction of a common accounting language has greatly increased the capacity of ESMA to identify enforcement issues across Europe.

Europe has adopted almost all of our standards lock, stock and barrel. The one exception—the carve-out of IAS 39—is only used by around 20 out of more than 9 000 European companies.

Does this near-complete adoption of IFRSs mean that Europe has relinquished its sovereignty in accounting to the IASB, as some seem to think? That is certainly not the impression if you are sitting in our office in 30 Cannon Street.

The EU has retained the prerogative to adopt IFRSs Standard-by-Standard and it takes its endorsement procedures very seriously. In fact, it can be argued that Europe has by far the most stringent endorsement process of all jurisdictions that have adopted IFRS. A myriad of European organisations are involved in the adoption of IFRS: EFRAG, national standard-setters, the Accounting Regulatory Committee, the European Commission, the EU member states and finally the European Parliament.

Many jurisdictions have much lighter adoption procedures. As you may know, we have recently published the first batch of country profiles, which detail how jurisdictions are adopting our standards. Our research shows that more than 40 percent of these jurisdictions adopt IFRSs automatically as they are issued by the IASB, without any endorsement procedure. Most of the others have relatively light endorsement procedures that only involve professional accounting bodies and/or securities regulators. Apart from the EU, only in New Zealand and Australia do parliaments play a role in endorsing IFRS.

It is also important to note that the European Union is not the exception in adopting IFRS without making significant adaptations. Our country profiles show that most jurisdictions do the same. This should not come as a surprise. After all, the G20 has repeatedly stressed the goal of a single set of global accounting standards. If every jurisdiction were to make local adaptations of IFRS, this goal would never be reached.

It is true that some big economies have not yet fully adopted IFRS. However, most of them have made a great deal of progress towards IFRS adoption and progress continues to be made, often behind the scenes. In Japan, for example, in the near future a sizeable number of companies representing around 20 percent of the total market capitalisation of the Tokyo Stock Exchange is expected to be using IFRS. Although the American SEC still has to make up its mind about the use of IFRS for domestic firms, it is important to note that over 450 foreign issuers, representing trillions of dollars in market capitalisation, are using IFRS in the domestic markets. This makes the US a very significant stakeholder in IFRS.

Finally, the European Union plays a very proactive role in the standard-setting process of the IASB. In fact, there is probably no other jurisdiction in the world that devotes so many resources to outreach, fieldwork and input to the standard-setting process as the EU does, through EFRAG and national accounting standard-setters such as the DRSC here in Germany.

This effort does not go unrewarded. EFRAG itself has pointed out many instances in which it was able to make a positive impact on the standard-setting by the IASB. This proactive role by Europe will be further enhanced by the strong voice of Europeans in the recently created Accounting Standards Advisory Forum.

Finally, I can assure you that in other parts of the world, the EU is not perceived as having little influence in the standard-setting process. Indeed, some of our many constituents around the world are sometimes worried that the EU through its sheer size has too much influence.

I believe that the relationship between the European Union, the IASB and its Standards is overall well balanced and constructive.

We will welcome any proposals that enable Europe to deepen its co-operation with the IASB in pursuit of our shared objective of global accounting standards.

So what of the Standards themselves? How is our current programme of work progressing? Later today, Martin Edelmann, our German Board Member, will lead you through the details of our financial instruments Standards. Let me give you a broader sketch of our major projects this morning.

Convergence

In the last few months we have taken several major steps towards completing the remaining convergence projects.

First of all, we expect to release a new Standard on Revenue Recognition this autumn. We are still tackling some challenges with drafting, but we are confident we will get it done soon. We have taken our time because this is a very important Standard.

it is about the top line and will affect all companies. It replaces American standards that contain thousands of pages of application guidance and IFRS Standards that provide too little guidance. That is why I call it the jewel in the crown of convergence with the FASB.

Lease accounting

Second is lease accounting, another difficult but very important area. Currently, the vast majority of lease contracts are not recorded on the balance sheet, despite the fact that they usually contain a heavy element of financing. For many companies, such as airlines and railway companies, the off balance sheet financing numbers can be quite substantial. It has been estimated that the hidden leverage in leases leads to an underestimation of long-term debt by some 20 per cent. So we are not talking about small fry.

What's more, the companies providing the lease financing are more often than not banks or subsidiaries of banks. If this financing were in the form of a loan to purchase an asset, then it would be recorded. Call it a lease and it simply does not show up in the books.

In my book, if it looks like a duck, swims like a duck, and quacks like a duck then it probably is a duck. So is the case with debt-leasing or otherwise.

Right now, most analysts take an educated guess on what the hidden leverage of leasing is. Some underestimate and some exaggerate the true level of leverage implicit in the leases.

That is why the vast majority of users have told us time and again that they need our leasing Standard to provide rigour and comparability.

We are aware that this change will not be without cost to preparers. We have made some pragmatic decisions to keep costs to a minimum, such as the exclusion of short-term leases and variable lease payments. In addition, much of the information is already required in the notes under IAS 17. Companies that are in full control of their leasing commitments should have most of the information at their fingertips.

I am also convinced that bringing leases to the balance sheet will have benefits to preparers themselves.

I would not be surprised if many CEOs are only vaguely aware of the full extent of the hidden debt in their leasing contracts. By making this hidden debt clearly visible, companies might be able to make more rational decisions on capital allocation. Leasing will certainly not disappear. But companies will be able to make better-reasoned decisions between purchasing and leasing.

Impairment

On impairment, the IASB and the FASB have found it more difficult to stay converged. The fact is that both boards have struggled with impairment. In the past three years, the two boards have developed between us no fewer than six different models and we have still not finished.

We both agree that the current incurred loss models gives too much leeway for banks to postpone the recognition of inevitable loan losses for too long. It is a question of too little, too late. We therefore agree that the incurred loss model needs to be replaced by an expected loss model that is more forward-looking.

However we have found it difficult to agree on the mechanics of the expected loss model. The FASB want all possible loan losses to be recognised on Day 1; we think the bulk of the losses can only be identified and recognised once a significant increase in credit risk has taken place.

One reason why we find it difficult to come to a common answer is that an expected loss model inherently has a relatively high degree of subjectivity, because it deals with uncertain outcomes in the future. There is no straightforward answer on how this can be done.

The good news is that the IASB eventually received very broad support for our latest model and we are certain we can bring it to a conclusion. At the same time, we still hope that the IASB and the FASB will be able to bring their respective models closer together. In September, we will have another joint meeting in London and we will see how far we can get.

Insurance contracts

The fourth area I want to discuss is insurance contract accounting. The insurance industry is a hugely complex and important one, with a collective investment measured in the trillions. There can be no doubt about the systemic importance of the insurance industry.

Because of this, it is unacceptable that we do not yet have a proper Standard to account for insurance contracts. As a result, there is huge diversity and complexity in how insurance companies report their numbers around the world. Investors talk about insurance accounting being a "black box".

Many insurance companies rely on outdated assumptions when measuring their liabilities. Indeed, some use interest rates from many years ago, while we know that the current low-interest environment makes life very difficult for the industry.

EIOPA, the European Insurance regulator, recently raised the alarm bell about the effects of persistent low interest rates on the industry. EIOPA is concerned that some insurance companies will not be able to meet their capital requirements. EIOPA refers to Japan, where persistent low interest rates caused some insurers to fail, while others had to lower the returns they had promised to their customers.[1]

If the insurance industry is a victim of the crisis, it has been a rather silent victim thus far. Part of the reason why it has not made more headlines is that the problems cannot be fully seen, for lack of a proper accounting Standard.

Fortunately, the end to this unacceptable situation is in sight. Recently, we released our second and final Exposure Draft for a new insurance Standard. In our proposals, we require measurement of liability using current interest rates. This will allow investors to gain a much more realistic view on the true performance of the industry. Markets will gain much more insight into how effective insurers are in matching their liabilities with assets. Where our proposals lead to more volatility, it is probably a reflection of real economic risks.

At the same time, we have worked very hard to ensure that the new Standard minimises, to the extent possible, non-economic, accounting-related volatility. Our revised proposals go a long way towards addressing concerns in this respect about our first Exposure Draft. We do acknowledge, however, that there has been a trade-off of increased complexity. We think that we have got the balance about right, but we are keen to hear views before moving to finalise the Standard during 2014.

Future agenda

In July, we published for public comment a Discussion Paper on the Conceptual Framework. We decided to discipline ourselves both in terms of time and scope. Thus far, we have been able to meet our deadlines even though they were very ambitious. Despite these tight deadlines, I think we were able to produce a Discussion Paper that is both readable and thought-provoking. I trust it will serve as a solid basis for a profound public debate.

The Discussion Paper sets out our preliminary views on some fundamental accounting topics, such as measurement and the use of Other Comprehensive Income.

It makes clear we continue to see Profit or Loss as a key indicator of financial performance and that we do not focus solely on the balance sheet. I also think the Discussion Paper gives the beginning of an answer to the question of the significance of OCI, and how its use could be disciplined. We do not pretend that this Discussion Paper will give a definitive answer to all accounting problems. Even if we took ten years and a thousand pages this could not be done.

A topic that is related to the Conceptual Framework is our work to improve financial reporting disclosures. For many companies, the size of their annual report is ballooning. The amount of useful information contained within those disclosures has not necessarily been increasing at the same rate.

Many agree that the disclosure problem is in many ways a behavioural problem. For example, many preparers will throw just about everything into the disclosures to avoid problems with the regulators. After all, no CFO has ever been sacked for producing voluminous disclosures, while restatements may be career-limiting.

Moreover, excessive disclosures can even be very handy for burying unpleasant, yet very relevant information!

And sometimes it's just easier to follow a checklist, rather than put in the effort to make the information more helpful and understandable.

In summary, understandable risk-aversion on the part of preparers, auditors and regulators leads to a ticking-the-box mentality. The communicative value of financial statements suffers as a result. So what can we do to change this culture? What can we do to break the boilerplate?

Well, first of all, we decided to give a good example ourselves. We managed to reduce the size of our 2012 Annual Report and the accompanying disclosures by 25 per cent compared to the previous year. At the same time, we actually increased the amount of useful information in the report and made it easier to read. It took some intensive discussions internally and with our auditors; but I assure you, it can be done!

Recently, I presented a 10-point plan to deliver tangible improvements to disclosures in financial reporting. Many of them are simple, such as making it clearer that when information is immaterial it is better to avoid giving it, even in the notes.

We also want to give entities more freedom to give a more prominent place to important disclosures or accounting policies.

With these simple measures, we hope to take away all excuses for taking the easy rout of just publishing boilerplate disclosures. I really think this can help companies to communicate more effectively about their strategy. They will certainly help to ignite the much-needed change in mindset of preparers, auditors and regulators that is so sorely needed. The IASB will continue to engage with these constituents and also, very importantly, with users, to facilitate the joint effort that is needed to make disclosures less indiscriminate and more meaningful.

Ladies and gentlemen, I will now draw to a close.

The global financial crisis provided a stark reminder of the interdependence of capital markets and the need for a globally consistent language of financial reporting. This is a responsibility that we at the IASB take very seriously. We are immensely grateful for Europe's continued support for our work, and your commitment to us is fully reciprocated.

I wish you a successful conference and thank you all for your time.

---

[1] EIPOA. Supervisory Response to a Prolonged Low Interest Rate Environment, 28 February 2013.

Strengthening Institutional Relationships

Speech by Hans Hoogervorst at IFRS Foundation
World Standard-Setters Conference in London, UK
23 September 2013

Introduction

Ladies and gentlemen, fellow standard-setters, I would like to welcome you to this annual meeting of world standard-setters.

The first meeting of world standard-setters took place in 1991, predating by ten years the creation of the IASB. Back then, the ambition of the national standard setters was limited, namely to reduce the differences in their respective sets of accounting standards.

Today, that mission has evolved to be a single set of high quality, global accounting standards. That mission is supported by the G20 and it is a mission that we are fully committed to achieving.

However, a single set of standards does not mean a single accounting standard-setter. IFRS has long been a joint effort by the worldwide standard-setting community. There is no way the IASB with around 60 technical staff and 16 board members can adequately engage with stakeholders across more than 100 countries. Without your help, we would struggle to identify the practical, gritty issues companies and investors would face when applying the new standards.

Our new agenda shows clear traces of our collaboration. For example, the proposal to amend the accounting for agricultural bearer assets might not have happened without the work undertaken by members of the

Strengthening Institutional Relationships

AOSSG, particularly Malaysia. And last week we started discussing business combinations under common control. Our starting point was the work of the Italian Standard-setter, EFRAG and the standard setters who form our emerging economies group. We have many similar stories.

So while a single set of global standards means a single arbiter of the standards, ensuring that those standards are high quality requires close co-operation between the IASB and the people in this room.

We have a similar challenge when it comes to consistent implementation and enforcement of our standards. We do not have the resources to support the implementation of our standards nor the remit to enforce their use.

Over the last ten years, much of our work with partners around the world was done in a rather informal way. In the 12 months since the last world standard-setters meeting, we have made important strides towards strengthening our institutional infrastructure. Let me walk you through some of these developments.

Jurisdictional profiles

First, one of the most frequent questions I am asked about IFRS is: who actually uses the standards? Until recently, we were at best able to make an informed guestimate. But it always felt somewhat unsatisfactory that the IASB was not able to come up with precise information to chart our progress towards global accounting standards.

In last year's conference, we presented the preliminary findings of our first endeavours to get the full picture of IFRS-use around the world. Since then, our team, led by Paul Pacter, has made great progress. With your help, Paul has been able to complete 81 jurisdictional profiles and more are to come soon.

The results of the survey are very encouraging. For example, of the 81 jurisdictional profiles now completed, 78 have made a public commitment to a single set of global accounting standards. More than 85% of jurisdictions have adopted IFRS in their capital markets. Those adopting jurisdictions made very few modifications to IFRS, and the few that were made were mostly temporary steps in the jurisdiction's plans to adopt in full IFRS.

Paul Pacter will provide you with a more comprehensive briefing on this work later in the programme, but this really is a very important initiative that would not have been possible without your support. By the way, Paul will approach those of you who have not been able to provide us with full information yet, and I warn you he will not let go of you before he has everything he needs.

IOSCO

A second important development is the joint agreement that we reached with IOSCO, the global organization of securities regulators. This agreement between the IASB and IOSCO describes a series of steps that will see the two organisations working more closely together to support high levels of consistency in the implementation of IFRS globally.

Consistency of application is just as important as the standards themselves. This agreement provides the IASB and IOSCO with the necessary institutional arrangements to stimulate work in this area. Securities regulators tend to be among the few friends that accounting standard setters have and we intend to make the best of this friendship.

ASAF

Third, the introduction of the Accounting Standards Advisory Forum, or ASAF, provides an important mechanism to strengthen our cooperation with the international standard-setting community. The ASAF has now met once in person and a second time via video conference, with the third meeting ASAF meeting to take place in London later this week.

I view ASAF as a very positive development, and I note from recent speeches by some ASAF participants that they also share this this view. Thanks to ASAF, giving feedback to the proposals of the IASB is no longer primarily a bilateral event, but a multilateral endeavour. ASAF members do not just discuss with the IASB, but also with each other. ASAF members do not only have to convince the IASB, but they will also engage with each other on the merits of their arguments. The end result is that participants will understand much better the competing views, while the IASB is better able to incorporate this feedback into our deliberations.

It is important that the ASAF reflects not only the views of the organisations sitting around the table, but of the entire standard-setting community. The regional standard-setting bodies such as the AOSSG, EFRAG, GLASS and PAFA serve as representatives of the entire region. This is extremely important to ensure that the ASAF is not seen as an exclusive club.

Inclusiveness is also the reason why we continue to need the World Standard Setters, because that is the only platform where all standard setters meet. I know there is some meeting weariness among members of IFASS, especially amongst those who are also members of ASAF. We will be happy to discuss with IFASS how we can minimize overlap and travel. However, I think we have a joint responsibility of keeping WSS as a vital platform, since it is the widest and most inclusive platform that we have.

The role of standard-setters

The final topic that I would like to discuss is what I call the paradox of standard-setting. Throughout the history of accounting standards, it has often been the most needed improvements to transparency that were the most controversial, and the hardest to drive through. For example, expensing stock options was obviously the right thing to do. But vested interests were so strong that the economic myth that these options basically were for free could be kept up for a very long time. If you believe that the role of accounting is to keep capitalism honest, then these are the battles worth fighting. This is the way we deliver material improvements to transparency and how we help to protect investors.

At the same time, not all controversy is the result of lobbying by vested interests. After all, most standard-setters have at some time proposed changes that were not sufficiently developed or that had unintended consequences not obvious at the time of proposal. Our due process provides an important quality control mechanism and this is something to cherish. Le-

On Global Accounting Standards

gitimate technical or practical concerns about our standards need to be addressed and that is what we do.

The difficulty comes in trying to distinguish between these two. It is not always obvious what is lobbying by vested interests and what is public interest feedback whose purpose is to help us deliver a high quality standard. More often than not the vested interest is packaged in public interest arguments. Sometimes even users do not want change. Analysts are sometimes so much in love with their own models that they do not want our standards to shed light on complex issues.

Helping us to make this distinction between legitimate concerns and the conservatism of the status quo is a central role of all standard-setters, including national standard setters. We need you to identify technical and practical flaws in our proposals. But we also need your help in pushing back on vested interests. This is difficult, often unpopular work, but it is essential and we cannot do it alone. If we are to deliver standards with the necessary rigour and discipline we need all the help we can get.

This is particularly important in the coming year as we seek to finalise the four major projects of insurance, financial instruments, leasing and revenue recognition. In each of these cases, we will do everything possible to minimise the possibility of unexpected consequences. High quality feedback and field testing is invaluable as we complete this work. However, we must also guard against being lobbied off course. Standard-setting is an exercise in change management, and change is rarely popular, even if it is change for the better. We need your help to get these changes done.

Ladies and gentlemen, I wish you a very successful conference and I look forward to discussing these challenges with you in greater depth over the next two days.

Expectation of US Commitment to Adopt IFRS in a Timely Manner[①]

**Opening remarks by Hans Hoogervorst at AICPA
Conference on Current SEC and PCAOB Developments
04 December 2012**

This time last year I provided an update on our work to establish IFRS as the global language of financial reporting. Today, I am happy to report continued progress around the world. Over 100 countries now use IFRSs, including three quarters of the G20. Almost all of Europe, including non-EU countries such as Russia and Turkey are now on board. Africa is increasingly committed, as are big parts of Asia and the Middle-East. In the Americas, we have almost all countries applying IFRSs, including Brazil, Argentina, Mexico and Canada. Of course, there is one country sandwiched between Mexico and Canada that has yet to commit, but more on that later.

When the IASB and the FASB signed the Norwalk Agreement in 2002, IFRS was considered by many to be a bilateral project between Europe and the US. Today, the standard-setting environment looks different. Many emerging economies driving global growth are supporting IFRS. Understandably, they want a seat at the table of accounting standard-setting. We are seeing the emergence of regional accounting standard-setting forums in Asia and Latin America to complement that of Europe.

As the convergence projects are coming to an end, the IASB is looking at new, multilateral ways to engage with such groups. Last month, we published proposals for a new mechanism to allow the global standard-setting community, to be more deeply engaged in our standard-setting processes.

---

① The title was added by the translator.

We would like and expect the FASB to become a fully engaged partner in this new global forum. We will continue to need the greatly appreciated expertise of our American colleagues.

Recognising the tide of globalisation, the G20 has called time and again for global accounting standards. The United States has had a proud role in this pursuit of a single set of global standards. In 1973, the United States played a crucial role in creating the IASB's predecessor. When the organisation was restructured to become the IASB, the SEC made sure that the IASB looked very much like the FASB. The first Chairman of the Trustees was Paul Volcker. A quarter of my Board and a third of our Trustees are North Americans.

Recently, we have appointed some prominent Americans to our organisation. Mary Tokar from KPMG, and formerly from the SEC, will join the IASB in January, while Heidi Miller, a highly respected executive from JP Morgan, will become a Trustee. Apart from this direct participation, the United States has had enormous influence on our standard setting through the decade of convergence between the FASB and the IASB. As a result, our own analysis shows that the US is very well prepared for a successful transition to IFRS.[1]

All of this has been done in the expectation that the US would become a permanent participant in the development, application, and enforcement of a single set of global standards. In 2007, a comment letter by the FAF and the FASB to the SEC said it all: "Investors would be better served if all US public companies used accounting standards promulgated by a single global standard setter as the basis for preparing their financial report. This would be best accomplished by moving U.S. public companies to an improved version of IFRS."

In my speech to you last year, I recognized that it would not be an easy task for the SEC to make up its mind about adoption of IFRS. I was not so naive to expect wholesale adoption of IFRS for all companies from day one. But there was a reasonable expectation around the world that the SEC would plot a course towards IFRS.

Expectation of US Commitment to Adopt IFRS in a Timely Manner

Yet, as you know, the SEC's intention to make a decision, originally planned for 2011, was postponed again in 2012. Self-imposed deadlines frequently slip, as we standard setters know all too well. I also recognize that the enormous pressures of Dodd Frank and the elections were not a perfect background for the SEC to make up its mind.

Five years ago, a standstill in the United States would have had very serious consequences for the IASB. The risk was that without the US on board, Europe would go its own way and Asia would develop its own regional standards. Today, such talk has gone. For the many countries I referred to, the cost of transition to IFRS is behind them. There is no appetite to undo this work and revert to national or regional standards. IFRS already has a global impact and that will not change. So there is no longer any risk of IFRS disintegrating as a result of a standstill in the United States.

Nevertheless, there is much concern about strong and continued US leadership in our work and processes if the US is not going to come on board in some shape or form.

I believe the United States should remain an important participant in our institutions and activities. But obviously, US influence will be commensurate with its commitment to our standards. To give just one example: it will make a huge difference whether the FASB will be in a position to endorse our standards, instead of being a national standard setter without a role towards IFRS.

Indeed, the status quo harbours a big risk of slipping back. The uncertainty about where the SEC is going to land is not a helpful backdrop for our work on the remaining convergence projects. Already, on some issues it is getting increasingly hard to find common solutions. If we cannot achieve converged outcomes within a convergence programme, then how will we maintain convergence once the programme has ended? The risk of increasing divergence will be enormous. What a waste that would be.

After a decade of progress, after tireless and sometimes painful work by the boards to bring about convergence between IFRS and US GAAP, after two years of analysis and report writing, many people around the world expect a clearer perspective of this country's intentions with IFRS.

That is why we really need a tangible sign of continued US commitment to a single set of global standards. Merely striving for greater comparability between standards will not do. We tried that during the 1990s and it was a failure[1]. In the absence of a credible, tangible step on the part of the United States, international concern could turn into international scepticism. The G20 calls for global accounting standards would start to ring increasingly hollow. We cannot allow that to happen.

Ladies and gentlemen, in the past decade, IFRS has de facto become the global accounting language for the greater part of the world. Investors around the globe rely on our standards to make the world safe for their investments. I do not know of any global economic standard or organisation without a leadership role of the United States. For this reason, I find it hard to imagine IFRS without a leadership role for the United States and the SEC. But leadership requires vision, mettle and tough decisions. All of these qualities should be in ample supply in the United States.

Please excuse my frankness during these opening remarks. The Dutch are infamous for their straight-talking — and I am very Dutch. But as a Dutchman who has lived and worked in your country I know that Americans like to talk straight as well. I truly appreciate your attention.

---

[1] IFRS Foundation staff analysis of SEC Final Staff Report on IFRS, www.ifrs.org.

---

① The International Accounting Standards Committee (IASC) was created in 1973 by nine "sponsoring members", with the AICPA representing the US. The idea was that national standard-setters would base their national standards on the IASC's standards, thus delivering greater international comparability. Yet, after 25 years of effort, none of the original nine sponsoring members used anything close to international standards. Each country would only take the parts of the international standard that they liked and modify those that they didn't. The model was a failure. The international community came together once again to see what could be done, and in 1997 published a strategy report that recommended the mission of a restructured IASC change to a single set of global standards.

Why the Financial Industry is Different: The Relevance of Current Measurement for the Financial Industry

Speech by Hans Hoogervorst at the Joint ICAEW and IFRS Foundation Financial Institutions IFRS Conference in London, UK
03 December, 2013

We at the IASB cannot get enough of setting standards for financial instruments. We love it so much, that we simply refuse to get it done! We have been working on IFRS 9 since 2008 and are still happily plodding on.

On a more serious note, the end of the tunnel is-fortunately-now in sight. IFRS 9 will get done and it will get done soon. But there is no denying that we have at times been struggling. And it is not just the IASB that is struggling with financial instruments, but also our colleagues at the FASB.

There are two reasons why standard-setters are wrestling with financial instruments. First, they are inherently very complicated. More importantly, the financial industry is extraordinarily sensitive to accounting rules. Relatively small changes in accounting rules can make a big difference to banks. Enthusiasm for greater transparency in accounting is greatly tempered by the possibility of this leading to further bank bailouts! So every change the IASB proposes is subject to intense scrutiny.

Why is this the case? What is it that sets the financial industry apart from other sectors of the economy when it comes to accounting? To be able to answer this question, I will first make some observations on accounting for non-financial entities.

The IASB has often been accused of being too focused on the balance sheet and on fair value measurement. This could allegedly lead to lack of prudence and excessive accounting volatility.

I have always thought this criticism to be largely unjustified. In our Discussion Paper on the Conceptual Framework, we make perfectly clear that we view Profit or Loss as a key indicator of performance and that we do not give precedence to the balance sheet. Nor do we give precedence to fair value accounting, although we certainly do not demonise it either!

It is for good reasons that we have chosen a nuanced approach between the balance sheet and the income statement. The truth is that the importance of the balance sheet differs greatly from industry to industry. For most companies in the manufacturing and service industries, the balance sheet gives only a partial view of the financial situation of an entity.

The current value of many of their assets is not of primary importance if they are being used in combination with other assets to produce goods or services.

In most situations for going concerns, the fair value of Plant, Property and Equipment, or PP&E is of limited relevance. For example, it is not extremely relevant for a car-manufacturer (or its investors) to know the present market value of its robots if the company intends to keep them producing cars. Moreover, valuing PP&E at fair value would in many cases also be very costly and would possibly open the door to earnings management. If profit or loss included frequent adjustments in the fair value of PP&E, an entity's earnings performance could become seriously muddled.

This is not to say that cost-based accounting does not have serious drawbacks. Especially in an inflationary environment, historic cost quickly loses its relevance. In addition, a cost-based balance sheet may prevent investors from seeing hidden treasures, such as the value of the land under an otherwise decrepit office building. But by and large, historic cost, adjusted for depreciation, is generally considered to be a cost-effective way of measuring many of the assets of non-financial companies.

The accounting treatment of intangibles is another reason why the balance sheet only gives a very partial reflection of many companies' true economic position. For high-tech companies such as Apple or Google, intangibles such as technology, design or sheer market power, are much more important to their future earnings power than the value of their PP&E. Because most intangibles cannot be measured reliably, they are not included in the balance sheet even if it is clear that they are there.

All this does not mean that the balance sheets of non-financial companies are unimportant. The balance sheet contains important information on the gearing of an entity. That is the reason why we are spending so much energy on our upcoming Leases Standard. The balance sheet should also inform the investor about the state of inventory and PP&E. But for the prediction of future cash flows, the investor will in many cases need additional analysis of earnings and intangibles.

The IASB is fully aware that an uneven focus on the balance sheet would not provide the investor with useful information.

The financial industry is different. Banks and insurance companies have huge balance sheets and those balance sheets matter hugely. Relatively small changes in the balance sheet can have an enormous impact on earnings. Future cash flows are very much dependent on the financial instruments on banks' and insurance companies' balance sheets.

For many financial instruments, it is their current value that counts. Some are actively traded on financial markets and are therefore subject to market fluctuations. So the balance sheet and current measurement techniques, which include fair value accounting but are not limited to it, are much more important to the financial sector than to the non-financial sector.

It is exactly this undeniable importance of current measurement techniques that makes accounting for the financial industry so controversial. Current measurement is much better at picking up mismatches between assets and liabilities. It is also much more sensitive to market fluctuations.

As a result, current measurement is more likely to lead to volatility. In this respect, bankers and insurers are no different from all other preparers: they all hate volatility!

And they especially hate volatility that they perceive to be induced by accounting.

At the height of the financial crisis, there was a widespread belief among the banking community that they were the victims of artificial volatility caused by fair value accounting. They argued that relying on market prices exacerbates the economic cycle in both upturns and downturns. These critics believed that fair value accounting thereby strengthened procyclicality and created artificial volatility.

The fact is that most banks were exposed to fair value accounting in a limited way. Fair value accounting was mainly limited to the trading book and derivatives. Most people will agree that for such instruments there is no alternative to fair value accounting. Moreover, for the majority of banks, most of their banking book consists of traditional assets, such as loans, which have continued to be measured at amortised cost.

So it no surprise that most academic research has concluded that fair value accounting did not have a major impact on the crisis.

Where fair value did play a role, it was often beneficial. Banks that carried poisonous CDOs at fair value were often more quickly aware of the dangers that confronted them. While the use of fair value may be associated with lack of prudence, using fair value as an indicator of impairment can be quite the most prudent thing to do!

The truth is that the accounting merely reflected the very real economic volatility that is at the core of the business model of the banking industry. In fact, it is hard to imagine an industry that is as prone to real economic volatility as the financial sector.

Both sides of a bank's balance sheet are vulnerable. Its assets can be very sensitive to the economic cycle, whether they are derivatives or loans backed by bricks and mortar. Traditional bank loans, such as mortgages, have long seemed solid, cut and dried business. Since 2007 we have known that long-term trends in house prices and delinquencies can be extremely misleading. Even gold-plated, triple-A government bonds can turn sour very quickly, as we have seen in the case of Ireland and Spain.

The banking industry's liability side is also notoriously vulnerable.

Funding, whether it is wholesale or retail, can evaporate with the speed of a mouse-click.

As if all of this is not risky enough, the banking industry has operated on the flimsiest of capital margins. Just before the crisis, tangible common equity of many banks was negligible. It was generally only 1 to 3 percent of the balance sheet, and some banks even had a negative net tangible equity.

Thanks to our stringent consolidation requirements, the extreme leverage of the banks was there for everybody to see. The fact that market participants chose to ignore this information is one of the most astounding cases of collective cognitive dissonance in economic history.

Despite the, at most, peripheral role of accounting in the crisis, both the FASB and the IASB were put under severe pressure to further reduce the impact of fair value accounting. The changes that were made were not very big, but the banking industry was in such bad shape that every improvement, no matter how small or cosmetic, was considered to be helpful. It was a classic example of bending the rules to make things look better because the reality was too ugly to be faced up to. If the banks had been properly capitalised, this ugly episode in standard-setting would never have been necessary.

There was one aspect of our Standards — namely the issue of "own credit" — where we agreed that fair value accounting could lead to counter-intuitive results. At the height of the crisis, the fair valuation of own credit sometimes led to bizarre results, Banks under severe stress would report profits as a resurt of the fair value of their own debt going down.

We fixed this problem in IFRS 9 and recently decided to make this fix available in isolation as part of our general hedge accounting changes.

The financial crisis also made it clear that the current impairment model does not work well. The current incurred loss model was designed to prevent earnings management through "big bath" provisioning. During the crisis, it became clear that the model was vulnerable to a different kind of earnings management, namely excessive postponement of loss recognition, even when it was abundantly clear that losses could not be avoided. That is why we decided to replace the incurred loss model with an expected loss model.

We have now developed a model that is operational and much more forward-looking than the incurred loss model.

As soon as a financial asset has experienced a significant increase in credit risk, the expected lifetime loss needs to be recognised. The new impairment model will address one of the main pitfalls of amortised cost accounting, which is that it lends itself more easily to the masking of inevitable shortfalls in future cash flows. Our field work shows that it will lead to a significant rise in the level of provisioning.

The financial crisis also led the IASB to accelerate its work to replace IAS39 with IFRS 9. In this Standard, the IASB is continuing with a mixed measurement approach, but we have tried to put the criteria for classification and measurement on a more objective footing.

The classification of a financial instrument depends on both the nature of the cash flows and the business model. To put it roughly, if an instrument has basic loan features and the business model is to hold it for collection, it is measured at amortised cost. If an instrument does not have basic loan features and the business model is to trade the asset, it will be measured at fair value through profit and loss. If an asset is held both for selling and for collecting the contractual cash flows, it will be measured at Fair Value through OCI.

IFRS 9 will not drastically change the present situation, in which most banking assets are carried at cost. So does this mean that the banking industry can continue to live in the blissful stability provided by amortised cost? Obviously, this is a rhetorical question, because we all know that reality is much more complex than that.

The savings and loan crisis in the 1980s in the United States is the classic example of the limitations of amortised cost accounting. In the early eighties, the savings and loan industry was, de facto, bankrupted by a terrible interest rate mismatch between their deposits and their outstanding loan portfolios. As the Federal Reserve Chairman of the time, Paul Volcker, increased interest rates dramatically, the savings and loan industry had to pay a lot more interest on their deposits, while their interest income on long-term mortgages was largely fixed. It is clear that amortised cost accounting did not show the full extent of the losses that were inevitable. It gave a false portrayal of stability which everybody knew to be untrue.

More than thirty years later, protecting the interest magin is more than ever before, a central task for bank managers.

The reality of banking is much more intricate than taking in deposits with one hand and collecting contractual cash flows with the other. The name of the game is to earn a stable net interest margin, which requires very dynamic and sophisticated Asset Liability Management.

While the loan officers of a bank are quietly collecting their contractual cash flows, their colleagues at the treasury department are very actively monitoring the interest rate markets. They manage their interest exposures on a daily basis. These activities are based on current measurement of interest rate exposures and require massive use of financial instruments such as derivatives, which are measured at fair value.

So if collecting contractual cash flows is only part of the business model of a bank, it is also clear that amortised cost in isolation cannot give a faithful representation of its financial condition. In fact, the instruments used to manage interest exposures are usually measured at fair value. The inevitable result of this mixed measurement approach is that a bank's financial statements are rife with accounting mismatches between amortised cost and fair value.

These accounting mismatches make it very hard for banks to explain their financial performance to investors, so most banks actively use our general hedge accounting Standard to address this issue. This way, they succeed in avoiding a part of accounting volatility. However, it is no secret that the existing hedge accounting requirements deal with some hedge relationships, but not others, using rather arbitrary criteria. More importantly, current hedge accounting is not capable of properly reflecting the management of net positions in open portfolios.

For this reason, the IASB is currently developing a Discussion Paper on a new macro hedging model. This model will make it possible to better represent in the accounts such risk management activity relating to open portfolios, rather than restricting hedge accounting to specific financial instruments. Accounting for macro hedging would basically make it possible to match the current value of interest rate exposures that are embedded in open portfolios with the fair value of the derivatives that are used to hedge those exposures.

When I recently read the memoirs of Bob Herz, the former chairman of the FASB, I realised that our macro hedging proposals are very close to his thinking on financial instruments. In this very readable book[1], he recounts his efforts to convince his colleagues at the FASB to adopt a measurement model for financial instruments that would be based on the present value of cash flows, discounted at current interest rates.

His proposal was in essence a "third way" of accounting, which tried to avoid the pitfalls of both amortised cost and fair value accounting. A discounted cash flow model would give much more insight into interest rate and maturity mismatches than amortised cost, while ignoring some of the "noise" of fair value accounting, which is caused by general market and liquidity factors. At the time, Bob Herz did not succeed in convincing his fellow board members, but I think he will certainly recognise elements of his thinking in our forthcoming Discussion Paper on macro hedging. The present value of cash flows is indeed central to the risk management of banks and also to our macro hedging proposals.

If this accounting is properly conceived and applied, it could much better reflect the actual business model of banks and it could result in a significant reduction of accounting mismatches. I do emphasise—if properly conceived and applied—because if it is not sufficiently disciplined, macro hedging could also degenerate into custom-made accounting without rigour or comparability.

Our objective is to improve transparency, not to mask economic volatility. For that reason we are treading very carefully in developing our proposals.

Since it is clear that it will still take significant time to finalise our possible proposals on macro hedging, we have separated it from the rest of IFRS 9. IFRS 9 is practically finished and will soon be ready to be endorsed. Because of the significant improvements that IFRS 9 makes in classification and measurement, and also in general hedging and impairment, I have no doubt that it will be endorsed around the world.

For reasons of time, I have spoken very little about accounting for insurance contracts. Those who have been following our efforts to create a new Standard know that our building block model also has features of what I just now called the "third way" of accounting. It is neither cost-based, nor fair value-based. Instead it is a discounted cash flow model using current interest rates.

While there is still a lot of public discussion about many aspects of our proposals, most market participants agree that the only way to achieve a meaningful presentation of the insurance liability is through current measurement. Especially in the current macroeconomic environment, in which interest rates are being suppressed over a prolonged period of time, the use of historic interest rates would obviously result in misleading information. So, current measurement techniques are also of the utmost importance for the insurance industry.

Ladies and gentlemen, I now come to the conclusion of my speech. I hope I have demonstrated convincingly that in general the IASB does not give precedence to the balance sheet over Profit or Loss. I am also sure that I was preaching to the converted when I argued that for the financial industry, the balance sheet does indeed matter very much.

I also hope that most of you will agree that current measurement of many financial instruments is absolutely crucial to risk management in the financial industry. Indeed, bank managers who do not do so on a daily basis, certainly warrant close scrutiny by the regulators!

We are working hard to make it possible for your accounts to better reflect these risk management activities. We will need your views and support to make our proposals work. So I encourage you to be fully engaged with us as we finalise our proposals on financial instruments and insurance contracts. Thank you for your attention.

---

[1] Bob Herz, Accounting Changes, Chronicles of convergence, crisis and complexity in financial reporting, 2013.